LOTTA

LOTTA

and
The Unitarian Service Committee Story

CLYDE SANGER

First published in 1986 by
Stoddart Publishing Co. Limited
34 Lesmill Road
Toronto, Canada
M3B 2T6

Canadian Cataloguing in Publication Data

Sanger, Clyde.
Lotta: the Unitarian Service Committee story

Includes index.
ISBN 0-7737-2072-3

1. Hitschmanova, Lotta, 1909-   2. International relief −
Canada − Biography. 3. Unitarian Service Committee of Canada.
4. International relief − Societies, etc. I. Title.

HV28.H48S35 1986   361.7'63'0924   C85-099662-7

Cover design by Brant Cowie/Artplus Ltd.

Cover photograph by Charlie Chew

Printed and bound in Canada

Contents

1. The Chain of Poverty   1

    A Rotary International honor
    The new generation
    Monuments...and people

2. The Road From Prague   12

    Childhood
    Paris and literature
    Writing against Hitler
    Refugee through France
    Under the Vichy regime
    Initiatives from Boston
    Lisbon and the wider world
    The long voyage
    Montreal and censorship
    UNRRA and back
    War's end, new home

3. Getting Started   40

    Launching USC Canada
    Westward the land is bright
    France, from the ashes
    Picasso's little people
    Homes in the castle

4. Eastward Alone   54

    Children in Czechoslovakia
    Canadian Club in Vienna
    Limbs and clothes to Italy
    USC Boston under attack
    Emergency in Macedonia
    The widows of Mesovouno
    Homes but few jobs
    Training for girls
    Sequel of the priest's quarrel
    The CAP approach
    The "eagle's nest" villages

5. Into Asia 81

   Korea: The largest program
   Long-range focus on children
   Norwegian partners and Mokpo
   Gaza and the "layette lift"
   Vietnam from both sides
   Hanoi and the hospitals

6. India From Four Sides 109

   India from four sides
   Beggar boys to carpenters
   The life workers of Bangalore
   Planting skills in Bihar
   False start in family planning
   Karnatak and the Gandhian heritage
   From the back of the bus
   Awamma Mulla's drinking well

7. Building the Canadian Constituency 134

   A memorable address
   Branching out
   Unitarians and the USC
   The veteran campaigners
   Her bridge of words
   Back at Sparks Street
   The golden media
   A decade to decide
   Bilingual by-and-by

8. Population and Progress 161

   Hong Kong
   Resilient refugees
   Indonesia: women in charge
   The Klampok experiment
   Lighting lamps with water!
   Transmigration of doctors
   Regreening of Sabu
   Sampans, wells, and fishponds

9. The Art and Science of Aiding People   186

A rare occasion
The art of giving aid
Adding the personal touch
The science of aid
Local people know their needs
Making a real impact
Stretching the dollar

10. Breaking the Pattern of Poverty   202

Bangladesh
   Years of frustration
   Devious route to RDP
   Focus on 50 million poorest
   Organize and reconcile
   Literacy first, loans later
Briefly in Cyprus
Nepal: beyond single-need projects

11. Southern Africa   226

Triplets with differences
The gum trees of Botswana
Lesotho: erosion and egg circles
Swaziland: change and the cyclone
Making a life in towns

12. The Fifth Decade   241

The long journey
South Asia partnership
The bottom line: fund raising

Appendices   252

Index   257

Acknowledgements

THERE WAS ONE OBVIOUS AUTHOR for this book: Dr. Lotta Hitschmanova herself. She had been the mainspring of the agency for almost all the forty years the book reviews and, besides, she was a most skilled communicator and writer. Indeed, Dr. Lotta started on the task of writing her own book when she gave up the day-to-day direction of the Unitarian Service Committee (USC) in 1982. Sadly, her health soon deteriorated, and board members looked for someone else to take over the research and writing. They chose me, remembering (I suppose) that I had visited USC projects in Korea and written of them in another book*.

I was glad to take on the job, because it gave me an opportunity that was intriguing for one who has been involved with several Canadian nongovernmental organizations. This was the opportunity to describe in detail the transition of a remarkable NGO from relief work in postwar Europe to fullblown development assistance for large rural communities in Asia and Africa. It also allowed me to satisfy the inquisitiveness, which I think I shared with many Canadians, about this extraordinary personality and to dig into the roots of Dr. Lotta's earlier life. She had never talked much about her past, because her immediate work was all-absorbing and always looking toward the future. But her lack of vanity was not matched on our part by lack of curiosity.

I have many people to thank for help with this book, starting with Dr. Hitschmanova herself. Because of her illness I could not interview her satisfactorily, but the USC files in the National Archives are full of her vivid reports of overseas trips and accounts of fund-raising tours in Canada; and I have quoted often from them. The USC board formed an editorial committee of Gordon Merrill, Bower Carty, Harry Bolster and Jack Todd, to be both guide and goad to me. To everyone's mild surprise,

---

* *Half a Loaf: Canada's semi-role in developing countries*, Ryerson, Toronto: 1969.

the system worked harmoniously: the committee members improved my text and I met their deadlines. I also appreciated Peggy Bolster's quick eye for an irrelevancy, and Harry Bolster's unfailing concern to move the work forward.

I am particularly grateful for the generous support of Mr. Howard Webster, for making available funds through the RHW Foundation, which made possible more than a year's work on the book.

For much of the account of Lotta's life and career before she launched USC Canada in 1945, I was greatly helped by the memories of her sister Mrs. Lilly Steen, and also by George Skaller, Edgar Sarton, Lotte Heim and Marjorie Mader. Everyone on the present staff of USC Canada was extraordinarily patient with my visits of exploration and excavation; it is not, I trust, invidious to mention in particular Raymond ven der Buhs, Pamela Lee MacRae, Gloria Avery and Virginia Valenzuela. Among former staff members I was helped in several directions by Gilles Latour, Gérard Holdrinet, Lorraine Cameron, Deborah Cowley — and Shirley Plowman, who gave me a memorably cheerful interview shortly before her untimely death.

The USC branches across Canada have been a fountain of enthusiasm as well as hives of communal activity. I enjoyed visiting several branches and being splashed with the enthusiasm of Dorothy Legge in Truro; Elisabeth Lang in Montreal; Iona Pilowski and Euphemia Tainsh in Winnipeg; Jack Jefferson and Margaret Donald in Vancouver; and Ida Weisse, Hazel Woodward, Art Mann and Frances Nicholson among others in Victoria, Duncan and Nanaimo. In their quite different ways, the Rev. Philip Hewett, Mamie Maloney Boggs and Stuart Keate were most useful informants.

USC Canada began with considerable help from USC Boston, whose own colorful history has been gathered through taped interviews by Ghanda Di Figlia. She let me listen to these tapes and also, with Alan Seaburg, guided me round the USC files now in the Andover-Harvard Theological Library. I am grateful to both of them, and also to the Rev. Howard Brooks for a good interview. I am only sorry that the USC Boston section was drastically reduced during revision of this book, under pressure of space. It deserves a book to itself — by someone else.

Perhaps the most exciting part of writing this book came when I visited current projects in Bangladesh and caught up with what had happened to projects in Greece and India, from which USC

Canada withdrew years ago. Mrs. Jahanara and Humayun Reza were among many helpful USC Bangladesh staff, and Farida Islam was the best of traveling companions. For the return to Macedonia, Mr. A. Papadopoulos in the Greek embassy in Ottawa went to much trouble to locate the village of Mesovouno for me, and introduced me to friends in Kozani, lawyer Minos Papachristou and architect Demetrius Marmaras, who after overcoming suspicions that I was a Bulgarian spy could not have been more helpful. In proper Greek style, Tony Trimis "tired the sun with talking" about community development one afternoon against the wonderful backdrop of the Acropolis, while Bruce and Tad Lansdale were splendid hosts during an Orthodox Easter weekend spent at the American Farm School.

As for projects in India, Swami Yuktananda brought up to date the tale of success in agricultural training begun at Ranchi in Bihar, and M.S.S. Nambudiri was the most invigorating guide any visitor to Madras might wish. Of my three-day visit to the Karnatak Health Institute, I would simply say that the wisdom, warmth, and dedication of Dr. M.K. Vaidya, his wife and children leave an impression that will last my lifetime.

Finally, back in Canada, I am grateful to David Walden and other guardians of documents at the National Archives; to Ed Carson, Publisher of Stoddart Publishing, for his speedy planning of this book; to my editor, Lillian Goodman, for her incisive and intelligent work; and to my wife Penny for many friendly and helpful comments.

But the book properly belongs to Lotta Hitschmanova. Charles Dickens, who also started work as a journalist, wrote lines that can serve as tribute to her: "The hill hath not raised its head to heaven that perseverance cannot gain the summit of in time."

Clyde Sanger

To that dauntless little figure

who strode up many hills,

I dedicate this book.

CHAPTER 1

The Chain of Poverty

A Rotary International honor

PHYSICALLY, THE FRAIL and tiny figure is dwarfed by the great arena. And of course she is conspicuously out of place in a hockey stadium. For she stands there, on an improvised stage, behind a plastic lectern, in a uniform that is as dated as doodlebugs or gas masks. Her peaked cap seems American, but "Canada" is firmly pinned on her lapels. She wears five rows of medal ribbons, but her cap badge is no eagle or grenade; it is a sliver of a chalice with a lick of flame above it. She is a woman of discipline and devotion, obviously, but never of war.

Yet she has seen many wars, even sought them out continuously. She grew up in the midst of what Europeans called the Great War, missing her father who was away with the Austrian army trying to organize provisions for Russian prisoners. She suffered as a refugee on the run, almost died of starvation on a street in Marseilles during the second and greater war, until a three-year journey brought her from Czechoslovakia to Canada.

That would be enough war for most people, who would start building a secure career, a summer cottage, and other comforts, especially if they had a Ph.D. as she did. But Lotta Hitschmanova kept going back to wars, or to the wreckage left by them, for the next thirty-five years: to Europe with its thirty million displaced persons and thousands of mutilated children; to Greece struggling out of civil war and ravaged by drought and famine; to Korea and the Middle East; and, much later, to Vietnam, and to Bangladesh after its bloody Caesarean birth. She also went many times, with her shoulder bag ready to hold the thick notebook she was always filling with names and numbers and quotations, to countries where war, in the words of their political leaders, meant the national fight against malnutrition and disease. She often found that this extended to a guerilla struggle against an uncaring bureaucracy and local power structures, to rebellion against male conservatism and the despairing passivism of the utterly poor. It was a fight she

1

Lotta

joined in India and Nepal and Indonesia, and in the little
hostage states that border on South Africa: Botswana, Lesotho,
and Swaziland.

Now, after thirty-five years in these battlefields, delivering all
manner of help and meticulously gathering from the dusty
ground ammunition for all the speeches ahead of her every
autumn to Canadian audiences, she is worn out like any old
campaigner. She is grown as frail as the hill-women to whom
she used to take milk and saris in the Kodai district of south
India. She seems tiny as she stands on the stage in front of
well-breakfasted Rotarians, under the dome of Maple Leaf
Gardens. But only in physical terms is she dwarfed. Stature has
more to do with deeds than with centimeters, and the morning's
business is to honor what she has done all these years.

Maple Leaf Gardens, the heartland of hockey in Toronto,
has had other big occasions out of season: evenings of opera
and a historic political convention in October 1967. But in June
1983 the Gardens hosted a quite different scene. This was the
presentation of the Rotary Award for World Understanding, in
honor of her many years of humanitarian work as executive
director of the Unitarian Service Committee of Canada (USC
Canada). Rotary International had only made this presentation
twice before; in 1981 to Dr. Noburu Iwamura, a Japanese eye
specialist who worked in Nepal, and in 1982 to Pope John
Paul II. It carries a one hundred thousand dollar award, in the
form of ten scholarships to be given, in the recipient's name, to
students from developing countries to study abroad for a year.

The theme of this seventy-fourth annual convention sounded
like a Chinese slogan: "Mankind is One: Build Bridges of
Friendship Throughout the World." And the 16,800 Rotarians
who had gathered in Toronto from 102 countries were working
on it, with cheerful encounters and plans for later meetings.
Guest speakers talked about wider horizons of concern. Dr.
Bernard Lown, a Harvard cardiologist who was also president
of the International Physicians for the Prevention of Nuclear
War, said it would take only one-tenth of the world's military
expenditure to feed all the hungry children in the world.
Pictures of the Hiroshima attack were flashed onto a huge
screen after the president, Dr. Hirojo Mukasa, a psychiatrist
from Kyosho, told of the agonizing experience of leading a
medical team into the city's ruins.

Dr. John Evans, of Toronto and the World Bank, spoke of the "silent human tragedy" of disease and malnutrition that over the next ten years would almost certainly take the lives of 150 million children, as many people as might die in a nuclear attack. Yet half of them could be saved by "relatively simple, inexpensive measures used routinely in industrialized countries."

By the final day of their convention, the Rotarians were in need of some positive relief. It was also a time for this all-male organization to remember the other sex. Lapels blossomed with rosettes that proclaimed "Rotary Wives are Beautiful People." A warm-up quartet from Ontario, the North Bay Rotary Songsters, swtiched to the rollicking desiderata of South Pacific sailors: "There is nothing like a dame." And then, in mid-morning, came the presentation to Dr. Hitschmanova.

Onto the broad stage, in front of lines of Rotary officials, came this diminutive figure in a new uniform. The screen, that the day before had shown the horrors of Hiroshima, was turned into a checkerboard of happier scenes; young people of Asia and Africa with the woman who now stood by the lectern, shyly clutching her shoulder bag, as a short citation was read: "...born in Prague, from where she fled in 1938,...worked in France until 1942...in 1980 appointed a Companion of the Order of Canada..." The citation over, she was handed a crystal sculpture, which looked almost too heavy for her to receive. At seventy-three, even gifts of honor can be too weighty. Raymond ven der Buhs, once her assistant and now her successor at the helm of USC, who was standing alongside, took it on her behalf.

But all nervousness was gone when she stepped forward to speak about her years of service to "some of the neediest, the most forgotten." In a clear strong voice she said:

> Your organization and ours are truly walking on the same path. I completely share your belief that the little ones and the elderly must be given as much assistance, protection and love as possible... and thus we are all brothers and sisters, aiming at one single goal: to help make this torn, crying, bleeding world of ours a peaceful shrine for everyone – whatever his or her language, background or color.
>
> Let us promise to remember this important gathering that has brought us together from many parts of the world...some of you will say that mine is a Utopia, and that may be so; but are we not on earth to make it a better, a kinder, world for all?

3

Lotta

> With all our might we must avoid another holocaust, which would be a catastrophe. Instead of destruction we must aim at construction – and very little time is left...

As well as the citation there was a message of congratulation from Prime Minister Pierre Trudeau:

> I am sure the spiritual rewards you have received from a life of selfless service to others are plentiful...It is also most appropriate that [this award] is one which gives to others the opportunity to build a better future for themselves.

Afterwards, there were a half-dozen interviews for radio and television in the chairman's lounge. She was tired, but she emphasized to each inquirer that she would continue with the USC "as long as I can be helpful." But in the last three years, she added, a new team had taken over the project work that she previously had done virtually on her own. "A new generation of brilliant young people...It is different now. We have passed a turning point."

The new generation

Five months later, at Nanaimo on Vancouver Island, Gilles Latour, USC's chief projects officer and one of "the new generation," was nearing the end of the annual fund-raising campaign. He was beginning to look exhausted.

Never someone who relished early morning appointments, he had girded himself for a breakfast-time interview with the local radio station. But the station sent its sports reporter to the Malaspina Hotel. The mistake was soon explained. He had thought Mr. Latour was on a cross-Canada run. No, said Gilles, a cross-Canada fund-raising tour. The reporter left, asking no questions. Despite getting two phone calls later in the day, the station found it had no other reporter available, or else no interest. Fundraising requires stamina – much like a long-distance runner.

No one knew this better than Dr. Hitschmanova. For thirty-five years, she used to set off in late September for a three-month trek across Canada to tell young and old about the conditions of hunger, ill-health, and deprivation in other

4

countries, to give a detailed account of what their help the previous year had done for others, and to appeal anew for clothing and funds. It was a mighty effort. In 1949, for example, she traveled seventeen thousand kilometers (in those days by rail and road) and spoke ninety-six times in thirty-three communities. The fund-raising target was fifty thousand dollars and she found that "money was scarce and people confused by contradictory reports about conditions overseas." In fact, receipts fell just short of the target.

By the 1983-84 financial year, USC's total income had risen to $5 million. The Canadian International Development Agency (CIDA) would provide about half of this total, through matching funds. Yet that still left an enormous sum to raise. But, instead of a single woman crossing the whole country within twelve weeks, USC was now deploying five people, whose workdays on speaking tours added up to some thirty weeks. None of them would hope to have the drawing power, the charisma, of Lotta Hitschmanova in her heyday. Instead, they could compensate by fanning out into a greater number of communities and by giving a more measured, and probably more comprehensive, picture of the "chain of poverty" which holds hundreds of millions of people down from developing their full potential in today's world.

To glimpse this team approach, let us follow one of them as he makes his presentation.

Gilles Latour has led an adventurous life of a thoroughly modern kind. As a child he lived in Paris, where his father was studying radiology. He has been a taxi driver in Montreal and also hunted up ancient volumes for a bookseller. In the 1960s he flung himself into the hippie world of Haight-Ashbury and emerged to join the well-connected and flamboyantly optimistic Jacques Hébert, who was organizing youth exchanges through Canada World Youth. He came to USC in 1980 after a sober stint with the Canadian Teachers' Federation. He was a high school teacher himself for four year while earning money for his M.A. studies.

He faces a sedate evening meeting at St. Andrew's United Church in Nanaimo, on the hillside above the harbor where the salmon boats are tied up for the winter. Nanaimo people should make a good audience, for many of them have known uncertainties and hardship. The Pacific fishing industry is today "at a crisis point," as the first words of the 1982 Pearse Report declare. And earlier generations were hammered by the disasters that hit a coal-mining community. Nanaimo must be the only city in Canada where the central monument, on Front Street, is dedicated to "100 Years of Coal," while the war memorial is tucked away in the background. But there is every reason for this. More men died in the "Black Tuesday" explosion at No. 1 Mine in May 1877 than were killed from the area in two world wars. There is a weathered strength in the faces of the small audience, and a sympathy for Gilles's message about Third World problems.

He builds his message around eighty color slides taken in the last few months in the six countries where USC is working today: Bangladesh, Indonesia and Nepal in Asia, and Botswana, Lesotho, and Swaziland in southern Africa. He has a script, which if read straight through, would contain his talk within fifteen minutes. But, like any teacher, he elaborates.

The talk is entitled "Children in Developing Countries – the First Victims," and it starts with some slides put there to shock: a woman lying on a sack in the street, her infant propped against the wall behind; a naked, potbellied child photographed against the bare earth; some young boys astride a stone wall on a cold Lesotho hillside, staring at the camera. Gilles gives the World Bank statistics of misery: 800 million people living in absolute poverty and 200 million children suffering from dire hunger. Children are the first victims of a polluted environment and the illiteracy of their parents, and it is often a harsh, cold, isolated environment in countries like Nepal and Lesotho.

Scenes of pollution follow; a contaminated waterhole, used for all purposes, in rural Swaziland. "And many thousands migrate to the cities without jobs, where life is more hazardous as there is no family system to support them." A shot follows of young Indonesian women washing clothes, which looks almost idyllic until he explains they are standing thigh deep in a main Jakarta sewer. He shows a line of handsome Bangladeshi children close up and staring, and adds: "Of all those born in 1979, which the United Nations declared the Year of the Child, 50 million will be dead by 1984. Not dead of cancer or rattlesnake bites, but dead of poverty that can't be cured by doctors and drugs. It's more insidious than that. Poverty begins in the wombs of malnourished mothers." Then there follows a crisp explanation of how an illiterate mother endangers her child's life by overdiluting bottle formula to make it last longer

6

and by using dirty water and a contaminated bottle; and of the risks of malnutrition when the child is weaned onto solids lacking in protein.

"And if the child survives to five years, access to literacy, primary school, and skill training is severely restricted." A slide of a mud-hut school in Swaziland follows; no furniture and the children sitting on the floor, few books, and no equipment. "In Lesotho 95 percent of the education budget goes to teachers' salaries." In any case, the struggle for survival is already joined, and the child has many household jobs, gathering fuel, caring for animals, to keep him or her from school.

"This is the chain of poverty," says Gilles Latour, and the USC believes in attacking the whole chain. So a series of more cheerful slides follows: Nepalese women terracing some farmland, filling pots with clean tap water, and operating a sweater-knitting machine; a nutrition class in Swaziland; and another slide, which often raises a giggle from Canadians, of two dozen Swazi matrons standing around a model toilet which is mounted on a concrete slab. Gilles explains that "these are the groups we seek out and help, because they are already involved in improving their communities." They have by now installed one thousand such latrines, lining the pits with stone, and are organizing communal vegetable gardens. "This year in southern Africa I saw many distressing things. But as long as you meet such groups, they give you hope with their self-initiative."

People remain poor, though their health may improve. Income-generating projects are important, and nearly all of them involve adult education for women. Most agricultural training has in the past been aimed at men, while women did the work; anyway, 60 percent of Lesotho men are away working in South Africa. For the USC, the training of women has priority and produces results; lower birthrates, greater food production. This claim is capped by a slide of Lesotho women harvesting wheat in a scene as bountiful as the luscious canvases of Gustave Courbet.

Throughout, he has talked about revolving loan funds rather than grants. "The best way to help is not by constantly giving. Indeed, money usually comes at the end of the process. Loans are better, for when a loan is reimbursed, and the family has improved its earning situation, they're proud of the achievement."

This leads into a brief description of the largest project USC is supporting; a rural development program among share-

7

cropping families in northwest Bangladesh.[1] "After two years of this program, studies have shown that the fifteen hundred Bengali families involved have increased their income to $400 a year – some $250 above the national average." Gilles adds: "We are very excited about this project, but it was not dreamed up overnight." Indeed not. It grew out of the experience, good and bad, of over ten years at village level, of Humayun Reza, its director.

It's time to sum up. "We may be guardedly optimistic about the communities we're helping. But there are thousands and millions beyond." (Some quick slides of other malnourished, disabled children, and one of a ragged couple of "hardened street-urchins, living from trash can to trash can")..."Most problems are the result of poverty. As long as two-thirds of the world is in poverty, we cannot have security or real economic advancement..." But the message at the end is one of hope: "it is a drop in the bucket, but it is making ripples."

Over the next week the presentation is repeated in oddly different settings along the coast of Vancouver Island: in a bleak church hall in Duncan, warmed mainly by the cheeriness of the chairman, Art Mann; in the gymnasium of Chase River Elementary School, where the principal has on his office wall a poster of gophers, chomping dandelions, over the slogan, "Learn to Eat Problems for Breakfast." By Sunday the campaign has shifted to Victoria, to the Unitarian Church, where the family planning issue is squarely raised, and to contrasting high schools: Lambrick Park, whose students have been studying population questions in Grade 11; and to Norfolk House School for Girls, whose traditions and motto Do Thy Best were transferred from England seventy years ago by the intrepid Miss Dora Atkins. This is not Gilles' best moment; it is too early in the morning. The sun slanting through the library window is fading his slides, and the girls are whispering noiselessly to neighbors, a skill soon acquired at private schools.

Finally, at the big meeting in the Crystal Ballroom of the Empress Hotel in Victoria, the Pearson College of the Pacific choir from twenty-two countries, from Kenya to Kiribati ("the sardine choir tonight," said its director Edgar Samuel, "since we're rather closely packed") sang songs from around the world: a Liberian lullaby, a Russian ditty, the Huron carol, and a Swedish

---

[1]A fuller description follows in Chapter 10.

song *"Vem kan segla?"* whose words seemed hauntingly appropriate to the whole story of the USC and Lotta Hitschmanova:

Who can sail without wind?
Who can row without oars?
Who can leave a place one loves without tears?

Monuments... and people

So much has changed in forty years of attempted development: the people, the ideas, the methods. It is an open question, though, how much has been learned beyond the undoubted fact that development is a far more complicated business, with many interwoven factors, than seemed the case in 1945. Not many of the methods used to clear the ruins of Europe, and build it again in shapes both familiar and new, were transferable to other parts of the world. Too much infrastructure is lacking in them: the systems of schools and training, of investment and savings and credit, of distribution of goods, and division of labor.

Where then to begin? For different reasons political leaders in developing countries and directors of the World Bank plumped for monuments: big dams, heavy industry, large-scale irrigation. Politicians liked visible projects and the equation of industrialization with development. So India built its steel mills, and Kwame Nkrumah put the reserve funds from Ghana's cocoa exports into the Akosombo Dam and Tema harbor and the bauxite industry, rather than into improving basic agriculture. The World Bank liked big projects because they involved less staff-time per million dollars invested, and because a prompt return on its loans was more probable; with a hydroelectric dam for example, its operators would collect revenue at once from its users. The government agencies in industrialized countries (the adjective itself was persuasive) took a similar line in their aid policies.

There were, of course, nongovernmental agencies, that from the outset put people ahead of power stations. To them, human development was the important investment. They did not, in any case, have much money to disburse, which helped them to get their priorities straight. But they simplified the issues, too, partly because with limited energies, like a mountaineer at the bottom of a rock-face, they had to focus sharply on one aspect of a vast problem in order to get started; and partly because the

9

message for their supporters needed to be straightforward to make practical sense and to stir them into action. There was no point, indeed there was harm, in invoking the reaction, "This problem is just too big, there is nothing we can do." Drops of water do count, candles are worth lighting, a single oarsman can move a boat.

Lotta Hitschmanova focussed always on the development of people, starting naturally enough with the care and nourishment of children. Some of the slogans she coined for the early campaigns – Bread for Greece and the March of Diapers – sound unsophisticated today, but they produced results in their time. Tons of clothing were collected and sent off, thousands of dollars accumulated from small donations. And teams of volunteers in cities across Canada responded to the flow of clothing, gathering in firehalls and church basements every week to sort, mend, and pack.

From the outset, also, she emphasized self-reliance. The familiar image of Lotta Hitschmanova bending over some scrap of a child, ladling out milk, "white gold from Canada," she often called it, into a tin mug, gives the opposite impression of a mothering instinct that would promote dependence and might not let go as the child-country managed to grow. But the facts belie this image. She was insistent that all the USC representatives abroad should be from those countries and not from Canada, and that she work with local organizations as partners. She was let down occasionally by weak partners, but not often. She also insisted that the USC should not work in a country a year longer than it was really needed there, and her withdrawal of support was sometimes thought too abrupt by those left on their own. But while the USC was working in a country, she demanded the fullest accounting from the people running a project, so that she could in turn assure her Canadian supporters that their money was being well spent and their trust in the Service Committee was deserved.

Today, there is around Canada more knowledge and concern about developing countries. Take the three journalists who interviewed Gilles Latour in 1983 in Nanaimo. Chris Poole of the *Nanaimo Times* had worked in Fiji. David Watson, a host on cable television, was also managing the Global Village resource center. And Claus Muenter on the *Nanaimo Free Press* had been a prisoner for five years in Soviet labor camps, and came to know poverty and hunger like the Russian people he worked alongside. "We were always hungry. They kept two potatoes for a midday meal and drank warm water because they couldn't afford tea." Today, he asks after Dr. Hitschmanova and adds: "I am sick when I read of those people in Africa with nothing... It hurts me to the soul."

In 1945 nearly all Canadians were ignorant or innocent of the world beyond North America and Europe. There was then in Canada only half today's population of 25 million. It was a bold venture for a recent immigrant — and a woman, at that — to launch a relief and rehabilitation agency for Europe and who-knows-where-else at a time when a million Canadians were being welcomed home from the armed forces, and when they and their families were mainly concerned to pick up the threads of domestic life. Where did this boldness in Lotta Hitschmanova come from, and her drive to stir people to look abroad again, to acknowledge the good fortune of Canada and to give to more needy people? We should step back to her childhood in Prague and trace her own development up to the moment when, at the age of 35, she made these moves.

CHAPTER 2

The Road From Prague

Childhood

LOTTA HITSCHMANOVA was born into a secure and relatively prosperous family in Prague on 28 November 1909, during the last years of the Austro-Hungarian Empire. Fifteen months later a sister, Lilly, arrived. In contrast to Lotta, who was a strong and chubby baby, Lilly was born with jaundice and was a sickly child. But she survived some difficult years, spent all her high school years alongside Lotta, and qualified as an architect. In 1940 Lilly left with her husband Charles for Palestine and Egypt, and after a brief postwar return to Czechoslovakia, emigrated to Canada. Except for a dozen years of separation in the 1930s and 1940s, the strong-willed sisters have been the closest friends.

Their home as children was in a small apartment building at 36 Sokolska Ulice, near the center of the city. It was owned by their mother's father, who was a businessman with a lumber yard. Grandfather Theiner, Lilly recalls, was a well-educated man who looked forward to the girls' school days when they would learn Greek, his favorite language. But he died of stomach cancer when they were still young, and his widow, who had a weak heart, later moved to the country. His son Franzi inherited the lumber yard, but left Prague for New York with his American-born wife Viola in March 1939 when the Nazis moved in. Another sister married an architect who was the inspiration for Lilly's career.

Their mother, Else Theiner, was an elegant and socially ambitious woman who spoke several languages; among them, fluent Italian, French, and English, as well as German which was the language of government and society in the Austrian Empire. To her children she spoke German, but they had (besides a cook and a parlormaid) a live-in nanny, Ruzaena, who spoke Czech. Later, the beloved Ruzaena was replaced by a Swiss governess, to teach them French. The children were supposed to address her as "Mademoiselle," but to show their displeasure they shortened it to "Made," which in German means a grub.

Their father, Max Hitschmann, came of a poor family who lived in a village in Bohemia. Two of his sisters moved to Vienna and a brother, Ferdinand, left for the United States as a young man and settled in Chicago. So the girls saw little of their father's family. But he was of the greatest influence on their young lives, particularly on Lotta, and friends speak glowingly of his qualities of hard work, honesty, wisdom, and charity.

As a young man, Max was apprenticed to a malt producer. He learned the complicated process, the finger-tip control, of converting the barley they bought on the grain exchange: heating the grain, spreading it on factory floors, soaking it for germination, and drying the malt. After a time, he had experience and reputation enough to set up in business with a partner, and then alone. Until the Depression of the 1930s he made a good living selling malt to brewers in Bohemia and Switzerland. Photographs that survive show him in parks with friends, in brisk and confident pose, smartly dressed with spats and homburg hat.

In 1914, when Lotta was nearly five, he was taken into the Austrian army as a supply officer with the job of apportioning the meager food rations for thousands of Russian prisoners brought to camps in Austria. He is said to have done the job so scrupulously, in contrast to more selfish officers, that several former prisoners made their way to his house in Prague after the war to thank him. But meanwhile, the girls grew up in the charge of their mother and her parents to such an extent that, when Max appeared on leave in a handsome uniform, Lilly eyed him critically and then asked: "Papa, did you say thank you to Mama for the new uniform?"

Lotta's first six years of school were spent in what Lilly calls "a rather sissy ladies' school, very clean and nice." But then she was shifted to a coeducational high school, Stephans Gymnasium, a school in the classical tradition, with instruction in German. Lilly jumped one class, and for the next eight years the sisters shared the same school bench, which had three seats, and where their friend Emmy sat between them. Life became less sheltered. Boys in the row behind them dropped ink-soaked pens down the ringlets into which the sisters' long hair was coiled every evening with little leather garters, but this distressed them less than it did the washerwoman who had to deal with their ink-streaked dresses.

On the whole, classes were well behaved and hardworking. The students appreciated the particular qualities of some of their teachers: the little Latin teacher with his goatee beard, beautiful voice, and witty German puns; and "Father" Leppel who taught geography and was such an avid football fan that, to please him, students wrote congratulatory messages on the blackboard when his team won.

Lotta and Lilly both finished with honors in the final examination. This ordeal was called *matura*, and a panel of visiting teachers sat alongside the gymnasium's own teachers while they asked questions on every subject, from Latin and Greek, religion and chemistry, to mathematics and geography. The visiting teachers tended to keep silent, and even fall half-asleep, as long as the student did not falter. So the way to survive the long examination was to keep talking and talking.

Two stories from high school illustrate Lotta's early concern for others. There was a fifteen-minute recess in the middle of each morning, and she used to spend it in a public rehearsal of the day's assignment of Latin and Greek for the benefit of those classmates (usually boys) who had come unprepared for their lessons. They would cluster round her desk as she translated, and she let them copy down new words. On one birthday, the group gave her a tiny gramophone and a record they had made with a poem about Xenophon, in gratitude for her tutorials. But, when Lilly suggested that the two of them share their homework and halve the time each spent with a dictionary, Lotta would say they should take no shortcuts. Lilly could see no logic in this and got furious; the argument several times ended in fisticuffs, and Lotta always beat her.

The other episode, with a sadder outcome, showed at least her ability to organize, if not to check out facts. When she was sixteen, a rumor went round Prague that, if someone took the trouble to collect ten thousand used streetcar tickets, the Streetcar Commission would in return donate an artificial limb to some war-wounded veteran. Lotta set about organizing not only the whole school but also the employees of a nearby bank, to hand in their tickets every day and, after months of collecting them, she went off to the commission's head office with a suitcase full of carefully counted bundles. But the officials unhappily told her that the whole story was a hoax, and Lotta came home in tears.

Many years later, in a series of radio talks she wrote for a Canadian audience in 1943, she recalled some of the joys of school days in Czechoslovakia. She told how on every 28 of June, when school broke up for the summer holidays, students would go in their best clothes with a bunch of flowers for their teacher, to say goodbye and receive their annual report. The hilarious farewells outside the school building would end when their mothers arrived to take them, by an unwritten law, off to celebrate in one of Prague's many *glaceterias*. There, under great fans and beside a big window, the students would sit at marble-top tables and vie in ordering the weirdest combinations of ice-cream flavors. A double-decker of lemon and nuts, Lotta recalled, cost the equivalent of four cents and was topped off with whipped cream by the smiling Italian chef. This childhood memory may be the reason why Lotta Hitschmanova, fastidious and sparing in anything else she eats, has kept all her life a passion for apple pie and ice cream.

Her father laid heavy emphasis on their getting a thorough education. Lotta quotes him as saying: "Money can lose its value, my factories can burn down. But brains, training, a good profession – nobody can steal or destroy that. My children will learn what they like, to become independent, whatever may happen to me."

As reward for graduating with honors from the gymnasium, Max sent his daughters and their mother on an extended tour through medieval German cities and up into the Swiss Alps. There, in the Engadine, they swam in the lakes, climbed in the mountains, and picked Alpine roses. It was, Lilly remembers, an enchanting time. Other holidays they spent near Marienbad, where their mother drank the waters for her health and indulged a remarkable skill for sniffing out mushrooms, even the rare *Steinpilze*, in the nearby woods.

There were more serious expeditions. Max occasionally took them out to one of his malt factories beyond the suburbs of Prague. Lotta, in the style that became familiar on her tours overseas for the USC, asked questions of everyone: their salaries, their working hours, their problems. On the train journey home, she would discuss her findings with her father who ended by protesting: "But our conditions are better than in any other factory, Lotta. Our standards are above the requirements of the law."

Paris and literature

In 1929 she enrolled in the faculty of Philosophy at the University of Prague and plunged into the study of languages: ancient French, High German, old Provençal, and Spanish. After three terms, she persuaded her father to let her do the two middle years of her four-year course at the Sorbonne. Lilly had meanwhile entered the Engineering faculty of Karls University as an architectural student, and their paths diverged for the next five years, for Lotta spent four of them in Paris.

It was a big jump from the family apartment in Prague to the pension at 4 Rue Monsieur le Prince, in the heart of Montparnasse. The pension was run by Monsieur Catet, who taught at a girls' lycée, and his wife. Among the other lodgers were a Canadian student, an American woman, a Guatemalan girl called Elvira who laughed whenever she was addressed, and a Rumanian man whose dinner-time French did not extend much beyond asking for the cheese. And there was Hans Skaller, a mechanical engineer on an exchange program from Berlin, who with his future wife Ruth, was to become a lifelong friend.

Monsieur Catet strenuously discouraged any political conversations at his cosmopolitan table, and the main focus was on learning French. Simone, the lively daughter of the house, used to spend mealtimes correcting everyone's grammar. But she also led cheerful expeditions with Hans, Lotta, and the others out to Fontainebleu and Versailles, and was ready with lots of historical facts. There were other Sunday excursions to art galleries and flea markets, ending inevitably at a boulevard café. Compared with the modern theater of Berlin and Prague, French theater seemed to them old-fashioned, but Lotta became a faithful visitor to the Comédie Française and to the classic plays of Corneille, Racine, and Molière.

It was a broad new world, and only by studying day and night for the last few weeks did she cope with her final exams. In fact she coped well, taking first prize in 1931, with her diploma in French Civilization.

Over the years to 1935 Lotta accumulated diplomas in five languages – French, English, German, Spanish, and Czech –

from Prague University. She also gained a diploma in French studies, granted by the Sorbonne through the Institut Français Ernest Denis in Prague, in June 1932. This included a scholarship which led to her completing her work for her Ph.D. from Prague University, with a thesis on André Thérive, a literary reviewer and critic who she had met in her early days in Paris. Thérive was a leading member of a group of writers, poets, sculptors, and painters, whose views of the current state of French society and politics were sharp and astringent. For this reason she entitled her thesis "André Thérive, Critique du Temps." Another member of this group, who remained a good friend into the postwar years, while thirty years her senior, was André Mary, the poet, philologist, and "translator" of medieval classics such as *Le Chevalier au Lion* and *Le Roman de la Rose* into modern French.

Paris became for her the center of intellectual life, and she happily returned there in 1933 to enroll simultaneously in two schools at the Sorbonne: political science and journalism. She had by then decided to become a journalist, with the intention of later taking up a diplomatic career. These were years of increasing turmoil in France, as they were in Germany. Lotta was a discreet observer of political meetings, and of the scuffles that often ensued; her parents kept in close touch by telephone and urged her to take care. Her friends of that time remember the cosy coffee parties she used to give, the visits with her to art exhibitions, and the immaculate way she would dress with hat and white gloves, obeying the code prescribed for well-bred young ladies of prosperous merchant families.

She remained in Paris only a few weeks after completing her journalism diploma in June 1935, but in that time she fitted in a training period of three weeks on *Paris-Soir*, which was then the largest daily paper in France. When she left, the editor-in-chief, Gabriel Perreux, wrote that she had worked in all sections of the editorial department and had shown "the liveliest intelligence" in journalism.

Writing against Hitler

For the next three years, up to the signing of the Munich Pact on 30 September 1938, Lotta Hitschmann had plenty of scope to demonstrate this lively intelligence in political journalism back home in Czechoslovakia. She may have returned home abruptly to help her father in his malt business, and she did indeed work regularly in his office, but she soon had made arrangements to act as correspondent for several newspapers.

It was a period when Czechoslovakia, Rumania, and Yugoslavia were trying to give substance to their Petite Entente and stability to their fragile independence. Rumania had French language daily papers that reached outwards in this partnership, and Lotta was soon kept busy as the Prague correspondent for the largest of these, *Le Moment*, and also for the Rumanian government's own daily paper *L'Indépendance Roumaine*.

She also wrote for papers in Prague: the daily *Lidové Noviny*, the liberal intellectual weekly *Přitomnost*, and the periodical *Alliance Française*, which was advocating closer French-Czechoslovak relations at a time when President Beneš was building his broader alliance with both Paris and Moscow in the 1935 treaty. In April 1937 she traveled with President Beneš's party to report on the Congress of the Petite Entente in Belgrade. Lotta also wrote a literary column for the government's own *L'Europe Centrale*. Finally, she took on work with the Yugoslav government's news agency. With all these commitments, she was as overworked as she was underpaid. But her father gave her soothing advice: "Much more important than a large salary is practice and publicity. The reward in money will come later."

She was back at Sokolska 36 in the family apartment building. Her parents gave her a separate *garconnière*, or bachelor apartment, with a large living room and study for entertaining her friends. She kept a guest-book for all her visitors to sign, and Lilly is proud of being the first entry with this original couplet:

Für zwanzig Jahre waren wir Schwestern,
Aber Gäste erst von gestern.

(For 20 years we were sisters,
But host and guest only since yesterday.)

For Lotta, as the Nazi jackboots stamped ever closer, life was deeply serious, even somber. Men of her own age were uninteresting compared with the older intellectuals whose company she had so enjoyed in Paris. She had pleasure in visiting young married friends and their children, like Hans and Ruth Skaller who had fled to Prague from Berlin as early as 1933. But most of her emotions and energies went into work and writing.

The summer of 1938, as Adolf Hitler turned from the occupation of Austria to the intimidation of Czechoslovakia and the stirring of unrest among its 3 million Sudeten Germans, was a time of unbearable tension for anyone involved in, or on the edges of, politics. For Lotta, at the age of twenty-eight, it was a brutal coming-of-age politically.

Not only was she writing hectically for the papers in the endangered Petite Entente; she was also often serving as an interpreter in the gruelling meetings between Czechoslovak officials and the German minority groups, which fell increasingly under the sway of the Nazi leader Konrad Henlein and raised their demands for autonomy beyond any reach of compromise. She belonged to no political party, but her own views were plain. The strong stand in mid-May, when the Czechoslovak government ordered partial mobilization of its forces to counter German troop movements, when the British and French governments warned Hitler of the danger of general war, and when the French, supported by the Russians, reaffirmed their 1935 promise of immediate aid to Czechoslovakia — this, in her view, was the only way to save the peace.

But the events of the next four months were infinitely distressing. Hitler recovered from his humiliation and redrafted directives for Operation Green ("It is my unalterable decision to smash Czechoslovakia by military action in the near future"), and Britain and France slithered into appeasement. On the day of Munich she listened in tears to President Beneš's pathetic farewell speech, as he announced the surrender of 28,500 square kilometers of territory, including Czechoslovakia's main system of fortifications, and his own departure into exile. That very afternoon her latest article in *L'Indépendance Roumaine* was still pleading for an independent Czechoslovakia.

As she wrote later: "A world broke within me: my beliefs in international cooperation, in treaties signed by World Powers..."

Several officials in the Department of Foreign Affairs advised her to leave the country. They knew it was only a matter of weeks or months before Hitler's troops occupied all of Czechoslovakia, and she was undoubtedly on a German list of unfriendly journalists. After some hesitation, she went to the French consul in Prague, got a visitor's visa for France, and managed to book a flight to Paris amid the stream of Czechoslovaks already fleeing their homeland.

It was a different Paris from the one she had loved — or

maybe she had changed the more. She registered for a literature course at the University of Paris, but she found the whole atmosphere in the capital pro-Munich and collaborationist, and herself without close friends. So she obtained a month's visa for Belgium and left for Brussels where friends from her student days in Paris welcomed her.

Refugee through France

German troops motored into Prague on 15 March, the Ides of March. By then Lilly had destroyed all the newspaper clippings, documents, and articles that Lotta had left behind and that could possibly be incriminating. "I had only one coal-fire stove in the bathroom," she says, "and there I burned her papers. It took me days!"

Lotta herself went to live at the Brussels house in Rue de Neufchatel of René Golstein, who was then an advocate in the Court of Appeal and also a published poet and novelist. She helped him with his work and she also found a part-time job as secretary to Betty Barzin, the Brussels correspondent of *Time-Life*. Through Golstein's intercession she was granted refugee status, and through work with Mme Barzin she acquired a press pass that allowed her to leave and reenter Belgium. It was about this time that she began exclusively using the Slavic version of her surname – Hitschmanova, rather than Hitschmann – in a patriotic move to show her distaste of things German.

She also began writing for the Belgian periodical *Le Flambeau*, but she was unhappy and frustrated in finding it difficult to rouse the Belgians to the danger of war approaching their country, even after the German invasion of Poland in September 1939 and the declaration of war by France and Britain. The Belgians chose to believe that they, so battered in the First World War, would somehow be spared the blasts of the gathering storm.

At dawn on 10 May 1940, German aircraft attacked Brussels, and the German Army punched its way westward into Holland, Belgium, and France with eighty-nine divisions headed by at least a thousand heavy tanks. That first dawn attack on the sleeping city was traumatic. In Lotta's own words: "Crushing, tumbling walls and houses...contradictory instructions over the radio...desperate, ghastly faces in the street...and already the decision taken by an entire nation: we shall not undergo the horrors of a German occupation…this time they will find an empty land."

A stream of refugees soon began moving westward, by car and by cart, on bicycle and on foot. The roads became blocked and the stream sluggish. With René Golstein, Lotta joined it on 16 May in a small car, advancing a few kilometers a day, sleeping on the road at night, waiting to cross the border into a country she hoped would resist. She remembers an incident just short of the French frontier. The line of cars was halted inexplicably, and people were starting to shout and protest as a cart moved by, pulled by a pair of oxen. Bedding was piled high on the cart, and she could see the pale face of a young woman above it. Down the line of waiting cars a sentence of explanation was passed – "She's giving birth" – and there was a sudden, solemn silence. New life in the midst of despair and destruction; it was an unforgettable moment.

The Belgian army surrendered on 27 May, but by then Lotta was well across the border into northern France, its green summertime pastures offering an atmosphere of peace. This soon evaporated. There was a shortage of gasoline, and of night lodgings. And the German aircraft stepped up their low-flying attacks on the roads crowded with refugees. She wrote later that she would "never forget the cries of little children, frightened to death by the machine-gunning squadrons…children crying because no more bread and milk was left in village shops…the sinister voice of the [German] radio announcer reading bulletins of new Nazi victories…and the faces of French people, helpless, unbelieving, hoping for a miracle to happen…"

Paris itself was no place of refuge. She had had the foresight in February to send ahead a large suitcase containing a coat, two dresses, and shoes; and this she was able to recover. She also managed, on 29 May, to obtain a loyalty certificate from Dr. Hubert Ripka, the director of information of the Czechoslovak National Committee, then based in Paris. Paris fell to the Germans on 10 June, and by then she was nearly four hundred kilometers to the south, in Limoges.

Lotta spent nearly three weeks in Limoges, taking the place of an Austrian professor who had been teaching German at the College Fenelon and who had fled further south. The old city was in chaos, crowded with refugees of many nationalities. At night they slept in parks and gardens and on the verandahs of hotels. She remembers how a whole family was making a home for themselves in a hearse, near the Municipal Theatre.

She drove on southwest to Bordeaux and then to Bayonne, hoping to board a ship for Britain where the Czechoslovak government had taken refuge. She hoped that her Red Cross nursing diploma might gain her a berth. But the captains of any boats chartered for Britain were under strict orders to take only soldiers, and no women. This may have proved fortunate for her because one of the ships she tried hard to board was sunk by a German submarine while still in French waters.

All the exit points from France were closing. On 21 June Hitler came to the forest of Compiègne, where Marshal Foch had dictated peace terms to the Germans in 1918, and dictated his own terms of surrender to the French army commander. The Pétain-Weygand government, which had retreated to Bordeaux, capitulated. The terms left half of France, in the south and southeast, unoccupied and under the control of the Pétain government which set itself up in Vichy. But the Germans made sure that the occupied zone would include the whole Atlantic coast to the Spanish border, and also demanded that any anti-Nazi German refugees found anywhere in France should be turned in.

In the last week of June, Lotta tried to cross the border into Spain on foot, ahead of the Nazi arrival at the little village of St. Jean Pied de Port. But both the French and Spanish police stopped her, and the French police took her back to the gendarmerie building. She had carefully mailed on, to a poste restante address in Lisbon, all her certificates and letters of recommendation, and had destroyed any papers connecting her with journalism. The French police saw only her Czechoslovak passport and said they owed a debt to her country because of Munich. They warned her that the German troops were due to arrive the next day, but promised they would show her the way to Pau, across the new demarcation line. She spent a sleepless night in the police station, but they were as good as their word and guided her to Pau, in the foothills of the Pyrenees.

She stayed with a peasant woman in a farmhouse near Pau for two weeks, but no means of escape to Portugal offered itself. So she moved on to Marseilles, where the Czechoslovak consulate officials told her the Vichy authorities had stopped issuing exit permits. She tried a more devious route, buying first a visa for the Dutch East Indies for two hundred francs on the black market, then queuing for days for a Portuguese and Spanish transit visa. The final obstacle was a French exit visa. At the Prefecture, she was told to write directly to Vichy, where all Czechoslovak cases were examined individually. But that night, for the first time, armed police surrounded blocks of houses and arrested foreigners without valid papers. *Le Petit Marseillais* carried a notice the next day that refugee women and children would be sent to special camps for "protection." Lotta at once decided it would be folly, or else the swiftest way to a concentration camp, if she applied to Vichy for an exit permit.

Under the Vichy regime

At this point, when she was in despair, her Belgian friend wrote inviting her to move to Lourmarin, a little village near Avignon, in the beautiful Provence countryside. She found a job there, at five hundred francs a month, as a librarian for the Fondation Laurent-Vibert in the old Chateau Bastides. Her job was to catalogue the foundation's collection of fifteen thousand volumes, which belonged to the arts department of the University of Aix-en-Provence. She stayed there almost a year, until June 1941, and has called it a mortifying time. She lived in a boarding house that was run by enthusiastic supporters of old Marshal Pétain and the Vichy regime. The only consolation was that her landlady provided some protection against too many inquiries from the mayor and other officials – until the woman finally gave her notice, saying food was short.

She went to Seyssins, near Grenoble, where her old literary friend from Paris, André Mary, had a house, and stayed there several weeks. But by August 1941 she was back in Marseilles, trying to persuade the American consul to give her an emergency visa. While at Lourmarin she had spent a good part of her salary in cables to friends in New York about visas (the Skallers, among others, were there by then), but nothing had happened – she found out later than none of the cables ever arrived. The consul himself refused her request, saying that the state department had laid down the policy in order to protect any relatives left behind in German-occupied countries! She thought the reason absurd and the consul rude beyond description. Her fortunes were at low ebb; in Marseilles she had already sold all her remaining jewelry, except a pearl necklace her mother had given her at her matriculation.

But the tide turned quickly. Another refugee saw her look of despair, scribbled an address on some paper and said: "Go to them. Maybe they can intervene for you." The slip of paper read: "International Migration Service, 4 Rue Stanislas Torrents." Lotta found her way there and was sitting in a crowded waiting room when an elderly woman put her head out of the inner office and asked: "Does anyone here know French, English, and German?" Lotta was the only one to reply. In a few minutes she was translating for the director, Dr. Marie Long-Landry, a conversation with a German refugee and later drafting a cable in English to New York.

The next day she returned to hear that her request for an American visa had again been refused, but that Mme. Long-Landry badly needed a secretary-interpreter who was also fluent in Czech and Spanish. Within a month she had an official work permit (classified as an industrial worker) from Vichy, and for the first time in years she was able to forget much of her own pain by helping others.

She worked for the Service Social d'Aide aux Emigrants (IMS was its American affiliate) for five months at the tolerable salary of fifteen hundred francs a month. The work was hectic, but satisfying. She was compiling dossiers on refugees who had been drafted to labor battalions or to the internment camps at Gurs, Recebedou, Rivesaltes, and elsewhere; arguing with the Prefecture to obtain their release; pleading with the American consul for overseas visas; organizing food packages for those trapped in the camps on a desperately low diet. The Jewish refugees were probably in direst straits, although Spanish Loyalists had suffered the longest. But the SSAE, like most other agencies, tried to help all refugees, whatever their nationality or creed. All had, wrote Lotta, "one big cry on their faces: save us, help us leave this inferno of Europe. We want to live, and here we shall die."

She was living on the fifth floor of the small Hotel Pavillon with friends from the SSAE, among them the outgoing Marie-Thérèse Schinz who remembers companionable times drinking coffee and smoking endlessly. But there were dark hours: anxiety that the little hotel would be invaded by Gestapo agents checking papers and nationalities; the worry every month when her documents had to be presented at the Prefecture for extension; chilblains and loneliness; and a debilitating diet of beetroot and carrots.

One lunch hour, after queuing in the market, Lotta fainted from fatigue and hunger in the street on her way back to the office. She recovered consciousness to find blood running from her mouth and hands, her head aching, and one of her teeth broken. She struggled to the medical clinic that she knew the Unitarian Service Committee had recently started at 25 rue d'Italie; and there a doctor bandaged her up, gave her a tetanus injection and a tonic, and recommended a few days' rest.

It was her first contact with the USC. When, in January 1942, she was appointed liaison officer with the Czechoslovak relief agency, Centre d'Aide Tsechoslovaque, she came to know the USC and other agencies better. By stages over the next four years, her collapse that lunch hour in the Marseilles street led to her life's major work.

Initiatives from Boston

We should now go back a few years to trace the work of the Boston-based Unitarian Service Committee in Europe.

The USC was officially established at a meeting of the board of the American Unitarian Association (AUA) in Boston on 24 May 1940. But it had really been in existence since the day of Munich. Dr. Robert Dexter, who was then in charge of the AUA's social responsibility section, had made a lecture tour of Czechoslovakia and met Unitarian ministers there in 1937. He felt the capitulation of Munich as a personal blow and argued that they "had an obligation to aid our friends who had been so betrayed." With AUA blessing he visited Prague in December 1938, with a representative of the American Friends Service Committee, to assess the specific needs of the thousands of refugees who had fled to Moravia and Bohemia from the Sudetenland, Germany, and Austria. He came back with a government list of refugees and the idea for a Unitarian service committee based on the Quaker model.

The AUA quickly raised funds to send another minister, Waitstill Sharp from Wellesley Hills, Massachusetts, and his wife, Martha, as commissioners to Czechoslovakia in February 1939, to provide relief to refugees and to help in the emigration of intellectuals and others who were likely targets of the Nazis. They worked out of Prague for six hectic months, completing application forms for thirty-five hundred families seeking to emigrate to the United States and elsewhere, and traveling to London, Paris, and Geneva to secure job offers and sponsors for them. There were dangerous missions, as when Martha escorted thirty-five emigrants across Germany and Holland to England. They were supposedly domestic workers and dependents traveling to new jobs, but among them were the Prague correspondents of *United Press* and *Associated Press*. She finally left Czechoslovakia on 15 August, the day German troops started moving eastward to the Polish border.

In June 1940 the Sharps returned to do similar work in southern France. Waitstill was soon involved in a Scarlet Pimpernel adventure, spiriting the German novelist Lion Feuchtwanger out of an internment camp near Marseilles and over a Pyrenean trail at night. From Lisbon Martha organized a freight-car load of milk for children in Basque villages around Pau.[1] And in October the Reverend Charles Joy, a Boston-born minister and editor (he later published an anthology of Albert Schweitzer's writings), set up a USC emigration office in Lisbon, working out of a small room in the Hotel Metropol. In March 1941 he opened a USC headquarters in Marseilles and hired Noel and Herta Field to run it.

Under them a medical clinic was started four months later, and the doctors, dentists, and part-time specialists were soon doing remarkable work in cramped quarters, particularly for children suffering from consumption, tuberculosis, and rickets. The clinic was soon able to tell of many young lives saved and transformed, and by mid-1942 Dr. Joy was reporting that it had "probably the best-stocked pharmacy in all France today," with most of its supplies donated by the International Red Cross.

This was only part of the work of the medical director, Dr. René Zimmer, who himself was a refugee from Alsace. For he was greatly concerned about the appalling conditions in the internment (or concentration) camps which the Vichy government had set up for some twenty-nine thousand foreigners: fifteen thousand were Spanish Loyalists, eight thousand were

---

[1]Waitstill Sharp and Martha Sharp Cogan gave a discreet account of these and other adventures in the 1941 USC booklet *Journey to Freedom*, and elaborated on them in taped interviews with Ghanda Di Figlia in 1978-79.

German refugees, and the rest were from Poland, Czechoslovakia, and a dozen other countries. One of the worst camps was at Gurs in the Pyrenees south of Pau, where Jewish refugees were crowded in among aged people who had been removed from workhouses. The USC helped organize some drainage and also installed windows in the barrack buildings, and these measures brought the death rate down sharply. Other camps – Argelès-sur-mer and Rivesaltes among them – were on the windswept coastal plain near Perpignan; there were twenty-five hundred children held at Rivesaltes. At Noe and Recebedou camps near Toulouse there were many tubercular patients, segregated behind barbed wire.

Dr. Zimmer used to visit these camps as often as possible, delivering medical supplies himself. And by mid-1942 the USC was employing about thirty men and women to work in the camps, establishing local clinics, distributing food packages, providing farm tools and seeds. A sixty-bed hospital was set up in Toulouse, in cooperation with the government. But the winter of 1941-42 brought on a desperate situation, with an increasing number of deaths from what Dr. Zimmer called "la maladie de la faim," an epidemic of starvation. He persuaded the French inspector-general of the camps to let an investigating team of doctors from three agencies – the USC, the Swiss Red Cross Children's Aid, and the Jewish Children's Aid Society – do a thorough study of malnutrition, and by the early summer of 1942 the doctors had examined nine thousand internees and written a detailed report.

It was ready at just the time that Lotta Hitschmanova was leaving Marseilles for Lisbon, and she was given a copy of this remarkable report to bring to the USC headquarters in Boston.

Lisbon and the wider world

We had left Lotta in Marseilles, as she moved to work for the Centre d'Aide Tsechoslovaque in January 1942. Under the young director, Karel Dubina, her main job was to set up a school for Czechoslovak children who had been liberated from concentration camps in Vichy, France. This brought her into closer contact with the Quakers, from whom she got food for the children, and with the USC medical clinic, where cases of malnutrition were treated. It was a busy and positive time.

One day she received a brief cable: "Hitschmanova Canadian duration visa granted. Apply American transit visa." Ottawa had granted the visa by Order-in-Council, a special ministerial decision made on the recommendation of the Czechoslovak Government in London. "Duration" meant "landed for the duration of the war," after which her status would presumably be reviewed.

Her first reaction, she confessed in a note written in 1944, was of disappointment that she had not obtained an American visa: "I felt sorry not to join my friends in the States, and was afraid of leaving for a country that was entirely unknown to me. I also thought that I would be of no use to our refugees in Canada, and that I could make much propaganda in New York, by simply telling the tragic situation I had seen from so near, the last two years..."

It took three months, with several agencies working on her behalf, to obtain the American, Spanish, and Portuguese transit visas, but they were ready by the end of April. There were some sad-sweet farewells to make of good friends. Her guest-book frivolously records her friends' comments on a "sumptuous lunch" she prepared on 22 March at her little hotel, renamed "Restaurant du Pavillon:" among the six meatless courses were Beetroot hors d'oeuvre, Fondu d'épinard à la Praguoise, La carotte à la Long (in honor of her old SSAE director) and real Gruyère cheese. And a month later, her close friend Marie-Thérèse wrote of her departure: "It is the first step towards a better future, towards days of joy and hope." Lotta left Marseilles for Lisbon on 29 April to find passage on a boat leaving for New York, but also to organize from Lisbon an "expedition" of clothing, food, and medical supplies for Belgian, Czechoslovak, and Polish refugees still in French camps.

She found Lisbon beautiful and "strangely oriental." Charles Joy, then the European commissioner of the USC, let her use his office for sixteen days while she set about trying to get export licences for a supply of everything from sardines to shoes, to be sent to Marseilles through the Red Cross. (She ran into roadblocks in the Portuguese bureaucracy and tried to organize a similar shipment later from Montreal.) Dr. Joy was the first American with whom she had worked closely, and the bad impression she had gained from the U.S. Consulate in Marseilles was dissolved. "He was a revelation to me...I have for him unstinting admiration and respect."

Any agency dealing with emigration in 1942 had to face a rapidly shifting picture. In quick succession, Cuba canceled all visas from German-occupied countries, Jamaica refused to take seventy-two Austrians who had visas, and Spain suddenly refused to allow men between eighteen and thirty to cross from France. The Joint Distribution Committee, a coordinating body, was chartering old Portuguese cargo boats – the *Serpa Pinto, Nyassa,* and *Guiné* – for different destinations: Havana, Mexico, New York. But the number of refugees remaining in Portugal was drying up. Dr. Joy warned Lotta that the committee might not be chartering any more boats after the next voyage of the *Guiné* in late May. So she had to give up her efforts to send supplies to Marseilles and prepare to leave the country.

Before then, there were lighter moments in Lisbon, as Lotta was introduced to new manners. She wrote in a short memoir in 1944:

> ...Then I met Charles Wood, from the Quakers. I could hardly understand his English, and at breakfast the first morning in Lisbon in that luxurious hotel, I couldn't make out why he was knocking my chair into my knees, when I wanted to get seated.
>
> Another strange *faux pas* occurred the following Sunday when Mr. and Mrs. Howard Kershaw had asked me to a Quaker tea. I entered the saloon and went from one old lady to the other, trying to shake hands with each of them. Poor old ladies, they were more startled than I was (not to get any response to my outstretched hand and were unable to find out what this strange girl wanted from them!)

The long voyage

The voyage on the SS *Guiné* was unforgettable for its discomfort – and for a dramatic adventure toward the end.

She was a 2,402 metric ton twin-screw steamer, built in Middlesborough in 1905, and designed for carrying bananas rather than passengers. On this voyage she transported 500 refugees of many nationalities, including 250 Spanish Loyalists. The journey to New York took forty-six days, and the boat went via Casablanca, Bermuda, and Mexico. For the men, women, and children aboard, wrote Lotta, "there was not the least bit of privacy or comfort. And still, to those who had been released from concentration camps the day before, the cots filled with vermin seemed luxury and the fatty monotonous diet of the Portuguese cook the most exquisite meal ever eaten…"

For one passenger, an elderly Austrian lawyer, it was also his last. He celebrated too well on the first evening of his release from a labor battalion, taking three helpings of the heavy food; early the next morning he had a heart attack and died. There were other crises: water ran short, a baby was born under the most unhygienic circumstances, an epidemic of measles spread among the children, more and more passengers got seasick. "But," wrote Lotta, "in the evenings the air was filled with the songs of many lands."

Lotta herself was kept busy. One agency had asked her to carry a million French francs to its North African office in Casablanca. Also, there were interesting and attractive companions, including a thirty-seven-year-old Spanish Loyalist commandant just released from a concentration camp in Morocco. Manuel Casanueva, grandson of a general and a lawyer until he was swept up into the civil war and three times wounded, was also a painter, and he did a charming sketch of a Bermuda harbor scene in her guest-book. He left the *Guiné* at Vera Cruz and spent many frustrating months in Mexico trying to enlist in the Free French forces. He wrote to her sardonically of "going to the movies where I am contemplating the war actualities sitting in a comfortable arm-chair."

She was also reading the Zimmer Report on malnutrition among nine thousand internees in the camps of Vichy, France, which she had been asked to carry to the USC in Boston. It was the first such study done in Europe, and Dr. Zimmer compared the internees' condition of starvation with those witnessed during famines in China. Many patients had difficulty in standing erect and were subject to vertigo. Their skin was discolored from anemia. He concluded that about forty-five hundred people in the camps needed not only supplementary rations but also curative treatment of vitamin pills and other medical products. He included dietetic menus that had been established at Gurs and Rivesaltes for the worst cases.

The report was recognized as an important study and was edited and published in the *New England Journal of Medicine* in 1943. Meanwhile, Lotta wrote from Bermuda to Charles Joy in Lisbon:

You know that I was close to your service at Marseilles, but I never suspected the full amplitude and importance of the work which you are accomplishing under such difficult conditions. I am so proud to be taking this precious document to America...For my part, I have decided to put myself entirely at Dr. Dexter's disposition and I will be useful to him [Dexter was then USC executive director]. I have taken some rough notes while studying the report, and I shall ask permission to prepare several articles for publication.

Indeed, a report inspired by her appeared in the *Montreal Daily Star* on 3 October 1942.

Toward the end of the voyage, on the last leg from Vera Cruz to New York, came high drama. In Lotta's words:

One day, near the Mexican shores of the United States, an American air patrol discovered a Nazi submarine hiding under the SS *Guiné*. By radio messages, the Portuguese captain was invited to go ashore, but he refused. There was great excitement on board...Suddenly, the airplane started to machine-gun the water all around the cargo boat, without actually hitting it. Panic broke out on the boat, and desperate cries came from all parts. After a few hours, the excitement slowed down, when American sailors took over the boat and the pro-Nazi captain and his crew were put under arrest. They had tried to protect an enemy submarine in American waters, a few miles only from the shore.

Montreal and censorship

The *Guiné* arrived at New York harbor on 2 July, and Lotta and other passengers had to spend two days in immigration procedures on Ellis Island, sharing a dormitory with German civilian internees. She went to Boston to hand over the Zimmer Report and then, on 22 July, reached Montreal. She has said she arrived "exhausted, with a feeling of absolute solitude in an entirely strange country...I came with $60 in my pocket. I had an unpronounceable name. I weighed less than 100 lbs, and I was completely lost."

She was not lost for long. On her fourth day in Canada she was already at work, as a secretary dealing with French and English correspondence for Wood Lumber, a Montreal firm run by a Czechoslovak refugee who had known her parents in Prague. She worked there for three months while sorting out other job possibilities that suited better her strong desire to help the war effort, and meanwhile trying to organize relief supplies to Marseilles by visiting the Red Cross and other agencies on her lunch hour. Within two weeks she applied for the job of postal censor in Ottawa and took an examination in German. Then, before she heard the outcome, she applied to join the Royal Canadian Air Force. But word came shortly that she had been accepted as a postal censor in the Department of War Services, and she moved to Ottawa in October 1942.

She had already made some influential friends. One of them was Marius Barbeau, for many years Canada's leading folklorist who was then working at the National Museum. He noticed her standing alone at a party in Montreal and at once asked her who she was. They had much in common, including years at the Sorbonne and a love of literature – and laughter. He helped her in many contacts in those first years, and they remained good friends until his death in 1969 at the age of eighty-six. Another welcoming figure was Dr. Frantisek Pavlasek, the Czechoslovakian minister to Canada.

The censorship department had originally been set up in Ottawa to intercept the incoming mail to German prisoners-of-war and to scan their outgoing letters, mainly to gather information for intelligence purposes in Canada and Britain. It was linked to a military intelligence group in Bermuda through an inner circle of highly trained Englishwomen based in Ottawa. The censors were first recruited among German-speaking Poles, White Russians, and Czechoslovaks, as well as graduates of Canadian universities; later they were joined by German refugees released from internment. The directorate was divided into seven sections, related to the different elements of the German forces, and housed in No. 8 Temporary Building, near Dow's Lake. There were more than four hundred people working there at a peak period of the war.

Edgar Sarton, who worked in the section dealing with Merchant Navy prisoners, remembers it as very intense work, with seven or eight hours a day spent in concentrated study of letters, copying significant quotations in German on an information slip with an examiner's note appended. He had several Czechoslovaks in his section, but Lotta, who worked in the Army section, did not come to talk to them or go partying with the group. "She led her own life. She had other fish to fry," he says. But people noticed her, even in a room of two hundred people. "Always well dressed, and with that flaming red hair, like a flag."

She certainly did have other fish to fry. From December 1942 she was secretary of the Ottawa chapter of the Czechoslovakian National Alliance, and seized every opportunity to bring her homeland's cause before the Canadian public and to raise money for the Czechoslovakian War Services in London.

A climax to these efforts came in November 1943, the twenty-fifth anniversary of the Czechoslovak Republic. There was an exhibition of paintings by twenty Czechoslovak artists at the National Gallery; a piano concert in the Technical School auditorium by Rudolf Firkusny playing the works of several Czechoslovakian composers from Jiri Benda to Bohuslav Martinu; and finally, a grand bazaar and folklore exhibition in St. Andrew's Church with costumes and embroideries gathered from all over North America. Princess Alice, wife of the governor general, came to all these functions. Senator Cairine Wilson, who among many other activities had helped form the Canadian National Committee on Refugees, headed the planning committee. And Lotta, dressed in a hand-embroidered costume, celebrated by joining seven other women in the *Beseda* folkdance.

She was also busy broadcasting and writing. She gave a series of fifteen-minute radio talks in French on Czechoslovakian customs and culture over CKCH in Ottawa-Hull. Never one to waste anything, Lotta reworked her material for use on Uncle Ray's children's page in the *Ottawa Citizen*. And there were several film evenings at the National Museum, which she introduced.

She also became a central figure in the United Nations group that was formed in 1942, on the initiative of Irene Arnould, by the Canadian Women's Committee on International Relations. It was a high-powered group which held monthly meetings and drew a fair-sized audience to hear panels of speakers give prepared talks on weighty subjects: Countess Marie Potulika of Poland leading discussion on "Resistance in Occupied Countries," and Lotta herself chairing an evening on "Russia's Contribution to the Present War." The group plunged bravely into controversial issues. Aline Chalufour of France needed all her diplomatic skills as moderator during an evening on "Empires, Dominions, Colonies," when Colonel Dypenryxh was decidedly defensive about the Belgian Congo where he had commanded some troops in 1911 ("the Belgians did not stop the clock in Africa"). They were clearly stimulating occasions and they enabled Lotta to make a number of influential people more sensitive to the problems of her homeland.

For all this activity, they were months of personal loneliness. She was staying with a friendly landlady, Mrs. Milk, at 269 Breezehill and met interesting people at supper parties who asked her about her time in Europe. On the eve of her thirty-third birthday in November 1942, she was introduced to the King's Printer, Edmond Cloutier ("the high aristocracy of French Canada"), who got her talking about the voyage of the *Guiné*. That evening she bought herself a pale red cyclamen and thought sadly of all the earlier birthdays in Europe when friends and flowers surrounded her. And that Christmas she found the kind invitations to festive meals hard to reconcile with her memories of starving Europe, about which she still had nightmares. So she hurried away to copy documents about a project for the relief of European children that she and Dr. Marguerite Thibert, a Frenchwoman working with the International Labour Organization in Montreal, were preparing for the International Red Cross.

This was an impressive document,[2] its fifty-five pages full of tables detailing the rations that children were receiving in different countries of Occupied Europe, the rise in infant mortality rates (especially in Poland), and the average height and weight (by years) of two hundred French children who had been allowed into Switzerland compared with normal sizes — they were 4.6 kilograms lighter and 8.4 centimeters shorter. Their proposal was well received, and they were asked to develop it further with staff of the Canadian Red Cross Society.

Lotta was also working on two books about Czechoslovakia. One, called "Holidays in Czechoslovakia," was a children's book about customs at Easter, Christmas and other seasons. The other, "Happy Days in Prague," was a collection of a dozen vignettes of scenes and characters she had known. They show a gift of sharp observation and humor: Janda, the beggarman of Ruzova, whose daughter brings him spicy soup and who has collected enough coins to buy three buildings; the bookseller who despises the public and only displays trash in his window, while he reads Plato sitting on a ladder; and Mme Novotna the florist, who looks on her flowers "as incense, as the gift of God" and keeps chrysanthemums back for her most discerning customers.

---

[2] *Save the Children:* project of an international scheme of relief for European children victims of the war. January 1943 (unpublished).

Lilly, with whom Lotta had reestablished contact after making widespread inquiries around embassies and consulates, sent a set of sketches from Palestine to illustrate the book. Marius Barbeau found these "little tableaus" enchanting and wrote recommending the book to several publishers. But it was a time of severe paper shortage, and publishers were unwilling to take risks with a new author.

UNRRA and back

In January 1944, at Mme Thibert's suggestion, Lotta applied for a job with the United Nations Relief and Rehabilitation Administration (UNRRA) in Washington. She heard nothing until May, when she was suddenly offered the post of secretary to the director of the Industrial Reconstruction division at a salary of U.S. twenty-eight hundred dollars a year. Antony Fried was a former director of the Skoda works in Czechoslovakia, and she anticipated a lively partnership. But he left UNRRA soon after her arrival, and she was unhappy with his replacement, describing her job as being merely that of "a well-paid telephone operator," while she fretted about the incompetence and rivalry among senior staff.

She was transferred to the public relations department and offered an eventual posting in Europe – possibly in Yugoslavia – and finally given the position of field officer in the Western European Reserve. However, she was thoroughly dissatisfied with UNRRA, as were many other Canadians, including Mike Pearson.[3] Moreover, she had no assurance that she would be admitted to Canada or the United States after an UNRRA assignment overseas. So, in mid-September she took three months' unpaid leave and returned to her lower-paid job in Ottawa as a postal censor.

Back in Canada, she resigned from UNRRA and wrote to Charles Joy, who had become executive director of the USC in Boston; and in November she sent him a detailed proposal for postwar relief activity in Czechoslovakia. It began with a sharp

---

[3]See John Holmes, *The Shaping of the Peace*, University of Toronto Press, Toronto: 1979, pp. 34-104. UNRRA was wound up in 1947, and other organizations, including UNICEF and the International Refugee Organization, took over its functions.

criticism of UNRRA's apparent plan to send mostly American staff to European countries, where they would know neither the language nor the conditions. She suggested that it was inevitable that UNRRA would cede an increasing role to those agencies with experience in relief work, like the USC in Marseilles. She foresaw that Czechoslovakia would be "the crossing area of millions of people whom Nazi madness has displaced to East Europe." These millions would not wait for orderly UNRRA repatriation, but would trek through the mountain passes between Poland and Czechoslovakia. So she proposed three reception centers in Czechoslovakia, with dormitories and canteens for overnight shelter, first aid, and, if possible, a "family service" clearinghouse of information to locate relatives.

It was a significant document, but Dr. Joy replied that such work was "manifestly one of UNRRA's major responsibilities." Lotta was sceptical and disappointed; but the exchange led, in May 1945, to an offer by the USC to her to become its future representative in Czechoslovakia.

Her unhappy time at UNRRA moved her to appreciate Canada more. She wrote to a Czechoslovak friend in London that Canada was "the friendliest country in the world."[4] She was warmly welcomed back by her colleagues in the censorship directorate, particularly Marjorie Mader, a teacher from Nova Scotia, and Robert McBroom who had been a pianist in Montreal. The three had often relaxed over macaroni and cheese in their apartments. Marjorie recalls: "We were all poor, but Lotta was the poorest. I remember she kept her staple foods in orange crates with little curtains, and used to complain that I used too much soap in washing up."

Lotta signed up for the course on "The Human Geography of North America," which Marius Barbeau gave during the winter of 1944-45 at the University of Ottawa, and she enjoyed the sidelights shed on the Canadian character when she and her professor ate at an Ottawa hotel:

> Every time we have dinner at the Alexandra, I must smile. The same little incident occurs inevitably. In the lobby of the hotel there is a small checkroom where guests may dispose of their coats. Before we enter the dining room M.B. will go and place his overcoat there. He does not pay any attention to the big sign declining all

---

[4]Letter to Ida Young, 3 July 1944.

responsibility for lost objects – his Canadian confidence in the neighbour's honesty and his eternal optimism prevail. It would not even come to his mind that there might be a danger of not finding the coat again, an hour later. Happy people!

She was particularly pleased with the outcome of an interview with the director of immigration, Mr. A.L. Jolliffe, in November 1944. Beforehand, she was in a nervous state, after reading in Arthur Koestler's "Scum of the Earth" about foreigners lining up uneasily in a dusty Paris prefecture. She was worried that her special duration visa for Canada might be considered to expire when the war ended in Europe. But Mr. Jolliffe assured her it would last until the Japanese war was over, and after that she could apply for an immigration visa. "But I suppose you don't know yet what you're going to do yourself?" Lotta recorded in a memoir: "Such an intelligent, human remark...I felt so relieved and grateful. Good, good country where strangers are treated as human beings, with respect and kindness. If I were a Canadian, I would feel very proud. I know why Canada is the only country whose citizenship I would accept, if I could not go back home."

War's end, new home

As the Allied armies advanced across Europe, Lotta picked up the threads of old friendships, with a shuttle of correspondence across the Atlantic: to Marie-Thérèse Schinz, who had remained in Marseilles after the Germans occupied southern France in November 1942; to Dr. Marie Long-Landry, back in Paris; to René Golstein, now a major in the Belgian forces and busy preparing evidence for the war crimes trial that would take place in Nuremberg; to André Mary, recalling the café conversations in Paris as he patiently explained some literary turn of mind; and to Lilly, still having a hard time in Haifa in a dressmaker's job.

But there was no definite news of their parents. Lotta had known for some time that they had been taken to Terezin, a fortress town sixty-five kilometers from Prague that had been built in 1780 on the river Ohre by the Austrian Emperor Joseph II (and named for his mother, Maria Theresa). The Nazis, it was known, had turned the small garrison town into a swollen ghetto that was a collection center from which many were deported to Poland.

The full story of Terezin only emerged later, of course: how deportation meant the Auschwitz gas chambers; how 112,000 had died either in Terezin or after deportation; how Czechoslovak painters such as Bedrich Fritta and Otto Ungar had immortalized the ghastly experience before their deaths; how Rafael Schacter had conducted an amazing performance of Verdi's Requiem in front of Adolf Eichmann; and how the Germans had obscenely embellished the ghetto for a visit by a Swedish Red Cross commission and for a propaganda film. But Lotta did hear, in February 1945, that 1,200 of the older prisoners were being transported to Switzerland (in a cynical move designed to suggest to the Allies that such camps or ghettos were almost humanely run). She nursed the hope that her parents would survive.

In the summer of 1945 she was busy making plans for a Canadian section of the Unitarian Service Committee, which the next chapter will describe. But she was applying for several other jobs, foreseeing that the censorship directorate would be dissolved as soon as the war in Europe ended. (In fact, it closed in September.) She wrote to friends that she had five job offers. One was to work in Paris for the National Film Board of Canada. Another was the offer from the USC in Boston to spend about six months setting up a Canadian committee, and then to go home to Czechoslovakia to work on projects for the rehabilitation of children. She liked that prospect best, for she was eager to return home.

Then, in July 1945, direct communications were opened with Prague, and she cabled to a woman who her mother had long ago said would always have word of her and of Max. The saddest of telegrams came back. Lotta was desolated, although an escape to an enchanting part of Quebec, in the Ile d'Orléans, for a short holiday was some solace. She did not tell her desperate news to Canadian friends, because she could not bear their pity. But to a woman friend in Europe, she wrote in August: "If I tell you that nobody is waiting for me any longer, that I have lost the beings who are most dear to me, you will measure my despair, for you have the same sorrow. There's only one thing: to work, so that their sacrifice may not be in vain."

And to Marie-Thérèse, she wrote on the first day of 1946: "Because of my parents' tragic death, and unforgettable memories attached to Prague, I haven't any longer any haste to return to my country."

By then, Lotta Hitschmanova had been organizing the USC in Canada full time for nearly three months. She had been granted permanent residence in mid-December. Her decision was made; Canada was now her home.

CHAPTER 3

Getting Started

Launching USC Canada

FOUR PEOPLE ATTENDED the first meeting, on 10 June 1945, of the Ottawa committee that was soon to represent the other churches as the Unitarian Service Committee of Canada. They had been appointed by the parish board of the Church of our Father at Elgin and Lewis streets in Ottawa, and their job was to discuss the organization of a national committee.

The four got briskly down to business. Dr. Lotta, as chairman, was requested to write to the five other Unitarian churches in Canada "to secure their adherence as branches of a national organization." And, after she had described the difficulties of registering the committee under the National War Services Act, Elsie Borgford, as vice-chairman (and wife of the minister), suggested that she invite Senator Cairine Wilson, who was not a Unitarian, to act as honorary chairman. It was correctly assumed that Canada's first woman senator would ease their passage through the bureaucracy. Helen Sprague, as treasurer, was asked to tackle the customs department about importing promotional brochures printed in Boston. And Ronnie Whyte, son of a prominent firm of stationers, took on the role of secretary and began recording, in a little ledger book with green covers, the minutes of the twenty meetings held in the next three years.

At their second meeting two weeks later, the basic objective of the committee was agreed upon and noted: "The relief of distressed people, especially children, in France and Czechoslovakia, and help in their rehabilitation."

At the third meeting a work program was outlined: the collection of clothing, to start in January 1946; the shipment of medical supplies and "utility kits," both toilet and educational, for European schoolchildren from Canadian children; a foster parent scheme and the financial support of convalescent homes for children.

These ideas were not new; they had been discussed in correspondence between Dr. Lotta and the Unitarians in Boston since the beginning of 1945. Nor indeed was the collection and shipment of clothing an invention of the USC or other agencies in the last months of the war. Canadians had, at their own individual expense, begun mailing clothes to relatives in Britain in 1940. The following year, the women running the Central Volunteer Bureau set about coordinating these relief shipments, and the V-Bundles organization was born; the Prairie provinces shipping sixty-three metric tons of clothing through Winnipeg, and other centers, like Vancouver, contributing large amounts.[1]

In the United States, UNRRA launched a national week-long clothing drive in September 1944, and the USC Boston opened a clothing collection warehouse in New York in late November. By February 1945, Charles Joy wrote to Lotta, they had already shipped fifty-four bales of clothing and shoes to the USC distribution center in Paris and thirty-five more bales were ready — a total of fifty-two hundred kilograms. The target was to move two tons a week through the warehouse on East 35th Street. Wrote Joy: "Our offices in Lisbon and all over France are crying out for clothing as the need is beyond all computation."

Dr. Lotta herself hoped Canadians could contribute to this USC drive. She was encouraged by Unitarian friends, like Lotte Ulmann (now Heim), who also worked as a censor. Lotte accompanied Lotta to a meeting of the Women's Alliance on a bitterly cold night in January 1945, and recalls: "She was quite nervous, not being so used then to speaking in English. But by the end of the hour she had all twenty people there full of enthusiasm."

A month later, Lotta spoke to the Athenaeum Club in Ottawa on "Unitarian Relief in Europe" to such effect that its members decided to concentrate their annual drive on the collection of used clothing. But the Canadian government issued an order in mid-February stopping all clothing collections by voluntary agencies and private groups; the Department of National War Services was itself going to direct future collections.

When she reported this disappointing news to Boston, both Charles Joy and Henry Muller, in charge of the New York collection center, wrote resilient letters in reply, indicating a broader horizon. Joy wrote that they had for some time thought they should try to create a committee in Canada to

---

[1]See Gertrude Laing, *A Community Organizes for War*, Winnipeg: 1948. Ms. Laing wrote a colorful account of the Winnipeg center, where she was supervisor.

cooperate with Boston and with the USC in Britain. Clothing collection was "only the need that happens to be uppermost at the moment." There would be, he implied, many other tasks for such a committee.

Their letters prompted Dr. Lotta to discuss the idea of a Canadian committee with Dr. Ingi Borgford, minister of the Unitarian Church in Ottawa. She learned that he was keen to propose to the other five churches – in Montreal, Toronto, Hamilton, Winnipeg, and Vancouver – that they submit a scheme to their congregations to found a Unitarian Service Committee of Canada with an executive body in Ottawa. The churches were associated individually with the AUA in Boston, but he believed that a will had existed for months to create a body uniting the six churches in Canada. She reported this on 28 February to Charles Joy, who thought it an excellent idea.

Others were not so sure. Mrs. H.G. Barber, of the General Alliance of Unitarian Women in Ottawa, received a letter from Henry Muller in which he hoped that the Canadian churches could contribute clothing and added that, if the Department of National War Services insisted that a quota request be made by a relief agency, "we could perhaps consider to establish a Canadian Unitarian Service Committee." But Mrs. Barber was cautious about clothing drives in her reply of 1 March. She said there was a shortage of civilian goods for the thousands of young soldiers who would soon be demobilized. "The government's decision not to let goods out of Canada, until we have a national stocktaking, seems to me most reasonable...there is not much sense in leaving this country stripped."

On the question of a USC branch in Canada, Mrs. Barber thought it would do no harm to explore possibilities. "But," she added, "you must keep in mind what I always tell the Alliance: we in Canada do not work on a denominational, but on a national, basis." On this point she was proven right within a year, as the Unitarian Service Committee began to make many links beyond the church.

In April Dr. Lotta wrote to Boston, advocating a scheme of foster parents paying five dollars a month in "temporary adoption" of European children. This had worked well when Swiss people adopted French children after 1940, she said, and the money could be used to found children's homes. Dr. Joy replied that he hoped the Canadians might underwrite a children's home in Czechoslovakia, but warned that it would cost more nearly twenty dollars a month per child. His own committee planned to set up homes in the Basque region of France.

During this period, Dr. Lotta was still working a full day's shift at the censorship department and fitting in Unitarian work in the evenings and on weekends. On 8 March 1945, she had written to Dr. Joy that she, like many people in her department, was being asked if she was ready to continue her censor's job overseas, probably in Germany. She told him: "You know how anxious I am to do social work after the war, especially – if I could – for your committee...I would only consider to go abroad in my present function, if I cannot be sent overseas as a social worker."

Dr. Joy wrote back at once. He explained that it was USC policy to appoint an American as director of every important area of its work overseas. "This is also necessary because the government insists that all American relief operations abroad shall be obviously American, and wherever possible, headed by Americans." He asked whether she would be prepared to return to Czechoslovakia as a second associate director, if Waitstill and Martha Sharp went back as director and associate director to the country where they had worked so well in 1939. Dr. Lotta replied that she would not hesitate, if the USC personnel committee appointed her.

In May arrangements became more solid during a visit she made to Boston on a round trip to Detroit and Windsor, where she was to speak at meetings of the Canadian-American Committee on International Relations.[2] USC Boston formally asked her to organize a Canadian committee as a prelude to going to Czechoslovakia. The Detroit-Windsor trip was also useful in strengthening her friendship with Senator Cairine Wilson, for they were both representing the United Nations group from Ottawa. When Dr. Lotta wrote, on 27 June, asking her to become honorary chairman of the Canadian committee, Senator Wilson accepted at once.

It took another two months, nevertheless, to be granted registration. Dr. Lotta later described it as "a very difficult battle." But on 30 August 1945, Leon Trebert, Registrar of the War Charities Act, sent her a Certificate of Registration No.

---

[2]Those were days of cheap travel. Her railway ticket, taking in Boston and Detroit, cost $41.61, two nights at Boston's Hotel Bellevue were only $8.42, and breakfast, lunch, and dinner together a mere $1.90.

C-4036 for "The Unitarian Service Committee of Canada Fund," which allowed it to operate for one year. However, the certificate limited the fund-raising activities to members and supporters. Through the influence of Senator Wilson, who submitted details about the foster parent scheme and about the thousand dollars worth of medical supplies already shipped to Europe, the limitation was lifted in February 1946. Thereafter, funds were raised from the general public, as well as from the core support group of Unitarians. In August 1946, the certificate of registration was renewed without problems.

This timing, in fact, suited Lotta. She did not finish her job in the censorship directorate until mid-September. On 6 September, USC Boston had formally appointed her to act as executive secretary for Canada. Only then could she start traveling to meet members of the other churches that had elected committees, in Montreal, Toronto, Winnipeg, and Vancouver, and lay the foundations of an active organization.

Much was achieved in the last months of 1945. Canadian Pacific Railways was persuaded to offer free transportation for USC shipments, and Entr'Aide Française arranged free shipping from Canadian ports all the way to Paris. The assistant director of USC Boston, the Reverend Ed Cahill, came to speak at meetings in Montreal and Ottawa sponsored by the Canadian Women's Club and the Committee for Refugees, and this gave the Unitarians useful publicity. The Women's Alliance in Ottawa had a mammoth sale of six hundred dozen chocolate cookies. In Toronto, twelve women made a pledge to send regular food parcels to the USC office in Paris. In Montreal and Ottawa, Unitarian children painted wooden toys and made rag dolls. And sixty toilet kits, including a towel, toothbrush, comb, soap, a chocolate bar, and a personal letter were shipped to European children.

But for Dr. Lotta there were also moments of depression and anger. She went to a mass meeting on 2 October at the Capital Cinema for the opening of the National Clothing Drive. The keynote speaker was Grattan O'Leary, who was then assistant editor of the *Ottawa Journal* and much later was made a senator. She described the meeting in a letter to Marius Barbeau the next day:

> You wouldn't believe it but the speaker of the evening, in the mayor's presence, talked for 45 minutes in favor of Germany...that

we must help her because she was so destroyed and miserable...I have never in my life trembled so much from fury and shame. And the reaction of the Canadian public, will you ask me about that? Applause ...It was like a nightmare, but it has powerfully demonstrated that I should return to my own country without delay.

I am very alarmed at this "post-Munich" atmosphere that I sense again here among my friends – a desire to ally with Germany, because they are so afraid of the Soviets. You know that I have not been defeatist during the most critical times, but I am so now. This country has still so much to learn – and I dare not even think about the United States.

Her bitterness over the death of her parents was still raw. She did not know that Owen, one of the four sons of Grattan and Mary O'Leary, had been shot down and killed over Germany. But within weeks her mood of rejecting Canada passed, and on 12 December she became a Canadian landed immigrant.

Westward the land is bright

In January 1946, Dr. Lotta set off on her first trip to western Canada, to spread the name of the Service Committee in what was to become the most responsive region. It was a successful seven-week trip, sponsored by the Canadian Women's Club, to speak on "The Tragedy of Children in Post-war Europe." The club paid her travel expenses and organized good publicity along her route. And the journey started auspiciously, with a cable reaching her in Winnipeg on 4 February, just as she was about to record a CBC interview, to say that limitations on fundraising had been removed.

She spoke to fifty-three public meetings and did eleven radio interviews. After a Sunday afternoon CBC broadcast in Vancouver, she recalled, "money started to pour in. The following day I counted dollar bills until I could no longer distinguish the color of their denominations, and that day [was] one of the highlights of my life."[3]

The USC at that time had no office other than the apartment she rented in an old house at 668 Cooper Street, now demolished. But she had an obliging landlady with whom she had left a

---

[3]Address at the Royal Bank of Canada Award dinner, 20 June 1979.

bundle of envelopes, all addressed to her at the various hotels along her journey, "and, bless her…she forwarded all my incoming letters, many of them containing small cheques and bills 'for the hungry children of Europe,' and every night I sat down in my hotel room, gratefully writing tax-deductible receipts and little personal notes of appreciation and gratitude…"[4]

By early June the USC had collected forty thousand dollars and had eyes on an end-of-year target of one hundred thousand dollars. Street Car Advertising had accepted twenty-five hundred posters for free display during the summer. Already approaching the full year's quota set by government, thirty thousand kilograms of clothing had either been shipped or was ready for shipment. She sent very precise packing instructions to the branches, to "sort the clothing into winter and summer clothing…keep shoes separate (very tightly tied together); also bedding and rags. Wooden boxes…when packed should not exceed 150 lbs. [and] should be lined with waterproof paper… The boxes have to be strapped with 7/8 inch metal strapping…"

The organization was under way. In Ottawa and Toronto they got as many boxes as they needed from the breweries; in Montreal they used tea chests. The boxes were shipped to Antwerp, on their way to Prague, or to a French port for distribution from Paris.

As well, the Ottawa committee – the executive body at that time – had been enlarged. In October 1945, Dr. Robert Wickenden, a geologist and chairman of the Elgin Street Church congregation, had joined it, as well as Mr. T.A. McConkey, an accountant. His wife, Rita McConkey, came onto the executive in May 1946.

By midsummer Dr. Lotta was ready to embark on her first postwar visit to Europe. Her own salary was being paid by the Boston office, but it had no travel funds. So, with the Canadian branches, she raised the idea of investing two thousand dollars in a two-month trip to France and Czechoslovakia because, she said, she could not return in the following autumn to those western Canadian cities, "where I spoke so often, without being able to tell a new and appealing story." They agreed, and she sailed for Europe on 11 July.

---

[4]Address at the Royal Bank of Canada Award dinner, 20 June 1979.

France, from the ashes

The statistics of conditions in Europe in 1945-46 are appalling. Some 34 million people had been uprooted since German troops had marched into the Rhineland in 1936 and began tearing families from their homes. More than 10 million had ended the war in countries other than their own.

The figures for France alone are shocking. In February 1946, its Ministry of Reconstruction reported that 1,300,000 houses had been destroyed, and 6 million people were homeless. Among the wartime casualties, 100,000 had perished as refugees in flight – and most of these victims were children – and more than 60,000 had died in Allied air attacks. Of the survivors, most were undernourished; a study done in Marseilles showed that 70 percent of the men and 55 percent of the women were only seven-eights of their normal weight and had a badly balanced diet, with a shortage of meat and vitamins. The same was true of children. Remarkably, diseases were held in check: there had been a decline in TB deaths to 122 per 100,000 after the rate had doubled in 1941-42. But education was disrupted: some 500,000 children were not going to school at all, and another 1 million boys and girls were at least two years behind in their studies.

Let us focus on one little town in Normandy that had been built in a bend of the River Seine and was dominated by Richard the Lionheart's Chateau Gaillard: Les Andelys. In June 1940, German troops had pillaged and burned down the main part of town. Five years later, Mme Gwenydd Champsaur, a Montrealer whose husband, a local hotel-keeper, had been killed there, and who herself had worked for the USC in Portugal, wrote to Boston of her return:

> Today I have been trying to find my way through the once familiar streets. It would be easier to distinguish one street from another in ruined Pompeii. Houses and shops which once sheltered over 6,000 inhabitants have disappeared... The town hall, the post office are housed now in cramped little huts. Pitiful plaster and tar-paper barracks litter the square, each distinguished from its neighbor by the name of its occupant: Flamant, Tapissier, Leroy, Quincaillerie. The signs bear witness to the stubborn courage of the French people. M. Flamant has painted imitation timber beams on his walls and draped a remnant of tired brown velvet to simulate a shop-window.

Lotta

Mme Champsaur stayed on in Les Andelys and organized a welfare center, where two hundred schoolchildren came for a hot midday meal and an afternoon snack. It also served as a clothing distribution depot, and as a cheerfully decorated recreation center where the town's children could have showers and spend warm hours in the winter months – and celebrate summer festivals. For four years, from 1946, the USC Canada supported her work.

Picasso's little people

The problems of war-shocked and war-mutilated children were spread through many parts of France. Where should help begin? The Marseilles clinic, which Dr. Lotta had known in wartime days, might have been the logical start, but the focus of operations for USC Boston had shifted from Marseilles to Toulouse, and to the care of some of the 150,000 Spanish Republican refugees, who had fled in 1939 from General Franco's victorious forces and remained in southwest France. In Toulouse itself, a city then of 400,000 people, lived some 12,000 Spanish refugee families. Understandably, they were not the first preoccupation of postwar French governments.

Noel Field, who had become European director for USC Boston, went to Toulouse in 1945 to meet the local Spanish advisory committee, whose chairman was the painter Pablo Picasso, and to discuss the principal problems of the refugees. These were: shortage of clothing, even among young men demobilized from the French resistance forces; undernourishment and all the consequent diseases; war-mutilated adults and children; and destitute families who had lost their breadwinner. Their cause was well publicized in the United States by writers such as Martha Gellhorn (wife of Ernest Hemingway) and Dorothy Parker; and a broad program was started.

It was supervised by a doctor's daughter from California, Persis Miller, who became the refugees' steadfast champion after working for the Basque Boys Training Centre in prewar London and interpreting on behalf of Spanish immigrants held in wartime on Ellis Island. By February 1946, she was the USC representative in Toulouse, and she stayed there until she died in 1970, aged 67. She once wrote: "The nature of the Spanish refugee need is such that it cannot be answered by action in dibs

48

and dabs, now and then, a spot here and a spot there. The need demands sustained attention. Anything else is frivolous."

With Dolores Bellido, daughter of a former professor of physiology at Barcelona University, she ran a five-sided health and scholarship program; and they survived all the political turmoil that seems inevitable in exile organizations. The five parts included the sixty-bed Varsovie Hospital in Toulouse; a nearby dispensary dealing with three thousand outpatients a month; a forty-bed convalescent home for adults near Pau; a home for fifty or sixty physically deficient children at St. Goin; and a scholarship program of technical training for young people with ill or destitute parents (or else none at all).

Dr. Lotta put USC Canada's support behind the last two projects. The main purpose of the Maison des Enfants Déficients at St. Goin was to improve the health and increase the weight of young children, and the hope was to limit their stay to about two months. Many had to stay longer; a total of 174 children were cared for in the first two years.

The home was a well-built house with a garden in a tiny village overlooking the lower Pyrenees. The children's physical needs were for warm clothes and good food. The USC sent trousers for the boys, capes for the girls, and nightclothes. In 1948 Persis Miller wrote: "We thank the Women's Alliance for the nicest clothes any relief organization ever had." Food shipments included condensed milk, soup, sardines, sugar, and dried fruit, and helped give the children four meals a day – up to thirty-one hundred calories. These shipments made, wrote Miss Miller, "the difference between closing the home and surviving."

As visitors noted, the children had other needs; in particular, for security and affection. It did not help that the children were pressed by their teacher to think always of returning to Spain. Señor J.M. Alvarez recorded a rather quaint, and perhaps fanciful, conversation in class after setting them an essay on "When I grow up." His particular target was Pepito. While others had disclosed their hopes of becoming a movie star, an aviator, a lion hunter, a secretary and a pianist, Pepito had chosen the career of a sergeant in the Royal Canadian Mounted Police. The teacher harangued and mocked him, and the other students joined until one of them, Luis, offered Pepito an honorable way out by suggesting he could instead join the Spanish Republican Police.

PEPITO: I didn't think of that! That would be marvellous! I would go after the assassins of my father, to deliver them to justice.

TEACHER: Well said. You had forgotten Spain. But it really isn't your fault. It is the fault of Franco, who makes Spanish children languish in exile.

The patriotic but unrealistic Señor Alvarez was replaced after a time, and by 1949 several children were going to the village school, while French was being used in classes at the home. In September 1952, the French government offered to take the physically deficient into its own convalescent homes and give free tuition to Spanish apprentices – and French citizenship at the age of twenty-one. So the St. Goin home was closed, and Persis set about raising scholarship money for those apprentices whose parents could not afford to pay for books and meals and other expenses. Throughout the 1950s and 1960s, she raised enough for some thirty scholarships a year, of around eighteen dollars to twenty-five dollars a month, from USC Canada, Smith College, and a few private donors. In the mid-1960s, although some Canadians in USC branches had reservations about supporting people identified with the Spanish Republican cause, the USC was contributing enough for eight to twelve scholarships.

This was the first training program the USC supported, but Dr. Lotta had always indicated that she wanted to move beyond relief and welfare work. In a 1947 article, she told the story of thirteen-year-old Enrique Jordan, the brightest scholar and best football player at St. Goin. His father had been killed by Franco's soldiers, his mother died in hospital soon after bringing him into France, his three sisters disappeared in a convoy to the Soviet Union. "As a small boy he knew every kind of hardship facing an exile – misery, hunger and disease." But at St. Goin he thrived, gaining seven kilograms and growing ten centimeters in eight months. "He not only developed physically. According to his teachers, he has an extraordinary gift for mathematics, and in his free time he helps the director to keep the accounting books." Enrique's story, wrote Dr. Lotta, "shows how extraordinary circumstances may develop the very best qualities slumbering in a child."[5]

There was no doubt that the apprentices worked hard.

---

[5]*Phi Lambda Theta* journal, Menasha, Wisconsin; December 1947, pp. 72-73.

Among the eight receiving USC scholarships in 1967-68, Persis particularly commended Rosa Maria Achotegui, graduating from a school in Paris and about to take up a job as a technician-chemist at the University Hospital in Toulouse, and Emilio Ochando, who was starting a two-year course for electrical technicians. Rosa Maria's father, a former naval engineer, had a serious lung disease, and Emilio's father a weak heart after years as a prisoner of the Germans.

Homes in the castle

In northern France, Dr. Lotta had been working with Mme Jo Tempi, a German woman hired by Noel Field to run the USC Paris office, which had dealt with twenty-eight shipments of clothing from Canada (some forty-six thousand kilograms) in its first year of work. But she found two projects on her own for Canadian support. These projects were the sponsorship of 128 war-shocked children at Sèvres and 58 war-mutilated children at Villepatour.

The connection with the Maison d'Enfants de Sèvres began almost by accident, in June 1947. Hours before Dr. Lotta was about to leave for her second trip to Europe, someone at the National Film Board telephoned to say they had just received an unusual film, "Children's Republic," made with Madeleine Carroll, about a children's home outside Paris that needed financial support. Would she like to have it screened? She had no time, but jotted down the address. In Paris she spent almost a whole morning searching for this building before finding a big, dilapidated house that had once been a castle. Her reception there was brusque. After a lengthy wait, an extremely agitated woman appeared. She was the director, Yvonne Hagnauer. As Lotta wrote many years later (in 1980): "She shouted at me almost insultingly. Immediately I understood [she] was desperate for help and had been let down many, too many times."

Mme Hagnauer saw that Dr. Lotta was wearing a uniform made in the style of an American army nurse, and said words to the effect that "You Americans are all the same: you come and look, and do nothing. And now it's the end!" Dr. Lotta put her right on nationality and asked to look around. She learned that the children came from more than a dozen countries, and that Mme Hagnauer had risked her own life in saving some Jewish

51

children during the war by mixing them all up in beds during a search by German troops. The reason for her despair that day was that the government allowance per child had become quite inadequate. It was enough only for the cheapest food; as one child said later, "potatoes and potatoes forever."

Dr. Lotta was won over by Yvonne Hagnauer's approach in using art in every form as therapy for the terrible shocks these children had suffered in wartime. They had seen parents and friends shot or dragged away, and homes bombed. She inspired the children to paint beautiful things like butterflies and flowers, to write or copy poetry, to learn ceramics or weaving, to dance and play music. This appealed deeply to Lotta's own sense of beauty and culture, and Sèvres remained for her a favorite project, for which she recruited Canadian foster parents until 1980.

The USC provided equipment as well as food and clothes in the early days, and by 1949 the children were staging a Canadian Festival, with Mme Vanier the honored guest beside Dr. Lotta. They also sent ceramics and a book of their paintings to Ottawa, and these were exhibited in a USC display in Ogilvy's store. Dr. Lotta greatly enjoyed her annual visit to Sèvres, both for the strong friendship that developed with Mme Hagnauer and for the love of the children that lasted through their adolescence. Some of the early residents graduated to impressive jobs; of three girls she knew one became a civil servant, one a secretary, and one a nurse.

Then a new generation of children came to the Sèvres home. They had not known the trauma of war but had suffered from other tragedies, and they still wrote to her; Christmastime letters embellished with flower paintings and telling of visits to the nearby forest of Meudon. In the late 1970s, children were learning about lumberjacks and forest rangers, and also about the problem of hunger in developing countries; and Dr. Lotta continued her yearly visits to encourage this wider awareness.

At Villepatour, the needs were all too visible. The home had been started in 1940 by an energetic woman, Baronne Malet, who in the confusion of advancing and retreating armies simply requisitioned a spacious old castle near Paris. With help from the French Red Cross, she began looking after wounded children. The fifty-eight boys and girls there in 1947 had lost either an arm or a leg — and some had lost both legs — most of them after being wounded by Allied bombs. Their ages ranged from five up to eighteen.

There was no place in France that could supply these crippled children with artificial limbs which were modern and adjustable. So, besides supplying food and clothing, Dr. Lotta launched a special drive in September 1948 to raise $150 for each of the children. This would pay for a journey to Roehampton Hospital near London, and for the fitting there of an artificial limb.

The appeal met a swift response from Canadian cities and organizations. Saskatoon produced $150 for the first girl, eighteen-year-old Mathilde Capp, to be fitted with an artificial arm. The Girl Guides of Flin Flon collected for Jeanine Lemasson, the young people of Hamilton for Serge Buckthorpe, who was only thirteen when caught by a bomb. Very personal connections were made. The Alberta Women's Institute raised fifteen hundred dollars, and the Canadian Junior Red Cross the same amount. Within seven months thirty-five boys and girls had received limbs, and plans were being made for Villepatour to employ its own technicians to repair and adjust the artificial limbs on the spot.

The assistance with rehabilitation went further. The USC provided a machine for Dr. Bidou to give special electrical massage to his patients. And in mid-1949, a physiotherapist from the veterans' hospital in Saskatoon, Ruth McKinnon, volunteered to work at Villepatour; a mother and daughter in Toronto put up one thousand dollars to pay her way. It was a tough assignment for Miss McKinnon as accommodation was difficult, and the home surprisingly isolated. To her credit, she stayed eighteen months. But in all the forty years of USC operations, she was the only Canadian sent abroad as technical assistance.

The help to Villepatour ended in 1951, but a film survives in the Ottawa archives with some haunting scenes: armless girls undressing a doll; a young boy hanging from a wall bar with his artificial arm; older girls practicing in a shorthand class and writing lefthanded because they had lost their right hands; an early morning dormitory scene of boys helping each other fit their new limbs on again. The film has no commentary, and needs none.

CHAPTER 4

Eastward Alone

Children in Czechoslovakia

AS USC CANADA moved further east in Europe from France, first to Czechoslovakia and then to Austria, south to Italy, and finally and most enduringly to Greece, it took an increasingly independent line from the Boston body; and Dr. Lotta began to assert her own principles about local field representatives and technical assistance. Indeed, when the program started in Greece in 1950, it was a totally separate venture.

But in Czechoslovakia, the two committees – Boston and Ottawa – were still working in close harness. There is, in the Boston files, a dramatic cable that Charles Joy, USC executive director, sent from Paris during the bleak winter of 1945-46, which began: "Here is suffering Europe. The night descends upon us. The casualties of peace mount until they threaten to exceed the casualties of war... In Czechoslovakia almost a million children destitute, of which [one] fifth suspected of tuberculosis. In Poland indescribable unimaginable distress devastation anguish..."

In a letter from Prague on 11 December, he was more precise. Czechoslovakia had suffered a bad harvest in 1945, and the Germans had killed most of the cattle. They had also blown up nearly all the railway bridges, removed or destroyed half the locomotives and a good length of railway line, so transportation was disrupted at a time of acute food shortage.

Children, Joy went on to say, were suffering most. Some 800,000, out of 4 million, had serious deficiency diseases. The only children's hospital in Prague was unable to function because the windows were smashed, and no glass-making plant in the country had any soda. Around Opava, a city 80 percent destroyed, he came on 200 cases of typhus, and he found 400 children in two refugee camps without any shoes. Some 6,000 children in another district had no winter underwear. And on and on.

Many houses were taken over by public-spirited men and women to care for scores of orphans, but they were all short of supplies and trained staff. Dr. Lotta returned in September 1946 from her tour of Europe to tell her executive committee that, of all the eight countries she had visited, Czechoslovakia was the worst off. USC Canada worked hard to meet some of the needs of such homes. Within three months, two large shipments of concentrated food — liver oil, fruit juice, sardines, dehydrated vegetables — as well as of warm clothing, shoes, blankets, layettes, and "comfort kits" for children had been sent, with a total weight of eighteen thousand kilograms.

In addition, the foster parent scheme, under which a Czechoslovak child was "adopted" for three months for forty-five dollars, was being strongly supported, not only by church groups and service clubs but also by schoolchildren to whom Dr. Lotta spoke on her cross-country tour. By the end of 1946, more than seventy schools across Canada were subscribing to the scheme, and the USC was contributing to the upkeep of children in about thirty convalescent homes in Czechoslovakia.

The scheme continued to grow. By mid-1948, USC Canada had enrolled foster parents for 1,890 children in Europe, a large number of these in Czechoslovakia. In Canadian high schools, from North Bay to Saskatoon, there was enthusiasm about corresponding with hundreds of young Czechoslovaks through the Correspondance Scholaire Internationale organization. On her second speaking tour, Dr. Lotta was greeted at Vancouver's King Edward High School by students raising the Czechoslovak flag and singing its national anthem. "It made me almost cry," she told her branches.

But by February-March 1948, some months after being forced under Soviet pressure to reject participation in the Marshall Plan (the European Recovery Program), the Czechoslovak National Front government broke up. By June, a new constitution for a "People's Democracy" was promulgated, President Beneš had resigned, and the Communist leader, Klement Gottwald, prime minister since 1946, stepped up to the presidency.

These moves, and the death of Foreign Minister Jan Masaryk, shocked many people in the West. But the general trend was not unexpected by people who traveled and saw the misery. Charles Joy wrote, as early as February 1946: "Democracy is failing in Europe...because people are cold, hungry, weak and sick... It's nonsense to teach people to believe in the four freedoms while they starve to death. We are making corpses out of many, and out of the rest we are making disbelievers in democracy."[1]

Insiders were making their own preparations. Dr. Lotta had been cheerfully reunited with her sister Lilly and met her brother-in-law Charles for the first time, in Prague in July 1946. They had returned from Palestine by a gruelling route through Egypt and thence by coaling ship to Italy and finally a week-long train journey home. They never recovered the old apartment on Sokolska, but Charles found a reasonable job as a sales representative. After her 1947 trip, without telling her sister, Lotta applied for immigrants' visas to Canada for them. These were ready by February 1948, and Lilly and her husband left in June, after paying taxes for the year ahead. Many others left their homeland in the same bereft way.

Should the USC continue to send food and clothing and other gifts to Czechoslovakia? The need had not diminished, especially after a drought in 1947. In March 1948, Rev. Howard Brooks, USC Boston associate director, returned with the assurance that distribution was not being hampered, and added: "As a Committee, it is not our business to engage in political warfare, whether against Communism or anything else."[2]

Dr. Lotta herself spent six days in Czechoslovakia in July 1948 and called it "a sad but most necessary experience." There was, she reported, "a catastrophic food shortage...Our Canadian food and clothing have never been as much appreciated as at present." Health Ministry officials thanked her for the vitamin shipments to the homes. She wore Canada on the lapels of her uniform and wrote that "many people manifested their interest and sympathy, because of my Canadian insignia." But she had no problems with officials and no difficulty in leaving the country.[3]

However, by mid-1949 the picture was darker. For three months no letters came from Dr. Karel Haspl, the steadfast Unitarian minister in Prague, and Dr. Lotta did not visit Czechoslovakia on her trip to Europe. On 29 August she wrote a sad circular, saying with what difficulty and hesitation she was suggesting the suspension of shipments, at least until there was

---

[1]Report to USC Boston, 14 February 1946.

[2]Circular to all branches, no. 56, 19 March 1948.

[3]Circulars nos. 66 and 67, 14 and 24 July 1948.

some information on distribution: "Last year, after seeing the Canadian food and clothing distribution myself, I could honestly defend this program before any contributor. Today I cannot any longer."

The branches, which in three years had collected and shipped 11,238 kilograms of clothing and shoes to Czechoslovakia, approved the suspension. Mrs. Ransom, the Winnipeg chairman, wrote back at once: "I think you're wise...some of our committee have felt we should not send help there after the country became Communist-controlled; so your decision will ease their minds."

It meant the severing of many ties of friendship. In 1959 Mrs. J.R. Morgan wrote to Dr. Lotta, asking if she had any word of Rostislav Slovacek, whose foster parent she had been. "Though all your work means much to me, this boy comes first," wrote Marion Morgan. Lotta wrote to Karel Haspl, who was forced to reply that it was illegal to send such information abroad, but he guessed the boy was now in the army. Lotta wrote back to him: "What heartache that you couldn't trace this boy, for it would have meant a very great deal to someone who is slowly dying in Vancouver."

She herself kept in touch with Dr. Haspl, sending him special pills for his rare illness (myasthenia gravis). Mrs. Bladen of Vancouver went to Czechoslovakia in 1957 for the fifteenth anniversary of the Lidice massacre, to the rebuilt village and the rose garden with trees sent from many countries to symbolize peace and friendship. She spent some hours with Dr. Haspl, who told her that living conditions had greatly improved since 1948, that the Unitarian Church membership was increasing, with an average Sunday attendance of three hundred, and that he and the church were active in the peace movement. This fine, idealistic man died in December 1964, and with him went the remaining link with those early postwar years of generous assistance and heartfelt attachment to Czechoslovakia.

Canadian Club in Vienna

In the circular of 29 August 1949, in which she announced an end of the Czechoslovak program, Dr. Lotta suggested that there should be a general shift away from work in central Europe towards southern Europe, with a focus on Italy and Greece. Meanwhile, a modest program was begun in Austria.

Dr. Lotta revisited Vienna in August 1948 – she had known the city as a child – and was delighted to find it as charming as ever, and the people kind and helpful. Acute food shortages had been overcome with a good harvest. Instead, the foremost problem, in her eyes, was "the moral depravity of the youth": the rate of criminal offences had tripled in one year. There were many vagrant children, due mainly to a shortage of schools. Although three hundred bombed classrooms had been rebuilt, most still lacked basic equipment, from blackboards to benches. So different classes used the available rooms morning and afternoon, and most of the children were out on the streets.[4]

One solution, proposed by the city's school council, was to equip a large building in a factory district of Vienna as a recreation center for some three hundred children, aged six to fourteen. Dr. Lotta agreed to help equip rooms for sewing and carpentry classes and to provide food for a warm midday meal. But a year later, when she visited the center at 95 Grinzingerstrasse, tactfully named the Canadian Children's Club, she was taken aback to find only twenty children using the place. With a roster of forty-seven volunteer teachers, and with facilities for films, handicraft classes, and two gymnasia, it obviously needed better management. She found that it was election year in Austria, and the club's executive was politically divided and quarreling over everything.

In her strongest German, Dr. Hitschmanova demanded improvements and an increase of numbers within six months, under threat of removing four thousand dollars worth of equipment. They all, from the president of the board of education onwards, took notice. Just to make sure, Dr. Lotta got the local UNICEF representative to keep an eye on the executive. From then on, she had only praise for the club. "One of the most successful projects," she said in 1956, after being regaled with a program of folk dancing performed by the older girls, who had sewn and embroidered their regional costumes at the club.

Less spectacular was the support given for many years (two thousand dollars a year, on average) to two homes in Vienna run by Swedish and Danish Quakers for maladjusted children and young girls, victims of the war. These institutions, served by a poorly paid staff of social workers, psychologists and

---

[4]Circular no. 69, 7 August 1948.

therapists, who were doing pioneering work in using psychiatry and psychology in such cases, nevertheless received only a small subsidy from Austrian authorities, and were several times saved from closure only by the USC contribution. But it was not a project that appealed to many prospective foster parents in Canada, because the length of a child's stay in these homes was indeterminate, and the children were too disturbed to write letters.

Limbs and clothes to Italy

In 1949, USC Canada also moved into Italy at the request (according to an apocryphal story) of Maestro Arturo Toscanini, who was then based in New York. Whatever the truth of that tale, the practical link was made through Professor Egidio Reale, who had worked with USC Boston to reequip hospitals in southern Italy after its liberation and who was, in 1947-49, Italian minister to Switzerland. In April 1949, Dr. Lotta wrote to him asking about children's villages.

He put her in touch with his sister-in-law in Rome, and soon Mrs. Guiseppina Reale found herself enrolled as the USC representative in Italy, volunteering over the next seven years to sort out many problems, whether of food shipments gone temporarily astray or of priests who wouldn't answer letters. Mrs. Reale is one of a far-flung group of heroes (mainly women) who were captivated and captured by Dr. Lotta and, without question or complaint, worked for years afterwards to make sure their nearest wheel of the USC machine turned smoothly.

Some early USC assistance went to institutions run by Catholic priests for boys who were either orphaned or mutilated in accidents in the wake of war. Boys paid dearly for their inquisitiveness around recent battlefields; bombs and hand grenades exploded at their touch, and a boy trying to make a whistle out of a machine-gun bullet succeeded only in losing his hand. Father Jose Musso gathered many of them into his Opera Don Orione in Naples, 115 boys from five to eighteen in 1950, and wrote mellifluous letters of gratitude and pleading to Ottawa. Dr. Lotta raised money for artificial limbs for his boys, at $150 a limb. Appropriately perhaps, the Ladies Auxiliary of the Canadian Legion, in a half dozen towns from Exshaw, Alberta, to Deep River, Ontario, provided the most funds for this brief program.

On the whole, she found relations with the Italian priests rather difficult. Their letters, when they came, were long on God's blessings but short on case histories that she could use for fund raising. She foud it easier to work with two lay institutions, both directed by women: the Scuola Fabio Filzi in the Tiburtino Tre district of Rome, and three boys' homes grouped into the Colonie Dei Giovannia Lavoratori.

The school in this poor part of Rome, run by Professor Maria Guerrera, had fifteen hundred students, half of them girls, and most of them children of impoverished refugees from the Cassino region. Nearly one-third were said to be pretubercular. USC Canada shipped 1,360 kilograms of clothing to the school during the winter of 1949-50, and a group of ten-year-old boys responded by making a map of Canada which Dr. Lotta thought so wonderful that she wanted External Affairs to freight it back to Ottawa; the embassy officials demurred. The USC continued to send drums full of thousands of kilograms of powdered milk to the school until 1953.

Closest to Dr. Lotta's heart in Italy was the Colonie, run under great financial difficulties, by Dr. Olimpia Molina, who became a longtime friend. It had been founded in 1917 to pursue a progressive and democratic form of education, concentrating on agricultural training. When Dr. Lotta came to know it, there were one hundred young boys aged five to ten at Citta de Castello, another hundred aged ten to fourteen at Collestrada, both places near Perugia in Umbria, and a senior group of one hundred boys from fourteen to eighteen in the Bufalotta suburb of Rome. They were short of winter clothes and sturdy shoes and good food.

So the USC shipped appropriate clothing: eighty pairs of used lumberman's boots and fifty-six pairs of khaki trousers went in 1949. Later there were all kinds of nutritious foods: powdered milk, large amounts of honey, and a choice of fish, from Nova Scotia kipper snacks to British Columbia canned salmon. Surprising at first glance are shipments of twenty-three hundred kilograms of macaroni in 1952 and twenty-eight hundred kilograms of tinned bologna in 1956, but for boys unable to buy this staple food it made charitable sense. These gifts were supported for years by donations from foster parents, some of whom doubtless worried that they were only helping boys. On the other hand, these boys were learning some useful training, and the senior youngsters were nearing self-reliance through the sideline of growing and selling camelia and azalea plants in Rome.

USC Boston under attack

In 1946, USC Boston came under attack from several quarters on grounds that it had Communist affiliations. The attack only faded in 1947 after a new executive director, Raymond Bragg, took charge, after Mme Tempi in Paris was fired, and after Noel Field left the agency.

The first move was an attempt to smear Martha Sharp, who was the Democratic challenger in the 1946 election of a Republican congressman, Joseph W. Martin Jr. He persuaded the House Un-American Activities Committee to investigate the help which the Joint Anti-Fascist Refugee Committee had given to Spanish groups through the USC and Martha's wartime involvement with the committee. The trivial accusations were dropped as soon as Martin was reelected. Meanwhile, other charges that the European program of the USC was Communist-dominated prompted the agency to send its own special investigating committee to France to hear all parties. Its report concluded that the charges were unsubstantiated, but under continuing pressure from a conservative Unitarian group known as the Committee of 14, Jo Tempi was dismissed and Noel Field, in effect, squeezed out through a cutting off of funds.[5]

Dr. Lotta was a close observer of these convulsions. For years, her life and work had been affected by political eruptions. She knew she could not avoid them entirely, but she hoped to minimize the damage to her own USC Canada program and to escape, in particular, the dust of other groups' quarrels. She was already beginning to take a course independent from Boston. The bad experience suffered by Boston in 1946-47 must have persuaded her to diverge even more swiftly. The new program in Greece was one opportunity to do so.

---

[5] This is a bald summary of complicated events and controversial personalities. Two books that deal with the tragic life of Noel Field, including his wartime intelligence work for Allen Dulles and his much later imprisonment in Hungary, are *Red Pawn* by Flora Lewis (Arthur Barker, 1966) and *Operation Splinter Factor* by Stewart Steven (Lippincott, 1974). The report of the investigating committee, headed by USC chairman William Emerson, was published in *The Christian Register*, Vol. 125, December 1946.

Emergency in Macedonia

On her first day back in Ottawa from her 1949 trip to Europe, Dr. Lotta wrote a lengthy circular to the USC branches. Much of it had to do with northern Greece, where the civil war was coming to an end after three years of vicious fighting. By the time Marshall Tito closed the Yugoslav border, thus denying sanctuary to the Greek Communist forces, enormous damage had been done. Some 250,000 people were homeless, 30,000 children had been abducted to Bulgaria, and 750,000 people had become refugees, evacuated into government camps from vulnerable villages. She wrote:

> These refugees will soon leave their emergency tents and be repatriated to their destroyed villages. We could do a magnificent rehabilitation job if we shipped to them immediately blankets, clothing, shoes and kitchenware in as large quantities as possible. I am happy to tell you I was able to make the following arrangements, in case you will approve the proposed program in Greece...

Not everyone did approve. Some members of the Toronto committee thought that Greece itself should be prepared to take care of the destitute people, since it was receiving a large amount of military aid from the United States. But Dr. Lotta was not deterred. By February 1950, a four thousand kilogram shipment of new blankets and all sorts of clothing had been sent off, with ninety-nine boxes packed in Winnipeg. In April, another seven hundred kilogram shipment left Moncton. The Near East Foundation in Athens undertook to supervise distribution in the northern villages.

It was the start of nearly thirty years of USC association with Greece – the program was eventually phased out in June 1979. It began inevitably with relief measures and with large shipments of flour, clothing, and shoes. But it shifted as soon as possible to reconstruction work: loans to rebuild homes in Macedonian villages, gifts of crosscut saws and looms to communities that lived by forestry and weaving, and a famous tractor to the tragic village of Mesovouno. Later came the support of training institutions and the building of a model well baby clinic at Marathon. Most ambitious of all, three initiatives were launched to try out new concepts of community development among groups of villages.

Thirty years is a long time to maintain a program and it prompts the question, might it not have ended sooner? In 1949 Greece was in a desperate condition after a decade in which it had been invaded or fought over three times: by the Italians from Albania in 1940, by the Germans through Yugoslavia in 1941, and in civil war from 1946 to 1949. The picture of postwar recovery presented to tourists was deceptive; in the remoter areas where Dr. Lotta went, the scene remained stark. In 1957 as many as one-quarter of the 8,500,000 population had an income of less than fifty dollars a year. There were giant setbacks to development in the ugly form of earthquakes, and there followed in the 1960s the seven-year regime of the Colonels. The political tensions surrounding that period undermined efforts at community development.

Throughout those years, it was in fact a hard struggle for most Greeks with whom USC was working. Projects took longer to complete than anyone would have guessed. Yet the Greeks persevered, so the USC stayed by their side. And, it has to be added, Dr. Lotta was in no hurry to sever a connnection she had always cherished. A classicist by education, she wrote often of "my beloved Greece," and at the end of gruelling world tours she longed to retreat to the nurses' residence at the Marathon clinic, to write her reports as she gazed out over the blue Aegean Sea. For the last seven years at least, only a very small USC program continued. But it was enough reason for her to visit Greece regularly and maintain the links she so valued.

Relief supplies came first. By August 1950, some nineteen thousand kilograms of clothing, blankets, pots and pans, and school supplies had been taken into villages of Western Macedonia. With advice from the Ministry of Welfare, the representative of the Near East Foundation, Mr. A. Koskinides, chose twenty-six mountain villages that were considered the most isolated and heavily destroyed. The Greek army provided trucks, mules, and soldiers to take the cases up from the towns. Mr. Koskinides followed and supervised the distribution to the villagers, to 8,171 adults and children, in his careful enumeration. He wrote to Dr. Lotta:

> Your first shipment of blankets and clothing was distributed in the heart of the winter when the repatriated refugees needed assistance most. These refugees in Western Macedonia have suffered more than any other Greeks from the invasions...In many of the

border villages the men still stand on guard at night to watch for the enemy, while during the day they work on the fields.

That summer Dr. Lotta went to some of the mountain villages herself. She traveled with an interpreter in a jeep over roads marked with signs warning of the danger of land mines. Her driver knew only one word of English, "Okay," and his confidence was rewarded; there were no accidents. But the distress was evident, and the aid, though welcome, was insufficent. Most wretched were the tiny babies she saw, wrapped either in soiled rags or tattered newspapers. She had only two boxes of layettes, the gift of the Alberta Women's Institute, to distribute, and she vowed she would improve on that performance.

Back in Canada she launched a March of Diapers, appealing to all Canadian mothers to give one diaper, and to their husbands to give a dollar. The target of eight kilometers of diapers, or some twelve thousand in all, was easily passed. The Parents-Teachers Association at Campbell River, British Columbia alone promised two thousand, and dozens arrived from small Prairie communities in all designs — some had polka dots and others pink-and-white candy stripes.[6]

By January 1951, eight tons of diapers and other babies' wear had been collected for Greece. The dollars that came with them were used to buy soap, at fifteen cakes a dollar, for she had seen many babies and young children with skin diseases caused by lack of soap. Dr. Lotta became known among some Greeks as the "Diaper Lady." Anyone who has gathered twenty-nine kilometers of diapers deserves such a title.

In her speaking tour that fall, she landed a bargain in Charlottetown, where the firm of J.W. Windsor offered her twenty-five hundred cartons of fishcakes (total weight of 25,515 kilograms) at fifty cents a carton. Transportation cost another nine hundred dollars, but a warm letter from Mr. Koskinides in April, after he visited fourteen welfare centers in Macedonia and Thrace, showed how worthwhile it was.

He told of arriving, for example, in Grevena where the feeding station for five hundred poor students had run out of food — "not a crumb left" — and the Eparch said he was Godsent. He went west to Nestorion, from where one hundred cases of fishcakes were carried for eight hours on army mules

---

[6]*Western Producer*, Saskatoon: 30 November 1950.

up into three mountain villages on the Albanian border, where refugees had just returned and had no crops. He also went east to Veria, where St. Paul once preached in A.D. 49, to bring food to villages in the Pierian mountains which the guerillas had devastated.

Dr. Lotta traveled again through northern Greece in July 1951 and had a devastating tale to tell. Some five hundred villages in the whole country north of Athens had suffered a crop failure "due to excessive rains, floods, hail and hot winds just before harvest time." Normally, a farmer took more than 210 kilograms of wheat from a hectare, but "this year in many places their three to four acres [1½ hectares] gave only 120 lbs. [54 kilograms], all in all."[7] She flew back to Canada with haunting stories. One was of a woman in Thivounion, an impoverished village high above Kilkis, who told her: "If you find [one cent] in my house, you may have my head!"

So, in September Dr. Lotta launched her Bread for Greece Crusade across Canada. The response was overwhelming. In four months, seventy thousand dollars poured in, and on some peak days more than eight hundred letters arrived at the tiny USC office at 48 Sparks Street. Many donations were of one or two dollars, although some groups, like the Toronto Greek organization Ahepa, made large pledges. Despite a lengthy dock strike in New York, 365,000 kilograms of flour had been shipped by early February 1952, and by April had been distributed in villages in northern Greece. In June, another 225,000 kilograms went to twenty-seven villages much further south in the mountains beyond Karpenissi, and Dr. Lotta was there for a first sight of the difficult terrain where the Canadian-American Program (CAP) of community development would later be launched. She also went north to Grevena, where she enjoyed a welcome from schoolchildren "with flowers and a trembling little boy who had forgotten all his greeting-text for me, and trumpets and tambours and such an old-fashioned photographer! Our jeep was filled every night with all the flowers we received in the villages which we visited, because the news had spread all over Macedonia like wildfire that I love flowers!"[8]

She also received the Medal of St. Paul from the old archbishop of Athens, who told her he was "jealous of the record which

---

[7] Circular no. 7, 9 August 1951.
[8] Circular, 4 June 1952.

Canada possesses, doing so much good." The bronze medal was so heavy that, to avoid paying excess baggage (she carefully informed her supporters), she carried it in her purse during flights on the way home.

There were two more Bread for Greece crusades, in 1953 and 1956. The final campaign, which provided funds for a shipment of 264 metric tons was prompted by devastation she saw around the harbor city of Volos, where three-quarters of the houses were destroyed, and 110,000 made homeless in an earthquake.

To the end of its association with the country, the USC continued to send food to Greece in the wake of natural disasters; indeed, milk powder was sent in 1979. But, as early as 1952, Dr. Lotta was writing about moves to self-reliance. She had talked to village priests and teachers about steady ways for people to earn money to buy food, since the government had run out of funds for roadbuilding and other "work-relief" schemes.

The widows of Mesovouno

Mesovouno provided the first example of self-reliance. It is a small village on the lower slopes of the Vermio Hills, looking westward across a wide valley down which runs a main road from Yugoslavia to Ptolemaida and Kozani, and the heart of Macedonia. It is more than sixty kilometers north of the Aliakmon river line which British forces had intended to hold against a German invasion in 1941. When German troops surged through the Monastir Gap and down the valley in April 1941, Mesovouno was one of only a few villages in the area that decided to resist, and the men went up into the hills.

The resistance was not well organized, however, and the men became discouraged after some months. When the Germans sent word that they would not be harmed, only briefly questioned if they returned, they came down again. It was, of course, a trap. Within a week, German troops came after midnight and collected all the people from their homes into a field below the Church of the Prophet of Elias. There they separated the men and boys from the women and children, tied their hands, and took them to a field at the bottom of the village. At first light, they shot them all. There is today a simple marble slab in that field, with a flower bed and paving stones. Under the inscription, "Died for their country in the year 1941," are 140 names.

Mesovouno became a village of widows, struggling through the German occupation and then evacuated during the civil war. When Lotta first visited there in 1951 and asked how she could help, the black-clad women told her: "You cannot give us back our men who are gone forever. But you can replace their hands with a tractor."

She spoke about the Mesovouno request when she launched her first Bread for Greece Crusade that fall. The Women's Institutes of Ontario quickly raised ten thousand dollars, and a shiny red Cockshutt tractor from Brantford was bought, complete with plough and disc harrow. It was handed over to Dr. Lotta in a ceremony on Sparks Street in April 1952, in front of the Greek ambassador and Senator Cairine Wilson, and the president of the Federated Women's Institutes of Ontario, Mrs. R.G. Purcell, also passed on an extra one thousand dollars for fuel and spare parts. The next month, Dr. Lotta spent an "exciting and happy day" in Mesovouno, while the women organized a cooperative. They agreed the tractor was to be community property, to be used by every family.

Its arrival in Mesovouno, on 18 July, was graphically described by a Canadian woman, Julie Hanidis, who was secretary of the USC Advisory Committee in Greece. She reached the village an hour before the tractor, in time to meet the young progressive-minded women's leader, Mrs. Sophia Mavrina, whose husband was one of those massacred.

The tractor finally came. "There was great excitement. The boy scouts and home guards had formed a guard of honor. Mrs. Mavrina and I led the way to the tractor. Everything that could utter a sound did so. Birds twittered and hens squawked." And, of course, everyone made inspirational speeches, including a village humorist who said that, since the tractor came from Ontario, the home of the Dionne quintuplets, their own produce would naturally be increased fivefold.

Reading this saga in the USC archives and struck by an old photograph of widows with hollow eyes and worn hands, I planned to visit Mesovouno during a trip to Greece in May 1983. What had happened to the village in the thirty intervening years? Had the women made a go of it? Was a single tractor really all that important?

Mesovouno is not widely known, although I found the 1971 census list showed 724 people were legally resident there. So it still existed, but nobody in Ottawa or Athens could point to it on a map. Finally I found the village nestling between the hills (which is the translation of its name) by taking a bus from Kozani and a taxi from Ptolemaida. It was Good Friday in the Greek Orthodox calendar.

Five men, who had been sitting in the café, walked with me down the lane to the field of the massacre, telling me details of the story. I placed some red roses against the memorial and looked back to the church on the hill. An old woman was sitting, curled up on a stone beneath a hedge. Nobody spoke to her. I asked the men whether the tractor still existed, and the mood lightened. We climbed up the hill to the courtyard of Maria Polychronidou, who they said was custodian of the tractor. She first showed me the outside bake-oven in which her husband had hidden in 1941 and so escaped execution, and then she took me on to what she called "the museum."

It was, in truth, a corner of a stony field. The famous tractor stood there on blocks, with a broken axle, threadbare tires, and short of a gearshift and seat. The trailer the USC later provided was attached to it with barbed wire. Wild flowers were growing out of the battery.

We all laughed affectionately at the wreck. Vassilos slapped its flank, jumped on its platform, pointed to the still legible plaque "Gift of the Federated Women's Institutes of Ontario." Maria began clearing sticks away from around it, and when I gave her a color photograph of Dr. Lotta she kissed it. Then someone remembered that Antonios was a nephew of Sophia Mavrina, and we went off to find him on the far side of a wheat field, gazing into a hole where a pipe had leaked.

We all sat on the ground beside the hole and memories began to flow. One man, who had worked as a clerk in Cologne and spoke to me in German, said Sophia had had no schooling and thought Canada was something less than a country. So, on receiving the tractor, she had simply said: "Thank you, Mr. Canada." Antonios remembered his aunt explaining why, because of jealousies from a neighboring village, the progress of Mesovouno under her leadership had not been straightforward. She had told her young nephew: "You know about a camel and its crooked neck? Well, it's like that!"

But, in fact, Mesovouno had made much progress, and the old tractor played its useful part for many years. Antonios said it had been used to plough up to four hectares for each farmer, and it had been the basis for cooperation in many things.

And the village had prospered. It was not to be expected that such a crop of widows would go unhusbanded for long; men had moved in and married and helped work the land. That day there were green rectangles of young wheat quilting the valley, onions sprouting in house gardens, Virginia tobacco seedlings being grown under plastic, and blossom in the apple orchards. "If you taste the apples from Veria, you will know the difference," they said proudly.

Moreover, in 1983 the village was alive with tractors, speeding past the cafe on a score of errands with young people. I thought of the museum piece up on the stony hillside. Mesovouno had moved on, but the first one had given the village a timely push.

Homes but few jobs

There were other moves that the USC made to encourage or restore self-reliance. One was to provide 175 crosscut saws, costing only nine dollars each, to the men in lumbering villages whose tools had been stolen by the guerillas. This simple gift gave them back their livelihood. Another move was to provide building loans for villagers in Macedonia to rebuild their war-destroyed homes.

It was a pathetic incident − a baby freezing to death in his cradle − that led Dr. Lotta into her Houses for Greece campaign in 1955. In the village of Pyrgos near Ptolemaida, she met twenty-five-year-old Aspasia Serimis still grieving over her tragedy. Her makeshift hut had walls so thin that her four-month-old baby, though placed beside a burning stove, froze in the February winds. And there were, Lotta learned, more than four thousand houses that needed rebuilding in Kozani district alone. But because of the earthquakes further south in Thessaly, Volos, and the Ionian islands, the Greek government had removed all its available material to these new diaster areas.

Her first reaction was to donate Canadian lumber, but transportation costs were prohibitive; it would have cost the USC $10,000 to ship $20,000 worth of lumber from the Maritimes. So she followed the example of Aide Suisse à l'Europe, a voluntary agency which had set up a $17,000 revolving fund in Kozani district. The money went into loans, the equivalent of $330 each, enough to buy the necessary materials for a two-roomed cottage. The recipients bound themselves to repay the interest-free loans within ten years.

The USC raised $20,000 for a similar scheme in two villages near Grevena, Karpero and Doxera. The first loans of $300 each were made to sixty-five families in Karpero in 1956, and they had to find the other $500 that it would cost to construct a simple house from local stone. When the Karpero houses were completed, and their owners began to repay their loans, another twenty-six families in Doxera received their $300 loans.

Repayment became a problem. Partly this was due to bad luck; the earthquakes and poor harvests and lack of jobs. Partly it was psychological; since there was no interest to pay on the loan, there was no incentive to pay it off in a short time. After fifteen years, only half the total had been repaid. But Dr. Lotta was determined that it should be paid, and Mrs. Effie Goussi of the Hellenic Red Cross, although nearly eighty by then, was kept busy supervising the accounts. Through the 1970s, about $1,500 a year was reimbursed through the Agricultural Bank of Greece in Grevena, and the money was used for later USC training projects.

Doxera today has about one hundred houses (some built with Swiss aid) and three hundred people. During the German occupation it had sunk to five families. But no one would call it prosperous. The Grevena forests are famous for their oak and pine, but a factory that was built nearby never opened its woodworking operations, as the owner did not get a completion loan from the government. A farmer said to me: "We have the privilege of nature here: We breathe clean air and there's no pollution. But there's no work, either." Many young people had left for jobs in Germany, and their elders often relied on their remittance payments.

However, there was pride in the housing. One housewife, Eleftheria, whose earlier house had been burned by German troops, showed me around the two-roomed home she and her husband had built with USC support. It has a strong wooden floor and good furniture. She had six daughters and three sons, now grown up, and at one time twelve people had lived in the two rooms. A neighbor had a similar story: four children living away, her home a classic cottage with goats to milk, and onions in a little fenced garden.

At the café, an old man whose own four children had left for the cities, recognized Dr. Lotta's photograph and said kindly: "She helped revive the place."

70

Training for girls

The next logical step for the USC in Greece, after relief and reconstruction, was to support training. This is the pattern the agency followed in many countries, and in Greece, as elsewhere, the training was focused on girls and ranged from handicrafts to rural health. Three institutions were mainly involved: the Glifada Vocational School in Athens and the rural girls' school attached to the American Farm School outside Thessaloniki, both teaching handicrafts; and the Marathon clinic and nurses' residence.

The Glifada school gave two years training to girls of poor families, usually from villages. For nine years from 1950, foster parents in Canada sponsored twenty girls, out of a total enrolment of more than two hundred, at sixty dollars a year. As usual, the connection grew beyond simple sponsorship. The Calgary branch sent eight knitting machines, one outstanding needleworker was offered a job at the National Museum in Ottawa, and several Greek-Canadian foster parents were keen to continue sending contributions after the girls had returned to their villages.

Support of the rural girls' school near Thessaloniki took a different turn. For twenty years from 1947, a group of British Quakers, whom Dr. Lotta described as "rather austere," ran an orphaned girls' school in a building loaned to them by the American Farm School. The farm school itself is a wondrous place. Established as the Agricultural and Industrial Institute in 1904 by an American Congregationalist minister, John Henry House, on twenty-one hectares of "parched, waterless land in a bandit-infested area," it offers full-time training for more than two hundred boys and girls, as well as short courses for thousands every year, and it has the best dairy herd in Greece. But the rural girls' school in its first incarnation was not a total success. The Quakers put emphasis on baby care and homecrafts, and several of the girls preferred to find work in Thessaloniki's factories or in Germany.

When the Quakers left in 1968, the Farm School took over responsibility and turned it into a two-year program concentrating on dressmaking, tailoring, embroidery, rug making, and weaving, in addition to more academic subjects and home economics. It hoped that Greek village women could increase their income by supplying the growing handicrafts market in Western Europe, and these girls could become village instructors as well as setting up a small business. Those with weaving skills were given, on graduation, a locally made loom costing about twenty-one dollars, which they would repay from their earnings. Others received sewing machines and books of patterns.

Instead of sponsoring individual students, the USC for ten years paid the salaries of two Greek women who were instructing the girls in sewing and weaving. The contribution rose in that period from forty-three hundred dollars to nearly twelve thousand dollars as the cost of living climbed steeply in Greece. When some USC board members questioned the continuance of this program, Dr. Lotta defended it by saying that more than 140 of the 178 girls who graduated between 1966 and 1976 had gone back to their villages, and in any case, a part of the contribution was paid from "blocked funds," money reimbursed from the Grevena building loans, which had to remain in Greece.

But the Marathon clinic was her real joy. In January 1960, at the request of the president of the Hellenic Red Cross, she had gone to distribute layettes to mothers at the nearby village of Nea Makri. She was appalled at the condition of these families, only thirty-two kilometers from the outskirts of Athens. Many were the families of shepherds, who brought their flocks down from the distant mountains of Epirus to graze for the winter on the plains.

When she had seen their shacks made of sacking, small bits of wood and leaves, she went back to exclaim about the situation to the Red Cross president, Constantinos Georgacopoulos. Together they decided on the construction of a well baby clinic and a first-aid station on a six-hectare plot of land his organization owned nearby.

There were years of delay, mostly for political reasons. But in January 1965, Dr. Lotta officially opened the Nea Makri Health Center. She wrote to her board at the time: "I consider this one of the best and most far-reaching investments our organization has ever made in capital outlays." At that stage the USC had contributed fifteen thousand dollars to the ninety thousand dollars cost, but added another twenty thousand dollars for the nurses' residence later.

The health center had several purposes. Twice a week two doctors, a child specialist, and a gynaecologist held a clinic for mothers and children from ten nearby villages. By 1969 some twelve hundred families were registered, and in four years ten thousand immunization shots were given. There was also the first-aid station, increasingly used in traffic accidents. Even more important, the center became the base for student nurses – the Hellenic Red Cross ran the largest school of nursing in Greece – to do a month's public health training in rural areas during their first and third years.

The Nea Makri Health Center became a national model, and in 1978 the Hellenic Red Cross launched another with six doctors. The only ironic note was that the Marathon area, which seemed so impoverished in 1960, soon became comparatively prosperous. Two factories were established there, and children's summer camps on the historic site of Marathon provided a market for eggs and milk, as well as creating jobs for local women. Dr. Lotta questioned mothers attending the clinic in 1969 and found they had an average income of three dollars a day. She wrote: "While this improvement in itself is most encouraging, I would feel better if the Center with its magnificent resources were available to people in desperate need."

The links with the Hellenic Red Cross, with which Dr. Lotta felt a closer bond than she did with many other partner agencies, functioned in a dozen other ways. In 1958 she laid the foundation stone of a forty-bed dormitory the USC donated to the Red Cross preventorium for pretubercular children built at Aghios Demetrios, high up facing Mount Athos. And in 1957 the HRC became the distributor of most of the USC shipments of clothing, flour, and milk, as well as supervising the repayment of building loans. There was also some direct support of the organization; for example, providing material for summer uniforms for its two hundred trainee nurses. In 1969 Dr. Lotta calculated that in twenty years of association more than $1 million worth of Canadian donations, in cash and kind, had been channeled through the Hellenic Red Cross.

Sequel of the priest's quarrel

Greece was probably one of the most difficult countries in which to experiment with schemes of community development in the 1950s. And yet, for nearly a decade USC Canada was vigorously involved in supporting three extensive community efforts there. The results were mixed, for every sort of reason:

73

climatic, socio-economic, and political. But the lessons learned, both for the Greek participants and for USC Canada, were invaluable. Some of these lessons were later applied in India at the Karnatak Health Institute.

The predictable difficulties in Greece were mainly of attitudes among the rural population. Rugged individualism, inbred suspicions, even a lingering sense of inferiority after centuries of Ottoman colonialism, and a fatalism expressed in the phrase, "That's just the way it is with us" – all this made a poor basis for cooperation and initiative. They tended to wait for the government to act, and as Dr. Lotta explained, its structure was flawed:

> Greek administration is so centralised and at the same time so departmentalised that little overall coordination exists between the different Departments. Quite naturally, farmers are much less well informed than people in the towns about current legislation. On the other hand – and this was difficult for me to believe at first – the different village authorities never sit down together to discuss problems which are common to the entire community, or several neighboring communities, and to plan.[9]

Tony Trimis, the coordinator for seven years of the community development program in Thessaloniki, has written at length about these vertical and horizontal relationships, and he endorses Professor Roland Warren's definition of community development as "a deliberate and sustained attempt to strengthen the horizontal pattern of a community."[10]

Bruce Lansdale, director of the American Farm School since 1955 and the third generation of his family to live and work in northern Greece, says the idea of the Thessaloniki program was born when his associate director, Theodore Litsas, returned from trying to mediate in a squabble between the priest and the schoolteacher in a nearby village. The quarrel had split the entire village, and Litsas exclaimed: "Isn't it too bad these guys only get together to fight? Wouldn't it be great if we could get them together at some other time?"

When they sounded out leading figures in several villages about holding a meeting to discuss what could be done, the

---

[9]Circular no. 5, 8 May 1958.
[10]Roland L. Warren, *The Community in America*, University of Chicago Press, 1923, p. 324.

74

responses were almost all discouraging. "We can't do anything without government help" was followed by "We need to know what other villages are doing." Lansdale and Litsas accepted this challenge and planned a seminar at the Farm School with leaders from a cluster of six villages and also government officials. (The horizontal and vertical relationships, in effect). A set pattern was decided upon; each official spoke to the village leaders and then were subjected to questions. Later, the horizontal connections were addressed, and priorities agreed on for village projects.

The three-day seminar was held in May 1958. Says Lansdale: "We had no money and no clearly defined goals. All we had was a dream."

Dr. Lotta missed the seminar but spent two days visiting the six villages. She was struck by the different priorities of village leaders, according to their own functions as teachers, farmers, or priests, and surprised at the different levels of development within a cluster of villages. Some had no drainage or latrines, but others nearby had good roads, irrigated crops, a basketball playground.

The USC board was hesitant about supporting a dream. They wanted a well-defined project, like an irrigation canal or a training center. But Lansdale rejected (and still rejects) that view: "You don't provide buildings. What you do is provide inspiration. You get the villagers to realise what they can do, and you get the government to realise how much the villagers can do, and also to realise that, if they approach the villagers in the right way, they can inspire them."

It took a year, and the appointment of Antonios Trimis as coordinator, before the USC board was happy with this style. Lansdale says: "Tony Trimis was a perfect programmer, good with government and a fine researcher. But his real strength was relating to the people. He appealed to their child-sense and he used humor – and yet he pushed them."

Trimis certainly is a remarkable man. His grandfather was a shepherd outside Athens who acquired some wealth by buying land which was later incorporated in the spreading city. He set up a family trust to give scholarships for studies in architecture or agriculture. Tony's father took one to study agriculture in England and returned to build a model farm near the capital. Tony himself studied agriculture at Cornell University, where he first met Lansdale, and agricultural economics in Tennessee.

He then spent a year with a processing cooperative of Spokane pea-growers. After service in the Greek army, he came to the Farm School. The USC paid his salary as coordinator of the community development program for seven years. His doctoral thesis, based on the project, contains a full account of the work done in 151 villages, with a population of 170,000, during those years.[11]

He was, as Lansdale says, "a bear for work." As coordinator, he held 420 meetings in these villages and made 660 informal visits to them. Nearly every village – 140 out of 151 – set up a village development committee. Some 3,260 village leaders, both appointed officials and elected, came to one of 18 training seminars held either at the Farm School or in central villages. They planned 1,335 projects or group activities, and accomplished 714 of them. The success rate was higher in projects related to health and hygiene, village athletics, and the village church than in those linked to agriculture, fishing, or reforestation. And from 1960 the program received material recognition from the Royal National Foundation, the coordinating agency of all official community development programs in Greece, which agreed to underwrite 30 percent of the budget.

But, as Trimis emphasizes, "It's not the *what*, but the *how*." He tells the story of the village of Calamatou, with a population of 980, in semi-mountainous country about ninety-five kilometers from Thessaloniki. Its people bickered less over politics, co-operated more in farming activities, than most other villages. But there were moments of self-doubt. A few enthusiasts returned from a seminar inspired to complete, by their own efforts, a water-supply scheme that had waited three years for government funds. They led others up the mountain to dig a three-mile ditch and lay the pipes. By noon they had only dug a few feet in the rocky soil with picks and shovels.

One villager complained: "We can't do this by cooperation. It needs hard cash. Let's go back to the village – we are not fools!"

At this critical point, one leader said: "No, we are not fools. We can do it...with a mechanical digger. The secretary of our cooperative is here. Why don't we all sign for a loan through our cooperative and rent the digger?"

---

[11] *Community Development as an Element in Area and Regional Socio-economic Growth and Development, with Special Reference to the Community Development Program of Thessaloniki, Greece*, Montana State University: 1967.

The story ends well. Everyone signed for the loan, the digger was rented, the ditch dug, and the two thousand dollar loan repaid within two years, with profits from the extra vegetables grown.

A different example was of the village of Epanomi where, after a seminar, the athletic association decided to revive the annual festival of horseback races. It was a great success. Some fifteen villages sent riders to compete, five thousand spectators showed up, Epanomi had a profitable day, and everyone there – officials and ordinary villagers – felt good about this joint effort. Which is why Tony Trimis emphasizes the *how*.

The CAP approach

Many factors made the approach to community development in Evritanias prefecture in central Greece quite different. It was one of the poorest parts of Greece and had lost more than half its population between 1940 and 1958, when the Canadian-American program (CAP) began. Dr. Lotta was fond of calling it "the Switzerland of Greece"; but she once added realistically, "Karpenissi is one of the most needy areas…There are only stones, beauty and hunger – nothing else."[12] There were few roads into the fifteen hundred-meter mountain areas, and there were recurrent earthquakes and landslides to destroy a family's hopes. The isolation, the disasters, and the bitter winters were driving young people (and others not so young) into the more hospitable plains.[13]

Dr. Lotta first saw the Karpenissi district in 1953. It was neglected then, and when she returned in 1958 the only outside agency active there was the Congregational Christian Service Committee. The CCSC's operation was headed by Newell Steward, an American Quaker who had worked with black migrant laborers in the southern United States. Steward believed that a first step in community development had to be

---

[12]Report to the USC board, 1958.

[13]Place-names give a clue to the hardships. The village where a first CAP conference was held was called Laspi, or "Mud," until its inhabitants stirred themselves to change it to St. Nicholas. And the place chosen in 1967 as a center for further work was called Agrafa, or "Not Written on any map" – for it was five hours by mule from a passable road.

to increase the meager incomes of villagers. In 1958 in this district, a family's average income was the equivalent of $150 (U.S.); only one family in six had livestock, and the rest made some money from selling vegetables, fruit, and chestnuts.

Steward sorted out a program with Chrys Kehayias, the community organizer and an American Farm School graduate, to work with fifteen thousand people in thirty-one villages to use their resources to the utmost. Fruit and tomatoes had gone unpicked and meat had spoiled because food preservation was unknown. Again, most of the water flowing from the hills in ditches to the fields and villages was lost in seepage. So the first three-year program in three clusters of villages, to which the USC contributed $31,500, concentrated on covering such gaps and teaching new techniques. USC paid, for example, the salaries of a Greek social worker and a home economist, and also supplied sprays and stock medicines.

On her fourth visit, in 1961, Dr. Lotta could record impressive progress. In two years the people, working without wages, had lined eight thousand meters of water ditches with cement, and built latrines, laundry sheds, and slaughter houses – no easy matter when sand and gravel had to be brought from the plains by mule or on human backs. Chrys Kehayias trained a "mobile school" of farmers in pruning and grafting, and they toured the villages teaching others. Together they pruned ten thousand apple trees and grafted twenty thousand wild chestnuts. The home economist, with containers and pressure cookers bought from USC funds, taught canning indefatigably and trained at least one woman in every village to teach food preservation; no fewer than ten thousand jars of meat, fruit, and vegetables were canned in the first two years. A nearby animal station, built with CARE funds, provided bulls and rams to improve the quality of the local livestock, and Kehayias introduced cowpeas as a winter feed.

There was great enthusiasm at that time. Incomes rose in three years by an average 50 percent per family. Steward ascribed much of the success to the use of social workers, whose approach was to help individuals to help themselves, rather than follow the top-down direction of most government programs. "The people are coming alive," he said.

But there followed many disappointments. Plans to build a small tourist hotel in Laspi and link to it many small industries —from broiler chickens to handicrafts—soon collapsed. So did a scheme Dr. Lotta backed for an agricultural training school at Domnista. It was shelved partly because of earthquakes in February 1966 that damaged most of the villages nearby. The government began talking of shifting people from forty villages because the danger of landslides had increased.

Dr. Lotta refused to be discouraged. In 1966 she listed past achievements – irrigation ditches, food preservation, the introduction of Swiss goats and good seed potatoes, the perambulating "donkey library" of five hundred books provided with the dollars of Saskatchewan schoolchildren – and saw future opportunities in the relocation of villages. She hoped to build a women's training center at Agrafa and firmly told Mr. Steward, who had lapsed back into relief and welfare work, that he must return to community development schemes if he wanted any more USC funding.

Then, in April 1967 the military coup took place, and community development fell out of favor. The Greek colonels were prepared to double the old age pensions of farmers and to increase the support price of wheat. But they did not want dialogue or village democracy. The community development programs slowed to an eventual halt. And the bitter winter of 1968-69, when the mountain villages were snowbound from October to early May, sent villagers in droves to settle in the plains.

The "eagle's nest" villages

The third, much smaller, area of community development work was in Thesprosia district, close to the Albanian border and across from the island of Corfu. The program was entirely under Greek supervision. USC was led to this remote corner of Greece – "We live hidden from the eyes of God," one farmer's wife said – by Michael Zissis, a civil servant in the Department of Social Welfare who had accompanied Dr. Lotta on journeys around Macedonia. She described him as "one of those precious visionaries whom an emergency produces, who is able to come up with original ideas, for the good of a great many people."[14]

When Zissis was transferred from Kozani to Thesprosia, he came up with two ideas that USC supported from 1958. In the

---

[14]Circular no. 6, 15 May 1960.

first project, ten specially chosen families in two "eagle's nest" villages in this steep countryside were each given an artificially inseminated purebred Swiss cow, while six other villages received twenty-five beehives or hundreds of olive tree seedlings. The second project was to develop a tree nursery of olive, orange, and peach seedlings on a six-hectare plot donated near the harborfront at Igoumenitsa.

The total USC contribution was only eighty-five hundred dollars, but it was all a resounding success, according to a report in 1965. The quality of the local livestock had been decisively improved by the Swiss lineage, not to mention the vigorous supporting efforts of Jimmy, a bull imported in 1958. Thousands of tree seedlings were sold to farmers at cost price, and a competitor "who tried to undercut our prices with lower quality goods" went out of business. And the larger honey production from the "European" beehives introduced by Zissis was so striking that people in nearby villages switched to these more expensive hives.

By then Michael Zissis had retired back to Kozani, but a local partner agency — the "Committee for the Love of the Green" — was supervising what were, in every sense, model projects.

CHAPTER 5

Into Asia

Korea: The largest program

SOUTH KOREA was the scene of the largest program of the USC for more than twenty years from the early 1950s. When it came to an end on 31 December 1978, the agency had invested some $13 million in that country. This was at that time more than half the USC's total income in funds and gifts-in-kind (mainly clothing, food, and medical supplies). At the time of the withdrawal, Dr. Lotta called it "the USC's greatest success story during the past thirty-three years."[1]

It was not, however, the only large program there had been in Asia. Three other programs – assistance to Arab refugees, especially in the Gaza Strip, the programs in both parts of Vietnam, and the wide range of projects in India over a twenty-three-year period – were all considerable. They also carried many lessons: political problems, the importance of recruiting good field representatives and of moving from emergency aid to development assistance, the tricky question of when to withdraw from a major program. Mistakes were made, but on the whole these programs stand scrutiny well.

When the soldiers of North Korea crossed the 38th parallel on 25 June 1950, Canadians knew hardly anything about that divided country. Besides a few United Church missionaries, practically no Canadians had been there, and there was certainly no national interest at stake in the area. But the North's aggression was seen as a test of the fledgling United Nations, and with fifteen other nations, Canada sent troops to fight under the UN Command. By the time an armistice agreement was eventually signed in July 1953, nearly 27,000 Canadians had served there, mainly an infantry brigade, but also the crews of five destroyers and scores of fighter and transport pilots. In the cemetery above Pusan are buried 378 Canadian

---

[1] Report to the USC board, 14 May 1978.

soldiers. Many Canadian families had reason to feel a bond with Korea.

In July 1952, Dr. Lotta was invited by the UN Korea Reconstruction Agency (UNKRA) to make a fortnight's visit and investigate a possible program. Although the Greek program was at its height, she was keen to make the trip and told her directors that the agency could run both programs, and it would help the fund-raising campaign in the fall.

Her trip to Korea in August was a difficult assignment. The monsoon rains had been followed by increased Chinese probing and patrolling around the Imjin River, and Dr. Lotta found there was a severe lack of transport. Worse than this, however, was the absence of statistics and a noticeable lack of cooperation from officials, presumably unused to a visitor with so many questions to ask. But working with the YWCA was a Korean woman, Esther Park, who gave her helpful introductions, and Dr. Lotta returned by RCAF *Northstar* (keeping her total expenses down to $308) with three projects to help some of the children among the six million refugees adrift in the country. These were a Milk for Korea campaign to provide twenty-five thousand primary schoolchildren in Seoul with a cup of milk every lunchtime, a minimum of one thousand quilts as a Christmastime gift, and school supplies such as scribblers and pencils.

Brigadier J.M. Rockingham, who had been the Twenty-fifth Brigade's first commander, commended the Help Korea campaign, saying it was a unique opportunity to help children, the war's innocent victims. And the campaign went well. Within two months Dr. Lotta raised fifty thousand dollars, during a flying visit to New York she persuaded UNKRA to pay all the ocean transportation costs, and she ordered 31,750 kilograms of skim milk powder (half the price of whole milk powder, and it keeps better). In mid-November a first railway carload left the Gananoque milk factory, decked out with Canadian and Korean flags, for a ship in Vancouver that would get the milk powder to Seoul in time for distribution in seventy-six schools at the start of the January term. By the end of January 110,000 kilograms had been shipped, enough to continue milk distribution for the worst three months of winter.

At this stage the USC did something it never tried again anywhere: it sent a staff member abroad as its field representative. Theresa Potter, who had served in both the New Zealand Army and the British Red Cross, reached Seoul in February to super-

Dr. Lotta receiving the Order of Canada from Governor General Roland Michener (1972).

At highschool in Prague, 1924.
Front row, two in from left:
Emmy Irmenbach and Lotta.
Center: Father Leppel. Front row,
two in from right: Lilly, Lotta's
younger sister.

Lotta, dressed as a photographer, at
the wedding of an aunt. She and Lilly
recited poems to the guests.

Lilly with her husband, Charles Steen, on the seashore at Tel Aviv about 1941.

Lotta's parents, Max and Else Hitschmann on holiday.

Lotta and Lilly's grandmother, Rosa Theiner.

Marius Barbeau, great friend of Lotta and famous folklorist, translating native songs.

Maison d'Enfants at Sèvres, France. Teaching disturbed, war-shocked children.

*Canadian Ambassador George
Magann at Kotili in northern
Macedonia with a gift of
cross-cut saws.*

*Lotta in a traditional
Greek costume.*

Community development in Greece. Tony Trimis with Lotta in the audience (second from left) in Thessaloniki, Greece (c. 1961).

The widows of Mesovouno, Greece after the Germans had shot all the men and boys in 1941.

Dr. Lotta interviewing an old man with Cho Ki Dong, USC Korea director, looking on.

Dr. Lotta admiring the carpentry work of a young boy sponsored in a children's home.

vise the distribution and write some articles for Canadian papers that would sustain interest for a subsequent campaign. Mrs. Potter, in her honesty, found it impossible to give a detailed or glowing account of physical improvements among the children. They were not, she reported, weighed before and after the distribution period, the cups of milk they received were of different sizes, and they weren't fed regularly at noon. But their resistance to sickness seemed to be stronger. She came home early, after six weeks, as her husband was ill. Her whole trip cost $405.08.

The campaign for scribblers had a temporary setback. Dr. Lotta pursuaded the Queen's Printer, Mr. Edmond Cloutier, who was a wartime friend, to donate a ton of scrap paper for prisoners at Kingston Penitentiary to make into notebooks and pack in boxes. This inexpensive scheme (the only costs would have been box-lumber and the freight to New York) was canceled for lack of storage space at Kingston. Instead, teachers in Newfoundland came through in April with enough funds to buy twenty-four thousand notebooks and forty thousand pencils.

Dr. Lotta returned from a second visit to Korea in August 1953 (just after the armistice) with two priorities: to raise funds to provide barley gruel for the children and to gather shoes and socks to protect them against frostbite. But she soon found that her annual fund-raising tour was going badly across the Prairies, one of her favorite regions. Grain sales had been slack and there was little ready cash. She was depressed when she walked into the *Victoria Daily Times* and told her story to Bruce Hutchison, the editor-in-chief. This famous Canadian journalist rose to the occasion with a powerful editorial that began:

> Among Canada's major assets in world affairs we would nominate Dr. Lotta Hitschmanova, the tiny woman with the big heart who, at the moment, is trying to save 700,000 Korean children from starvation this winter.
>
> Back from a heart-breaking look at Korea, Dr. Hitschmanova says that many such children − victims of an international convulsion beyond their understanding, waifs in a world storm − will not see another spring if Canadians fail to feed and clothe them. When she tells us that last winter many children's feet had to be amputated because they froze for lack of clothing, the entire free world should take a good long look at the mirror of its conscience. And no one

---

[2] *Victoria Daily Times*, 5 December 1953.

should look harder than Canadians, who have food and clothing in abundance to spare.[2]

He contrasted the USC's "pitiful little budget of $125,000 for barley gruel" with the $2 billion that Canadians had already spent in fighting the Korean war, "the source of all this suffering." The paper launched a Christmastime campaign and raised nearly $12,000 in two weeks. It helped push her fund raising over the year's target in the last few days and was the first of many such newspaper campaigns.

Enough barley was sent, and mixed in Korea with milk, to provide 125,000 children with a daily bowl of gruel for the hungriest three months, January to March. It was, she reported, "the largest mass feeding project the agency has undertaken."

Barley was shipped to Korea for many years afterwards, but in her next year's fund raising (1954), she put the emphasis on sending dried salted codfish, because of protein deficiency among Korean children. Difficulties arose, however, about sending the 160,000 kilograms of codfish the agency bought in the Maritimes. It was learned at a late stage that only nonrefrigerated space was available on the sixty-day voyage from Halifax to Pusan. The USC board decided to split the cargo and spent nearly nine thousand dollars on freight charges for two-thirds of the fish to be railed to Vancouver for the shorter voyage, and then insured the smaller amount against spoilage. (UNKRA paid all ocean shipping charges, but CNR/CPR had ended free transportation in 1948). There was a send-off ceremony on Halifax's Pier 25, with Nova Scotia premier Henry Hicks presiding afterwards at a lunch aboard the SS *Leise Maersk*, consisting of − codfish. And the cargo sailed unspoiled to Korea.

This was not quite the end of the story. Dr. Lotta had agreed with the Korea Civil Assistance Command that the fish should go exclusively to children in orphanages and hospitals, just as fifty-five hundred kilograms of whole powdered sweetened milk, requested by a KCAC welfare officer in Seoul, should go to infants up to twelve months suffering from malnutrition who had been taken into that city's institutions. She complained forcefully to UNKRA when she found out later that the KCAC had allocated the codfish also to "welfare institutions and medical care facilities (including leprosaria) and other vulnerable groups of indigent persons," and that some of the milk had been given to fourteen-year-olds in Seoul's children's hospital who could easily have had UNICEF skim milk.

The whole operation had three consequences, one a light-hearted reaction and the others raising serious questions. The first of these consequences was that Dr. Lotta earned the odd nickname "Auntie Codfish" in Korea. The serious questions were the need it raised, in her view, to have someone in Korea who would act as supervisor of USC projects, and the importance, as expressed by the USC board, of a careful survey of Korean children's needs, so that the agency could decide whether to shift from this kind of emergency aid to long-term programming.

The solution to the question of a USC field representative was eventually found in 1957 when the agency teamed up with the Norwegian Korean Association (NKA) to enlarge a children's TB hospital in Seoul, and the NKA director, Gotfred Rekkebo, also began to keep a close eye on other projects for Dr. Lotta. Then in 1965, when Mr. Rekkebo had moved to the southern city of Mokpo, Cho Ki Dong became the USC director for Korea.

A man of driving force and stubborn determination, Mr. Cho spent his childhood in what is now North Korea before coming south in 1946. He studied electrical engineering before moving into social work, and he worked during the war with the Norwegians as an X-ray assistant in a field hospital. Later he was administrator of their hospital group under Mr. Rekkebo and also began doing voluntary work for the USC. When he became USC director, he was the first Korean to head any foreign agency in the country, and he went on to be chairman of the rather grand umbrella group of seventy organizations, the Korean Association of Voluntary Agencies.

Long-range focus on children

The board's question about long-term programming came at the right moment. In 1956, after Operation Codfish and the appeal for milk for malnourished babies, the USC program was reduced. In general, food conditions were improving. The wartime organizations, KCAC and UNKRA, were closing down. The future pattern of work was not yet clear, but it was certainly timely to look afresh at the people's persisting needs.

Dr. Lotta responded in her 1957 confidential report to the

USC board. The groups in Korea who were suffering most, she said, were orphans and beggar children, war widows, the refugees, and the very old.

Obviously, the USC could not tackle all these problems. It had, from an early stage, tried to help some war widows by shipping hundreds of Singer sewing machines (and soon only the heads, pedals, and wheels, for the tables could be made in Korea) from Hong Kong to the Women's Bureau of the Ministry of Social Affairs. When she thought the government-run projects were inefficiently managed, she organized later shipments through the Korean Church World Service. Many of the widows were helped on the way to recovery as they could earn up to forty dollars a month from their sewing.

But the concentration of effort, it was decided, had to be on children: in children's homes, in TB hospitals and rehabilitation centers, and in schools and clubs. Dr. Lotta came to call it "a daring and visionary program," with some good reason. For the USC was the first agency to employ a Korean team of trained social workers in this work – even before the government was doing so.

Children's homes and orphanages in Korea acquired a dubious reputation abroad in later years. Certainly, some directors were "on the make," drawing in funds from foster parents overseas and putting out the minimum to keep their wretched wards alive. Others were simply overwhelmed by the size of their task.[3] In the 1950s, there were about seventy thousand children in orphanages in South Korea. Some were indeed war orphans, others were abandoned children. There were many reasons for abandonment: a family breakup, the pressures of inflation, the child having an unwed mother who had slept with a foreign soldier. Only some twenty thousand of these orphans were sponsored by foster parents whose funding allowed the directors scope for improvements. Improvements were badly needed, and there was no dearth of Canadians wanting to be foster parents. Agencies, in fact, had lengthy waiting lists.

It was in these circumstances that Dr. Lotta looked for reputable children's homes that might be supported by Canadian foster parents through the USC. The program grew

---

[3] I wrote about the miseries and inadequacies of some Korean orphanages in an earlier book, *Half a Loaf: Canada's semi-role in developing countries*, Ryerson Press, Toronto: 1969, pp. 110-111.

rapidly to a peak in 1962 of some 640 children being sponsored at seven homes around Seoul and Inchon.

Dr. Lotta believed in making these homes much more than orphanages; they were to be foundations for the children's self-improvement. For example, at the Heimyung home in Seoul, Canadian foster parents were covering more than half the operational costs when they sponsored 120 children at sixty dollars a year. But she added many other things: some knitting machines, at thirty-five dollars each from Japan, on which the girls were given six months' training; scholarships for the most gifted half-dozen students; a grant of eleven thousand dollars to build three large cottages where 90 children could be relocated from an old Buddhist temple that was "utterly unfit for living quarters"; and — not to forget — thousands more kilograms of codfish. At Sun Ae home she found the children trying to do their evening homework by kerosene lamp; in the next year's budget she put in enough funds for electric light. Sun Ae was on land outside Inchon, donated by the director's father, and the children had planted thousands of pine and chestnut seedlings. The USC added funds for a sizeable greenhouse where they grew flowers for sale to defray their costs.

There were plenty of headaches, especially with certain directors. One, she discovered, was still sending letters to foster parents about four children who had already left. Another was a Seventh Day Adventist who so influenced some of his wards that one eighteen-year-old girl (offered a USC scholarship) would not attend university on a Saturday. Another director, having moved her orphanage away from the dangers of a government quarry to the foot of a mountain among ricefields, revealed her dream of running a big farm. Dr. Lotta reacted in two ways. She tried to bring her back to the job of caring for the children and maintaining a correspondence; and she also wrote advising her on better farming methods, suggesting how many goats the hill-pasture might carry and how to build a proper pigpen. Neither method of restraint was wholly successful.

The Sam Yook Disabled Children's Rehabilitation Centre in Seoul was a special case. When she first went there in 1956, to a ramshackle building near the center of the capital, Dr. Lotta wanted to help because of the war-mutilated children there, and Canadian foster parents were found for about fifty of them. Later, most of the children were postpolio cases, while others suffered from cerebral palsy or were blind. The facilities were improved when the U.S. Second Infantry Division raised funds for a center with modern facilities for physical rehabilitation on a new site. But Dr. Lotta had a series of differences with the director. He wanted to run lengthy vocational training courses in carpentry and other crafts. She argued that he should concentrate on physical rehabilitation and refer those who were able for vocational training elsewhere. She even wrote, in June 1962, to Dr. Howard Rusk in New York, an expert in rehabilitation, for his opinion, and he strongly backed her view.

The USC continued its support. In 1969, when I visited the center, 150 of its 220 children were sponsored from Canada, and the agency also paid a large part of the running costs. The director used to spend much of his time around government departments, which prompted criticism from Dr. Lotta. But his approaches paid off in 1974, when the government and Seoul City Hall became interested in making Sam Yook a showpiece project and together provided $700,000 for a model institution on the city's outskirts. Dr. Lotta, who attended the official opening, called it "the outcome of almost 20 years of careful investment of USC Friendship Dollars, of material aid, planning, guidance and" (she added with half-hidden meaning) "sometimes unwavering determination and diplomacy."[4]

In other quarters, she strongly pushed for more vocational training. One of the earliest projects had been to help the Salvation Army rebuild war-damaged schools. A nickel collection from every school class in British Columbia in 1955 provided thirty-five hundred dollars to reconstruct Son Nim school and to equip school workshops for such crafts as carpentry, tailoring, and tinsmith work. Wrote Dr. Lotta: "Education in Korea is still much too theoretical and impractical."[5] She favored the idea of all but the most exceptional students moving from middle school into three years of vocational training, rather than entering the "theoretical" high schools.

This was already in her mind in 1957 when she launched a scholarship fund with five thousand dollars in Kyonggi Do province, which surrounds Seoul. For, of the 102 boys and girls (90 of them orphans) who received awards, 30 were in primary school and 60 in middle school; only 12 were in high school. In 1959, as the exchange rate altered in favor of Canadian

---

[4]*Jottings from Korea*, July 1974.
[5]Confidential Report to the USC board, 1958.

dollars, she proposed that the USC spend six thousand dollars for three hundred scholarships in Kangwan Do province, which stretches up the eastern side to north of the 38th parallel into what the South Koreans called the "Soo Bok," or recovered area.

This northernmost part, near the demilitarized zone, tended to be an isolated and forgotten area, and the scholarship fund there was the first of its kind. Dr. Lotta went there in cold, snowy weather in 1963, to Kumwha Middle School, just three kilometers from the demarcation line. The propaganda loud-speakers were blaring from the North, she wrote, while the schoolchildren were in shabby uniforms and had no food for a noontime meal. Conditions were so poor there that she concluded it was the scholarship fund that was keeping thirteen schools going in this northern part.

Norwegian partners and Mokpo

But it was at the other end of the country − at Mokpo, in the southwest − that the USC had its greatest impact. The work in Mokpo centered upon the children's TB hospital, a collaborative effort with the Norwegian Korean Association − and that collaboration began years earlier, in 1957 in Mapo, the poorest district of Seoul.

Mapo had not always been so poor. It used to be a center for people who brought boats up the Han River to Seoul, but since the demarcation line placed the mouth of the river in Communist hands, this commerce had ceased, and by the mid-1950s unemployment was high among its 160,000 people. Some five hundred Norwegians had served in an army surgical hospital and formed the nucleus after the armistice for the Norwegian Korean Association (NKA). So it was natural that their first main venture was to set up a small hospital. They chose Mapo, and finding in the nearby orphanages an active TB incidence of 24 percent, they made it a children's TB hospital. The directors of Han No hospital were Gotfred Rekkebo, who was both a male nurse and a social worker, and his wife who was also a nurse. They had been in Korea since 1950.

When Dr. Lotta visited Mapo in 1957, she found the Rekkebos had plans to double the capacity of the main concrete building, to take in sixty patients, and to build an outpatients' department. She liked the latter project in particular. Tuberculosis was one

Lotta

of the worst enemies of Korea; estimates at that time were that
there were 300,000 infectious TB cases, and some 20,000
people died every year from it. There had to be hospital beds
for the most advanced cases (by 1969 there were still only 2000
TB beds in South Korea), but a bed case cost as much as 15 to 20
outpatients. So the USC provided funds for a six-room clinic
which was built alongside Han No hospital and was named
"Canada House." The well-equipped clinic became something
of a community center, for there was soon also a feeding station
where hundreds came daily for barley-and-milk gruel in the
hungry months. And, in order to try preventive measures and
attack the disease by home treatment, the USC paid for an
extension of Han No's services into the homes of Mapo
through a team of Korean health visitors and social workers.

So the foundations of collaboration between the two agencies
were well laid by May 1959, when the NKA president, Dr.
Herman Ramstad, traveled down to Mokpo with Dr. Lotta.
After asking many Koreans to name the area of greatest need,
the Rekkebos had found that Mokpo was indisputably at the
top of the list. For many wartime refugees, this city at the
southwestern corner was the end of the line. It was also a haven
for poor people fleeing from the seven hundred little offshore
islands in the Yellow Sea. But it had little to offer in jobs,
beyond a ceramics factory, a small shipyard, and a minor export
industry in shrimps to Japan. Some newcomers could find
shelter only in caves along the rocky coast. TB rates were
particularly high among the islanders and in the city's twenty
orphanages, yet there were no TB beds, even in the hospital
run by St. Columban sisters.

The visit started with a muddle as city officials had not
expected them so soon. But a good site was offered on a hill
with fresh air, where the ruins of an isolation hospital stood.
There was also plenty of excellent stone in Mokpo district. So
plans went ahead to build a children's TB hospital, although
with recurring doubts on the part of the USC. In the next few
years Dr. Lotta went three times to Oslo, and worried about
rising costs and the Mokpo council's wavering support, for the
city had six mayors within four years. She was also anxious
about the political situation, for in May 1961 General Park
Chung-Hee led a coup after the resignation of Syngman Rhee
and imposed an authoritarian state. The budget of the Ministry
of Health and Social Affairs had always been tiny, compared

90

with the funds for defence — about 2 percent of the total budget against 30 percent. Would the new government cut the health budget even further, and how would this affect such an ambitious project? In 1961 Dr. Lotta wrote with unusual pessimism: "This project was ill-fated from the very start...it is hard to muster the enthusiasm and faith that would befit an undertaking of such dimension or significance."[6] She recommended that the USC commitment to this project have a ceiling of $202,000 over eight years, after which it would be handed over to Mokpo council to finance and run.

Eventually, it worked out remarkably well. The American architect, whose services they borrowed from another agency, was disappointing, but two Korean architects compensated for him. When the hospital was formally opened in April 1962, she wrote that the three "have succeeded in blending Eastern style with Western efficiency, and the outcome is one of the most attractive hospitals I have ever seen."[7] The USC had at that point contributed $57,500 to the project, much of it collected in Victoria, British Columbia, and continued to help with running costs. The seventy-bed hospital took in about 350 advanced cases a year for totally free treatment, and the average stay was ten weeks. It ran smoothly for seven years under the gentle but alert direction of Dr. Park Chong Dal, while an outpatients' clinic was under the charge of a competent woman doctor. And in 1970, the administration passed into municipal hands without a hitch.

Just as important, collaboration with the NKA spread through Mokpo itself. Three public health nurses from the hospital followed up on the visits of a USC social worker, and every afternoon toured the shacks and lean-tos along the railway sidings and similar poor areas to find other family members of some little patient and try to stamp out the disease with them. The Norwegian contribution was to set up a control station for mass examination and BCG vaccination. The results, in seven years, were remarkable; the vaccine coverage of children under fourteen was twice as high as the national figure, and the prevalence of active TB was less than half.

But the work and the needs never ended. Dr. Lotta has written some harrowing descriptions of the conditions in Mokpo

---

[6]Report to the USC board, 1961.
[7]Circular no. 5, May 1962.

slums – cramped, unsanitary living quarters, hunger, damp-
ness, and cold – that were the ideal breeding ground for
tuberculosis. In particular, she wrote of visiting the tin-sheet
home, near the railway sidings, of Sung Ka, a three-year-old
patient in the hospital:

> The father, 41, is paralyzed. The mother, only 34, looks 20 years
> older, because acute pain is carved into her face: her left leg had
> to be amputated when a 180 lb rice bag fell from a lorry injuring
> her hip...Today, she is the only breadwinner for the entire family.
> The woman begs on the streets all day long, dragging herself on
> her crutches from door to door, but how much can neighbors spare,
> even if they are compassionate, when the lack of grains and ever-
> present hunger grip practically every single household in the town?
>   I stood in front of that shack, completely empty inside except
> for a few Canadian quilts on the mud floor and a cold stove. I saw
> the five-year-old boy munching a cold potato, and the quiet admis-
> sion by the mother, "No more food left," hit me like the most violent
> accusation...[8]

Another use for the Canadian barley was as an incentive for
family planning. The Korean government, looking at its 30
million people compressed into a small, mountainous peninsula, set out to bring the annual population increase down from
2.4 percent to 2 percent within five years. The USC played its
part in these campaigns by offering ten kilograms of barley
to any woman who came to the local health center for an IUD
insertion. In Mokpo during 1967, this doubled the number of
recipients to a total of 1024, and the governor of the province
awarded the agency a special citation during Family Planning
Month. In some cases, clothing was also offered. In another
area outside Seoul, where well baby clinics were held in villages
each month, Canadian milk was used as a similar incentive
for mothers.

Boy Scouts, seaweed and sashes

The culmination of this outreach work was the creation of
four social service centers. In the later years of the USC program in Korea, these became the centerpieces. In 1974-75,

---

[8]Circular no. 4, June 1968

the agency put $246,542 into supporting their wide range of activities, led by a team of nineteen trained social workers.

The longest established was the Mokpo center, whose staff were deeply involved in the family planning campaign and in casework in the poorest homes. They also ran a night school for working children, at middle school level, bringing in college students as volunteer teachers. And they worked, too, with that lively but often destitute stratum of the city's population – the shoeshine boys, ragpickers, newspaper boys, and other street entrepreneurs – giving them late-afternoon courses in "Korean Language and Social Life" and organizing them into Boy Scout troops. When the city council complained in its 1969 annual report about their ragged and lanky appearance, a youth worker persuaded the local barbers' association to give free haircuts to all the boys who had USC cards – 175 took up the offer!

The Mokpo staff also tackled the particular problem of the offshore islanders. Young girls arrived in Mokpo daily by barge and boat (and sometimes bus or train, if they landed elsewhere), fleeing from the poverty – or the boredom – of the islands, seeking a well-paid job, a husband, a more exciting life. Too often they found only despair, perhaps also prostitution. Some women of the local Presbyterian church launched a Hope Club for them, and a church worker, Mrs. Kang, took on the job of watching for these runaway girls at the pier, the railway and bus stations, to help them before they were lost in a miserable life. She developed a sixth sense at spotting such girls – in eight years she is said to have rescued 4,326 of them.[9] The USC supported her work by paying for their fares home, as well as a living allowance for the girls while things were being sorted out with parents. Quite often there were other expenses, like medical aid.

There were success stories in the field of community development. The forty-eight families who lived on Sindo Island, thirty-seven kilometers from Mokpo, had only a tiny area of

---

[9]Koreans may have been casual about baseline statistics, to Dr. Lotta's chagrin, in 1952. But, from whatever cause, they changed soon afterwards. I have never met a people so swift to quote strings of figures, or to flourish wall graphs and organization charts. I wrote in 1969: "Korea is a country where statistics hold a supreme place, and where anyone with claims to modernity seems devoted to the decimal point." (*Half a Loaf*, p. 114.)

arable land for farming and relied for their livelihood on gathering crabs, oysters and seaweed. As Dr. Lotta wrote,

> Their great problem was lack of storage to keep their sea crops from spoiling. A boat lands on the island only once a week in good weather and, when it is stormy, only twice a month…Thus it often happened that two-thirds of their people's catch would spoil or had to be sold at very low cost. The chief of the village community went to see our USC staff in Mokpo and obtained help in the form of 10,000 lbs of USC barley and 350 bags of cement. The fish storage building was completed on 30 March 1975 by village volunteers, and the village has become self-supporting. The 10,000 lbs of barley cost the USC $2,500.[10]

The other centers had their own special areas of work. The one in Inchon ran a project of stitching *obis* for export to Japan, where women wear these brightly colored sashes as belts. (For the statistically minded, 385 low-income women earned an extra $13,415 this way in 1974.) The staff also organized adult education classes, a job placement agency in local factories, four youth clubs, and a lending library for children. The Echon center, being in a rural area, concentrated on the development of eight villages, and helped organize a credit union club, a "rice bank," and cooperative stores. And the model center at Yung Dong Po, in a squatter settlement area of Seoul, took the place of the center at Mapo when the main part of that building was demolished in 1975 on the orders of the mayor, "Bulldozer Kim," to widen a highway to an elegant new part of the city.

These five centers were pioneering efforts. So, too, was the national conference of social workers organized by Mr. Cho in 1969. By 1975, other agencies had followed and set up sixteen more social service centers. And the government and Seoul city council became increasingly involved and more prepared to finance this work, as they headed into what had been proclaimed as the Social Development Decade of the 1980s.

By 1978, when USC Canada ended its assistance, and a newly registered Han Kuk Social Service Committee under Mr. Cho took over the continuing programs, South Korea was a very different place from what it had been in the desolate days of 1952. It had joined the small clubs of NICs, Newly Industrializing Countries, with a few other Asian and Latin American states. It had become one of world's major steel makers, and

---

[10]Report to the USC board, 3 June 1975.

was striding into new fields of science and technology. It boasted a per capita income approaching fifteen hundred dollars (U.S.). It had achieved these things while still pouring one-third of its budget into soldiers and armaments.

The flaw was in the widening gap between the wealthier classes and the poor in the city slums and the vulnerable countryside. The USC always stayed with the poor and it won some worthwhile battles. They can be indicated in the Korean way by statistics, such as twenty-five hundred children successfully discharged from USC homes in twenty-one years of sponsorship, or else illustrated by individual stories like that of Duk Kyoo, a war orphan with a hunchback caused by a TB spine, who got his vocational training apprenticed to a printer-engraver and found plenty of work. Expressed either way, and however small they are, these victories endure.

Gaza and the "layette lift"

By dictionary definition, the word *refugee* implies a temporary state: "person taking refuge or shelter," for it is derived from a Latin word meaning "to flee." When Dr. Gordon Merrill visited the Gaza Strip in 1975, as a special adviser for the USC, he noted that the babies being born in the camps there were the third generation of refugees. He felt obliged to remind his readers of the size of the Middle East refugee problem, as it had grown since the present grandfathers and grandmothers had fled from their homes in 1947-48:

> Today there are more than 1.5 million Palestine refugees registered with UNRWA, and more than 500,000 of them are housed in UNRWA camps, where they are provided with rations, medical services and educational facilities. Support is far from complete for the refugees who must obtain some income from employment that is difficult to find. For the record, there are 97,111 refugees in camps in Lebanon; 193,895 in Gaza; 155,280 in East Jordan; 73,850 in West Bank Jordan; and 50,179 in Syria...the USC supports medical centers in Gaza and West Bank Jordan, and pre-school centers and basic nursing training in Lebanon. The emphasis of USC assistance is clearly upon children and youth...[11]

---

[11]Report to the USC board, 6 March 1975.

The USC had by then been sending assistance to the Middle East for nearly twenty years. It was a program, that from its outset in 1956, caused debate and even controversy among the agency's supporters. There were board members who were worried about its political overtones; and a recurring question from branches concerned the shipment of basic layettes for Arab refugee babies: "Won't it just encourage their mothers to have more babies?" Dr. Lotta acknowledged this form of questioning, for she wrote in 1973, "the program for Arab refugees...is not very popular in Canada; although from a human point of view it is very much needed." She never wavered in her efforts to keep it going, or to support the officials of the United Nations Relief and Works Agency (UNRWA), who were forever struggling with a large financial deficit on top of the huge human problem.

She proposed an aid program early in 1956 for typically practical reasons. The USC program of sending clothing to Korea had begun to fade in interest for Canadian donors after three years — and after the signing of the armistice agreement at Panmunjon. She was also keen to find projects that would actively involve all those women supporters (and not a few men) with sewing skills. There were then nine hundred thousand refugees registered with UNRWA, and half of them were under sixteen. She took, to the USC annual meeting in January 1956, the plea of an UNRWA official for "any quantity of clothing, especially children's." There was a lengthy discussion, much of it circling around the political aspects. It was positively influenced by Dr. James Gibson, the chairman of the Ottawa branch, who spoke firmly in favor of a program. It had always been USC policy, he reminded the meeting, to help in the neediest areas.

In any case, people across Canada gave an enthusiastic response to a call from the USC to sew thousands of school uniforms from denim of a proper light blue color to please the United Nations, and to prepare layettes. For the uninitiated, a correctly assembled layette consists of four diapers, two nighties, two shirts or short jackets (often knitted from odds and ends of yarn, in unexpected colors), two knitted vests, one crib blanket, one towel, one cake of laundry soap, and four large safety pins. Nearly thirty years later, those who put them together can reel off the list, ending the incantation "...rolled all in a towel and fastened with pins."

The effort was tremendous. Some eighteen thousand meters of denim were cut and stitched into uniforms, Charlotte McEwen of Ottawa cutting the first nine hundred meters by herself. And by April 1960, the USC had completed what Dr. Lotta called its "Layette Lift," a pledge to deliver twenty-five thousand basic layettes to UNRWA. The mammoth pile – put all together they would have filled a warehouse of 180 cubic meters – was built up through the cooperation of thousands of women, often snatching a few minutes in a working day. One example was a Lethbridge widow, Mrs. A.C. Hinds, who one year made fourteen layettes by doing a bit of sewing or knitting every evening while waiting for a ride home from her job at Eaton's.

But large though the total was, it barely kept pace with needy babies in the Gaza Strip alone, where some ten thousand were born every year, and half the mothers were "hardship cases," unable to provide more than rags for their infants. In later years, the novelty of putting layettes together wore off, and although Dr. Lotta tried to set a target of three thousand a year, it was hardly ever met.

A great deal of clothing, however, continued to flow – interrupted only temporarily by the series of wars. The whole program began a few months before the American and British refusal in June 1956 to help finance the Aswan Dam and the subsequent events, including the nationalization of the Suez Canal, that led to the British-French invasion that October. It simply picked up momentum when those troops withdrew.

In February 1968, after the Six Day War, Dr. Lotta went to where the battle had carried some of its victims, to six temporary tented camps in the Jordan Valley, where fifty-six thousand new refugees had arrived from the West Bank. One of these camps had been shelled by Israeli artillery a few days before, killing six children and five women. She stood in another camp and watched as a truckload of refugees arrived from the Sinai desert, having left their homes in the middle of the night with few possessions. A refugee more than once herself, she gazed at an old tattooed Bedouin woman who was begging to be allowed to return. It was, she wrote, "a dramatic and heartrending sight."[12]

But help is worth more than pity, and the next paragraphs

[12]Report to the USC Board, 17 February 1968.

of her report set out new ways in which Canadians might come to the refugees' aid: teenage girls could make baby blankets from knitted squares, the British Columbia government could give a carload (16,300 kilograms) of evaporated milk originally offered for Korea, and Ontario should be able to provide four thousand pairs of shoes that were needed for Gaza refugees who had fled over the Canal into Egypt. (She added the caution that "Arabs have fairly broad feet.")

Dr. Lotta was deeply concerned about the provision of family planning facilities – probably more concerned than were those critics who had complained that sending layettes encouraged more babies. There were frustrations, though, to be faced. Alone of the Arab countries, only the Egyptian government had an active program of family planning; the Jordanian government allowed private clinics; and Syria and Lebanon flatly disapproved. And, as Dr. Merrill observed, "UNRWA is obliged to follow the policies of the host governments with respect to family planning, and the Middle East governments are not in the forefront of the movement. Also, a refugee population that feels itself under the threat of extinction is not predisposed to birth control, as nationalism and survival are at stake."[13]

So the USC concentrated its family planning support in the Gaza Strip, where UNRWA could follow Egyptian leads. It gave ten thousand dollars to a midwifery training program in 1958 and "topping up" amounts in subsequent years. Part of their training, and of the training of student nurses following a basic diploma course under the American University at Beirut, was instruction in family planning. As well, health education classes for girls in Grade 9 or above included such information. In 1972 the Gaza Strip had sufficient trained nurses and midwives for a total population then approaching four hundred thousand, and Dr. Lotta wrote, "I was radiant, for seldom has an investment of ten thousand dollars borne more tangible and far-reaching fruit."[14]

An even bigger effort began in 1970 with the support of a health center at Balata on the West Bank, a few kilometers south of Nablus, serving a camp of nearly ten thousand refugees. In the first years, this support of more than fifteen thousand dollars (U.S.) a year came from proceeds of the Miles for Millions

---

[13]Report to the USC Board, 6 March 1975.
[14]Report to the USC Board, 28 April 1972.

walks in Calgary and Ottawa. Besides a general outpatients' clinic, there were special rheumatic and diabetic clinics, and the care of mothers and infants was exemplary. In 1975 more than a thousand children up to the age of three were receiving monthly examinations, and nearly four hundred women were registered for prenatal care.

Two other innovative programs should be mentioned. There was a gap between the health care offered to mothers and infants at clinics such as Balata, and the care that children received once they were in an UNRWA school at six years old. So the USC supported four preschool centers in refugee camps in Lebanon that were designed to bridge this gap. (The Quakers ran similar centers in the Gaza Strip.) The children received supplementary food, were taught some hygiene and the beginnings of other learning by Palestinian nursery school teachers trained on the West Bank, and the mothers had some free time for work or for training themselves.

The other project was a rehydration clinic at Maghazi in the Gaza Strip. Recently UNICEF has popularized the idea of oral rehydration as the basis of a simple cure for the worst killers of children in the Third World, gastroenteritis and diarrhea. Back in the early 1970s, UNRWA had already established twenty-one rehydration/nutrition centers to deal with this scourge. There, infants suffering from malnutrition and dehydration resulting from diarrhea (and compounded by the long, dry summers) were given a special salt solution to restore body fluids and minerals, and also a high-protein, high-calorie diet. Maghazi was mainly an outpatients' clinic but had eight beds for those needing lengthy treatment. (In 1975 Dr. Merrill calculated that they were occupied each day by an average of thirteen children, which indicates the full use of facilities.)

One problem which the USC did not have to worry about in its Middle East program was the finding of competent field representatives. The health program funds and the continuing large shipments of clothing (up to 10,500 kilograms in 1975) and of milk and egg powder all went through UNRWA channels. Dr. Lotta had nothing but praise for these men and women. Somewhat wryly, she ended her 1971 report: "As I rushed off to be searched for arms – the newest device against hijacking in the skies – and boarded the plane, I said a silent thank-you for the excellent and devoted staff which UNRWA possesses."

Lotta

Vietnam from both sides

The USC program in Vietnam, although it had accomplishments in the health sector, enjoyed only rare periods when things ran smoothly. This was to be expected because dark clouds overshadowed the country during those ten years. March 1969, when Dr. Lotta first visited Saigon, was a time of waiting and uncertainty. President Nixon was about to announce the gradual withdrawal of U.S. troops, then at a peak of 543,000. And in April 1979, when her scheduled visit to Hanoi was canceled at the last minute, the Vietnamese had just been fighting on two fronts, in Kampuchea and on their own northern border against some 80,000 Chinese troops, and negotiations to try to settle that frontier dispute (still in active contention in 1984) were under way in the capital.

On her first visit, she described Vietnam as "without doubt the most difficult assignment" she had faced for the USC: "Unlike Korea in 1952...I had no logistical support and was forced to do everything myself – from trying to make appointments over an unreliable telephone, to securing background information and valid statistics in a country which consists of a sequence of armed camps."[15]

But, she added, there were advantages in relying on her own wits – and the French language: she came to learn something real from "the little people" – the taxi drivers, merchants, and refugees.

She sorted out a modest program to help handicapped children. This was very much in the tradition of assistance given at Villepatour, outside Paris, by the physiotherapist Ruth McKinnon in 1949; in Italy and Greece; and most recently at the Sam Yook center in Seoul. The successful parts were two study tours to Korean projects (including both Sam Yook and the Mokpo children's hospital) by staff of the Vietnamese Ministry of Social Welfare and support for Regina Pacis in Saigon, the only postpolio center for children in South Vietnam. Failure – for a time, at least – came in trying to add a special primary school and day-care center for forty handicapped children to the premises of the National Rehabilitation Institute, which served some twenty-five hundred adults, both war veterans and civilians. After a year's negotiations with NRI,

---

[15]Circular no. 5, July 1969.

Dr. Lotta suddenly decided she could not sign the twenty-five thousand dollar contract – the first time in twenty-five years she had said no to a project that had been planned in detail.

The problem over the NRI illustrates a common difficulty. The USC was to pay the costs of remodeling the building, including kitchen and toilets, the wages for support staff, and the cost of a protein-filled noon meal for the children. It was also arranging for an American psychologist, Mary Jo O'Connor, to act as a consultant to teachers who had never before worked with handicapped children and for her project assistant in the World Rehabilitation Fund, Miss Nguyen Thi Van, to be the USC representative. But this arrangement foundered in the antipathy increasingly being shown to foreigners by some Vietnamese officials. There was a change of directors at NRI, and the new one, Dr. Lam Van Thach, resented Mrs. O'Connor's presence and equally rejected Miss Van as having "non-Vietnamese manners." (The WRF is an American voluntary agency, and Miss Van had had part of her training in the United States.) When he insisted on running this specialized program himself (he was an orthopedic surgeon), Dr. Lotta backed out.

But all was by no means lost. The buildings had been reconstructed with USC funds, and Miss Van had translated into Vietnamese a handbook written by Mrs. O'Connor on the treatment of handicapped children. Even more important, Dr. Thach was stirred – challenged, perhaps – to carry the program through on his own. In 1971 Dr. Lotta made contact again with Dr. Thach and wrote that she was quite impressed by the tour he gave her of the day-care center. Its staff were caring for several mutilated children from the Me Linh Home, which had been opened after the 1968 Tet offensive to accommodate victims of that attack.

The support of the postpolio center had a better start. Poliomyelitis was particularly virulent around Saigon and the Mekong Delta because of the hot, humid climate and because it was difficult for health authorities to carry out a series of vaccinations and booster shots with so many civilians on the move as the war swept them around. Regina Pacis, a spacious place built in 1958 by the German Catholic organization Misereor, even had a therapeutic swimming pool. But the Vietnamese nun in charge, Sister Lucie (of the Order of St. Vincent de Paul), lacked funds to use the buildings to the full. She was running a primary and secondary school for two hundred day-scholars as well as training programs. This provided some revenue for the care of the seventy youngsters under her roof, but she found she was having to refuse as many as twenty appeals a week to take in other polio victims. Dr. Lotta agreed to support forty more children and to make use of an empty third floor. This was a popular project with Canadian donors; in particular, an Ottawa man, John Helliwell, gave fifteen hundred dollars to it in gratitude for having himself recovered totally from the disease.

In later years, Sister Lucie came up with some ambitious ideas, such as a five-year course for girls in social service and home economics. But Dr. Lotta would not offer help, having found, that while the curriculum was well planned and the course about to begin, nobody had worked out precisely how the heavy running expenses would be met. "This is a typical example of how much the Sisters are working on faith," she wrote.[16] She was worried about their other-worldliness in bookkeeping, especially when the USC was contributing more than fifteen thousand dollars a year, and paying for a social worker to visit the families of polio victims after their discharge and for a workshop to make special shoes and braces. She asked Sister Lucie where her accounts were checked, and hearing that the books were sent back to Paris, made a note to call on the mother superior there the following year.

Dr. Lotta searched for other ways to help handicapped children and found several. A British male nurse, Douglas Gray, who had once worked on an icebreaker in the Canadian Arctic, had ended up singlehandedly running a children's home for forty-one polio victims. The USC began paying the salaries of a nurse, an administrator, and a physiotherapist. The USC also supported twenty abandoned infants at Phu-My orphanage in the old part of Saigon, where without any regular income, a Swiss nun, Sister Rose Marie, somehow ran a haven for fifteen hundred people, old and young. Dr. Lotta arranged for Mrs. Mai, the social worker employed at Regina Pacis, to go to the orphanage on Saturdays. She helped a Vietnamese priest, Father Hoan, with fifty-five hundred dollars to make fifty hectares of land productive by clearing and planting, and so establish a self-help community − White Pigeon village by

---

[16]Report to the USC Board, 2 May 1970.

the sea – for two hundred orphans whom he had brought out of Saigon.

There was also support for the training of blind adults. Some were victims of the war; others, like Nguyen Thi Phuong who was blinded by smallpox when she was only three, had lost their sight in childhood. Miss Phuong was among thirty-two young people who were given free training one year at the NLRI to become X-ray technicians, morse code and telephone operators. But she and the others had to serve some months' unpaid probation before getting permanent, paid jobs, so the USC stepped into the gap with a monthly stipend.

Attempts to help other blind people outside Saigon – and there were an estimated thirty-one thousand in all South Vietnam – had mixed results. In 1973 Dr. Lotta drove out "a long way on very bad roads" to visit a mat-making project, only to find it abandoned because there were not enough sighted people to cut and split the reeds for the blind people who she found sitting dejectedly in bare barracks. On the other hand, a chicken farm cooperative launched that year with two sighted and ten blind men as partners was a great success. She confessed she had been most skeptical about investing twelve thousand dollars in the venture until she had checked with experts at the Government Experimental Farm in Ottawa to learn whether blind people could do such work.[17] Within a year, the project was self-reliant and paying everyone's wages from the sale of broilers and vegetables. And she raised funds for a mobile team of eight instructors from NRI to pay regular visits to other areas.

Uncertainties increased as the American troops gradually withdrew. But Dr. Lotta had eventually found a dedicated professional, Tran Dinh An, who could act as USC representative. Mr. An was the moving spirit behind the blind projects and could supervise the others. She wrote to the USC board in May 1973: "I am convinced that this is the time to invest to the utmost in South Vietnam, because the kind of services we supply must be extended, whether there is peace or the fighting continues."

The fighting did continue, of course, reaching its climax with the surrender of Saigon on 30 April 1975. The USC program, as it then was, collapsed. An American priest, Father Crawford, had one week earlier arranged the evacuation of

---

[17] *Jottings from Vietnam*, May 1974.

more than fifty children from the postpolio center to Oregon, and Sister Guillemine, one of the staff, wrote from there to Dr. Lotta, carefully enclosing the year's financial accounts and asking for help to set up a new workshop in Oregon. Another American who Dr. Lotta greatly respected, George Richison, had worked at Regina Pacis and strongly disapproved of the children's removal. He wrote to Dr. Lotta: "There was absolutely no reason to take them out of the country, as most of them had parents."

Two instructors in the mobile team escaped to California. But from the devoted Mr. An there was no word. His last messages had been pleas for help to feed refugees. Dr. Lotta began sending daily cables to his Saigon address after she reached Indonesia in June 1975 with Dr. Merrill on their world tour, hoping that by then the dust of battle and flight would have settled, and he might emerge. But no reply came from him, and she could not trace him when she was able to revisit Saigon, by then renamed Ho Chi Minh City, in 1978. Meanwhile, she and Dr. Merrill could not fly to Saigon.

Hanoi and the hospitals

Dr. Lotta was back in Vietnam, however, more quickly than anyone might have expected. At the outset of her 1976 tour, she stopped in Paris and Geneva to see representatives of Fraternité Vietnam, which was working to "heal the wounds of war" (their phrase) with projects in the south, and of the International Union for Child Welfare. She recommended that the USC board support a day-care center for children of working mothers, and in the north, a mobile ambulance to work in rural areas. She also had a cordial interview with Mr. Do Thanh, who was first secretary at the Vietnamese Embassy in Paris ("this typically French setting, reminding me of my student days a long time ago…"). Mr. Thanh, to her astonishment, was quite positive about her making an on-the-spot survey but said it would take time to arrange. She wrote her board, saying she hoped a visit would not interfere with the fund-raising tour in the fall.

But it all happened more quickly than that. Two months later in Jakarta, she received a cable from the ministry of health in Hanoi, inviting her to make an immediate, ten-day visit. After a scramble to get visas and catch flights via Tokyo and Peking, she landed in Hanoi in mid-May and had her arms filled with gladioli by a smiling girl-interpreter, Mai Huong.

Her ten-day visit, as the first Canadian invited to Hanoi to discuss aid projects, was a jumble of impressions. Thousands of cyclists crossing the bomb-damaged bridge over the Red River...elderly women squatting on the pavement to sell vegetables, shielded from the summer sun under big straw hats... the awful hotel with cockroaches (and rats, according to an East German) and dirty sheets...the tour around the Hospital of Traditional Medicine, where she refused to go into the operating room and see a patient being treated by acupuncture ("not a single smile of pity at my cowardliness").

She soon learned that her simple questions had to wait days for an answer and that decisions were made by a team, never on the spot by an individual. She also had an intriguing interview with a special delegate from South Vietnam (the two parts were not unified under one government until July 1976), Mme Nguyen Khanh Phuong: "Madame Phuong wore a dark brown silk blouse – somehow cossack style – and long black silk trousers; she could not have looked more austere and military."[18] They soon broke through the solemnity and found themselves to be sisters under their uniforms. Madame Phuong said she completely agreed with the USC policy of helping the neediest, and particularly the children – and threw in some words of congratulation to the USC for having been founded and directed by a woman.

Working out acceptable projects with Dr. Nguyen Van Dong, of the ministry of health, was not easy. She rejected a "much too nebulous" project in clinical research and also a request for a $200,000 cobalt bomb for cancer treatment. For his part, Dr. Dong said that mobile ambulances were no longer a priority. (Instead, the USC contributed through the IUCW in Geneva $17,700 worth of drugs for an existing mobile unit.) Finally, she and Dr. Dong agreed on a list. It was headed by an item of $200,000 to refurnish and equip the district hospital at Nam Ninh, 130 kilometers south of Hanoi. This would include 150 beds and all the linen, and also medical equipment for all departments. Dr. Lotta only received the request on her last evening and could not visit Nam Ninh. She realized they wanted

[18]Report to the USC board, 30 May 1976.

"to create a permanent memorial with USC funds as a proof of friendship between our two countries."[19] The Vietnamese ministry staff were totally inexperienced in dealing with Western agencies, and it took months of correspondence to sort out a detailed budget, and more than a year for Dr. Dong to shop around and finally order the equipment from Japan. But, meanwhile, local people rebuilt and transformed the old shabby hospital, and Dr. Lotta had a proud welcome from everyone when she visited it in 1978.

Other projects were simpler. An amount of fifty thousand dollars was allocated for the cutting and sewing of ten thousand pairs of hospital pyjamas. For some reason this project caused a good deal of speculation, even amusement, at USC headquarters, but it was a good, straightforward scheme. The striped cotton material was bought at a local textile factory, and Dr. Lotta visited the Hanoi sewing cooperative in 1977, where she marveled at the dexterity of the cutter who knelt on ten layers of the cotton and sliced through it with a huge knife. She also saw the first shipment of 45,500 kilograms of used clothing arrive in 1977, destined mainly for the Montagnards in the highland areas. And whenever she visited a hospital or day-care center, she came across 23-kilogram bags of skim milk powder from Alberta, parts of a donation of 163,000 kilograms from CIDA, for which the USC paid transportation costs. The single problem was delivery time; the ports of Haiphong and Saigon were so overcrowded that the milk powder took four months to reach its destination.

There was, finally, a hundred thousand dollars allocated for the Vietnamese to buy large quantities of four main drugs, in particular penicillin, for use in South Vietnam. Dr. Lotta made it clear that the USC wanted the penicillin used exclusively for children, especially those with respiratory diseases. But she sounded thoughtful as she informed the board, that according to Dr. Dong, penicillin was also urgently needed for the fifty thousand prostitutes in Saigon, "left behind by American imperialism." She ended her 1977 report with the assurance that "we may freely trust our partner, the Ministry of Health, because of its complete integrity." At the same time, the hundred thousand dollars allocated for drugs in 1978 went to the purchase in France of quinine powder, to be made into

---

[19]Report to the USC board, 30 May 1976.

ten-gram tablets in Hanoi and used to combat malaria among children in villages.

The Vietnam program continued to concentrate almost entirely on medical supplies. Among the few exceptions were the clothing shipments and a gift of laboratory equipment to a high school in Nam Dinh, which had been arranged by Dr. Lotta at the request of the British Columbia Teachers Federation. The USC provided a further forty thousand dollars worth of equipment to Nam Ninh hospital for an emergency unit that included an X-ray machine and an ambulance. And in 1977 it was agreed to spend two hundred thousand dollars on the equipping of a second district hospital, at Gia Lam near Hanoi airport. Dr. Lotta wrote that she was disappointed when Dr. Dong first made this request: "I had expected something more imaginative. After all, any agency can supply mere funds and to write out a cheque is not difficult for many." Then she was taken over this pathetically bare hospital, with 250 beds and little else. Bombing from B-52s had blown the roofs away and damaged the water supply. In addition, the single X-ray machine was unuseable and there was no laboratory equipment. "As I walked from floor to floor...I completely understood the urgency of coming to the rescue..."[20]

Nevertheless, she was determined that USC aid in 1978-79 should go into something other than the health field. But she ran into continuous resistance. Her request to stay longer than twelve days, to seek other proposals, was not approved. And much of her twelve days was consumed by being taken "from one war-destroyed hospital to another and nowhere else." Finally, during a drive back to Hanoi late one night, she told Dr. Dong very quietly that earmarking all USC funds for medical aid would alienate many Canadian contributors. She received the sharp reply that the USC had been put into the category of agencies expected to do health work and nothing else. A tense and unhappy scene followed, but the next morning a beaming Dr. Dong implied that the problem was solved. That afternoon she had a good interview with the president of the Committee for the Reception of Foreign Aid, Mr. Viet Thanh, who said the USC was now in a special category that allowed it to work in any field, provided there was a need. Unfortunately, Dr. Lotta had to leave the following day, too soon to obtain any project

---

[20]Report to the USC board, 7 June 1977.

proposals outside the health sector. "Thus in some ways Dr. Dong really did win his battle for this year," she concluded.[21]

Before the USC program in Vietnam was shelved in mid-1979, one large commitment in agriculture was carried out. In 1977 the worst drought in memory occurred, and then in August 1978 floods destroyed much of the rice crop and a great number of their basic vegetables. So there was an urgent request for some five thousand kilograms of vegetable seed, mainly cabbage, but also radish and bushbean; and, at a cost of $150,000, this was bought and shipped from Hong Kong in March 1979.

The decision to suspend the program came after the United Nations Security Council had voted for a cease-fire resolution that called for the withdrawal both of Chinese troops from Vietnam and of Vietnamese troops from Kampuchea; and the Soviet Union had, on behalf of Vietnam, cast its veto. Denmark and Australia at once stopped their aid to Vietnam, and the Callaghan government in Great Britain froze all but its humanitarian assistance. CIDA soon followed suit in freezing the aid it was channeling to Vienam through NGOs, while the British Columbia government canceled its program. The pressures on USC were heavy. Dr. Lotta canceled her two-week visit in late April "in order to protect our...absolutely non-political approach...and to avoid any possible misrepresentation of our presence in the capital during the negotiations between Vietnam and China," as she explained to the USC annual meeting in mid-June. On 30 August the board issued a position statement: "USC projects in Vietnam have been suspended for 1979-80 due to the political uncertainties in that country and the resultant inability of the USC to carry out on-the-spot investigation of projects. The USC Board of Directors will be prepared to look at the possibilities of re-establishing a program in Vietnam at a later date."

In the meantime, it spent more than forty-seven thousand dollars from the Vietnam budget to help some of the boat people, refugees who had reached Hong Kong, mainly with clothing. It was hard to escape the feeling that assistance to Vietnam had gone all the way round the circle, back to the beginning.

---

[21]Report to the USC board, 16 May 1978.

CHAPTER 6

India From Four Sides

India from four sides

WHEN DR. LOTTA made a farewell trip to India in March 1975, she called it "one of the most intriguing and beautiful countries I have ever worked in." But she had often been perplexed by India. She soon learned that it was hard to get a program started. "You cannot hurry India," she was told. Indeed, after the first year she wrote to board members: "...Does India want outside help? The task is so tremendous...but Indians are proud people, and were kept unfree far too long. What wonder now if they are greatly sceptical, and choose from whom to accept help?"[1]

In many reports she noted years of despondency in India, where the shadows of political conflict were long and darkened further by corruption. And, when food production began to improve dramatically, there were still concerns over labor troubles and growing unemployment as recruits to the workforce multiplied. The population explosion was at the core of her worried comments. In 1970, for example, there was a net increase of 13 million, when 21 million babies were born and eight million people died. She noted how government red tape, such as the frequent altering of survey forms, wasted precious time and prevented an all-out drive for family planning. In any case, she would say, that drive could only come after a well-planned program of maternal and child welfare had reached into the city slums and the six hundred thousand isolated villages and hamlets where welfare was most needed. And this was never a top government priority: "Following the usual pattern of developing countries, India has been placing emphasis almost exclusively on development, without paying the necessary attention to human problems and almost completely ignoring the needs of the most vulnerable, unproductive groups of citizens – the very young and the very old..."[2]

---

[1]Report to the USC board, 1954.

[2]Report to the USC board, 12 April 1970.

So the USC program came to concentrate on the needs of young people and their mothers in slums and isolated villages, on the leadership role that women could play in rural areas, and on the training of tribal farmers in northern hills. Wherever possible, she tried to introduce family planning as an element in a project.

One of the tasks she labored over was to make sure of a number of trustworthy partner agencies that were able to carry through projects vigorously. She soon appointed a remarkable woman, Mrs. Sarojini Aiyar, as USC resident representative, to visit the projects regularly for supervision and advice. But there were still occasional lapses: the misuse of funds at a girls' home (not actually USC funds, it transpired), and the theft of twenty-five bags of milk powder at another children's home.

These upset her, but they were minor affairs. When the program closed in 1975, the USC board approved outright grants, totaling some eighty-three thousand dollars, to four agencies as endowment funds to help the work continue, because these were seen as among the best projects it had supported in India. This chapter will mainly describe these four projects: the Saligram Boys Training Centre, Madras; the Deen Seva Sangha of Bangalore; the Agricultural Training Insitute in Ranchi, Bihar; and the Karnatak Health Institute at Ghataprabha.

Beggar boys to carpenters

The training center at Saligram, on the outskirts of Madras, was an outgrowth of the group of children's homes set up by the Guild of Service in the 1950s. The Guild of Service itself had been established in 1923 as a charitable group with a colonial tinge. Mrs. Waller, the wife of the bishop of Madras headed it, and its (European) ladies mainly engaged in hospital visiting. Among the first Indian ladies to join in 1936 was Mrs. Mary Clubwala Jadhav, who came from a rich Parsee family and was widowed when young. She had lots of energy and transformed the organization.

She tended to plan on a grand scale, and in eight years from 1950 she set up more than a dozen homes under Seva Samajam (the Indian name for the guild). She was a juvenile magistrate and had seen many destitute children being sent to government institutions for juvenile delinquents, for want of a more suitable place. A thorough study done by the Madras School of Social Work in 1956 estimated that there were five thousand beggars on the city streets, some fifteen hundred of them under the age of fifteen, even though begging was a punishable offence.[3] As a result, many of the children placed in the Seva Samajam homes had been found begging, but Mrs. Jadhav also often accepted the children of her friends' servants. Dr. Lotta was wary of the numbers piling into these homes and used to talk about the quality of the children's lives. It led to some sharp differences between these two strong-minded women.

At the Seva Samajam boys' home at Saligram, the first group of boys who had come in 1952 were over fifteen years old in 1957 and in great need of vocational training. The USC gave four thousand dollars that year to build and equip a training center there. When the president of India inaugurated the center, the equipment was modest: a loom, a sewing machine, some pottery and woodworking equipment. But by 1961 the carpentry section had been recognized by the government as a national training center, and the first twenty carpenters faced formal apprenticeship exams. Meanwhile, the boys in the weaving class gave Dr. Lotta a bedspread to use during her lengthy travels on dusty Indian trains.

A Girls' Training Institute was started the same year. The plan was to offer an eight-month basic course in home economics, to train girls in cooking, child care, and homemaking (in both Indian and Western style), and fit them for housekeeper roles.

While Dr. Lotta was the leading sprit in moving Seva Samajam into vocational training, she derived enormous delight from visiting the younger children USC foster parents were soon helping support, at sixty dollars a year, in seventeen homes in southern India. The warmth of their affection, a flood after the loneliness of their destitute years, enchanted her. To see them blossoming physically and mentally after a stunted period was deeply satisfying. She projected this pleasure in many circulars to Canadian donors. She especially enjoyed what she called "Canada Hour" when, after the official speeches of welcome

---

[3]*Report on the Beggar Survey in Madras City*, October 1956. Its authors eliminated from the survey "those found begging while proceeding on pilgrimage" and also fortunetellers and snake charmers.

were over, she would sit in a circle with the children (and an interpreter) and answer questions about the land of their sponsors. Many were about the conditions in Canada: "Do you have different houses for the winter and summer?" "In our country, trains run on rails; how do they run in Canada?" Some questions she recorded were more personal: "How long did it take you to study to become an executive director?" and (from a girl, of course) "You are taking care of so many children — but who is taking care of you?"[4]

In 1984 I visited Madras to gain some idea of how these institutions had fared in the nine years since USC support had come to an end. To outward appearances, changes come slowly in this part of India. As a visitor, you are soon taken to see a proud sight, the largest banyan tree known to be still growing. Its branches spread over a diameter of sixty meters, and little has changed since members of the Theosophical Society used to meet in its shade fifty years ago. Driving back into town, you dodge untethered cows nosing their way through the street garbage, until the roads suddenly smarten as you approach the old splendor of the Connemara Hotel and its Primrose Room. The Raj lingers on, with a main thoroughfare still named Commander-in-Chief Road and Queen Victoria still enthroned outside the university. But there are also brisk women police around these days, and beside a fishing beach the unforgettable statue of Roy Chaudury, of Mahatma Gandhi striding out to galvanize his people.

M.S.S. Nambudiri, the Saligram director, is certainly someone who has been galvanized. He came to Madras from Kerala and was the first specialist in social work to be hired by USC for Seva Samajam. He is also a shrewd businessman, for he contrives to run vocational training courses for about one hundred boys without drawing on outside funds. He has the support of Mr. N.E.S. Raghavachari, who became the effective, if unassuming, chairman after a distinguished career in the Indian civil service.

At one time, the USC was sending ten thousand rupees a year (about twelve hundred dollars), merely to pay for wood for the carpentry course. Since then, he has faced problems, and even a strike in 1979, in defence of his principle of not commercializing the institute. The work of the twenty-five students who are

[4]Circulars of 30 April 1960 and 31 March 1962.

doing a three-year course is never sold because, he says, that could lead to exploiting the boys. Instead, their costs are covered by a small production unit now employing fifteen carpenters and filling complicated orders. (When I was there, they were making drawing room suites, desks for different grades of bank clerks, and an enormous filing cabinet.) Their building was financed by a thirty-one hundred dollar gift from students at Forestburg High School in Alberta, who did chores on Friday nights and Saturdays to raise it.

The strike came when the carpenters in the production unit, then forty strong with apprentices on a stipend and senior men on piecework, formed a union to demand permanent contracts because of a feeling of dependency on Saligram and poor prospects outside. Nambudiri told them he could not keep anyone more than a few years; he was not running a factory but a training institute to fit them for carpentry work outside. Tempers rose for a week before a solution came from a friend who wanted twenty-five workers for a contract in the Libyan petroleum industry. Most of the strikers left, and he reduced numbers.

Nambudiri does not believe in expensive tools but in human ingenuity and skill, particularly in the case of school dropouts. He has found many of these dropouts, branded dull by some teachers, to be gifted craftsmen, and it is Saligram's achievement to have developed their skills. In the carpentry class some boys were using metal bars instead of hammers, and in a day's tour he will take you to an emporium in the Victoria Institute to marvel at some of the exquisitely hand-carved gods and goddesses, and then drive you to see another of Chaudury's fine statues – The Triumph of Labour – four men striving with poles to shift a huge rock. He is inspired by it. "What the ordinary human can accomplish!" he exclaims.

There are other accomplishments at Saligram. Ten or more boys get training in motor mechanics at an automobile unit and service station, built and maintained with local funds. A tailoring shop was built and equipped with a ten thousand rupee bequest in memory of seventeen-year-old Jennifer Coleman who was killed in a car crash in Ontario. On the wall is an epitaph written by Dr. Lotta on Jennifer, "who pushed harder than most, reached farther than most, lived more intensely than most." It is a bustling little place with thirty-five trainees. Three of them are chalking their drawings on the red floor, one boy with no left hand is using a sewing machine skillfully, another with a leg support is cutting cloth on the floor. Nambudiri rejected the idea that handicapped trainees should be in a separate unit.

An engineering unit that does subcontracts, such as lathe work on dynamo parts for large firms, had trained and found jobs for fifty boys in eight years. And there is a 1.2 hectare dairy farm, set up in 1971, through a USC grant. The pasture supports twenty cows and a part-Friesian bull, and boys from the Saligram home come over after school to milk the cows, supervised by the Nepalese farmer in charge.

When the USC gave Saligram a parting gift of twelve thousand dollars (or one hundred thousand rupees) in 1975 for an endowment fund, Dr. Lotta added one condition. This was that 2 percent of the turnover of production from the various Saligram activities should be added to the fund each year. The finances are succinctly explained to me by the honorary treasurer, Lt. Col. (retired) A. Vijayaraghavan, who in 1971 led a battalion in Bangladesh's liberation war. The present turnover is more than 5 million rupees, and the fund has now grown to 750,000 rupees. The interest from the bank, at nearly 11 percent, is used to cover the running costs of the two hundred boys now living at the Saligram home, half of whom are students in the regular school and the others who are enrolled in vocational training courses.

This is where Nambudiri the social worker tells of his next dream. He strongly dislikes the institutional side of Saligram, the four boarding blocks that each house fifty boys with one "parent." It has made them isolated and resentful – and also dependent. Nambudiri's dream is to break up the institution by building enough cottages on the edges of the farm to house the boys in family groups of eight with a foster mother. Knowing his determination, one can predict that he will find a benefactor. He has several copies of the blueprints.

The Girls' Training Institute has its success stories. Starting in an isolated spot on the airport road, it is now housed on the upper floors of Seva Samajam Girls' Home, behind the guild's head offices. In a dozen years, some six hundred girls have graduated from what is now a year-long course. A few go into nursing, some go on to jobs in the Gulf, more go into bakery, catering, and tailoring, and the largest number become housekeepers.

One of the first girls to graduate, Vimala, who was sponsored by Mrs. D.K. Doherty, the wife of a Canadian diplomat, has written a charming account of her travels to London, Paris, and Moscow as housekeeper with the family of Kewal Singh, who became foreign secretary. When his daughter Gita married, wrote Vimala, "I am very proud to say that she took another girl from our home to work with her, just because she found me so nice."

Nothing seems to daunt them. Mrs. Raghavan, who has directed the institute since 1962, talks casually about her six catering staff members who, with trainees, feed a thousand guests at receptions given by the state governor. And they have a regular engagement to cater at state cabinet meetings, for they know the varied tastes of the twenty-four ministers. In more plebeian style, other GTI graduates work at the Khadi bakery. The equipment used there is ingenious, a locally-made bread slicer is worked through a bicycle chain and a heavy weight.

The Guild of Service secretary, Mrs. Nirmala Gokarn, has her own dreams. She would like to see the two institutes combined into a coeducational center. The courses could be rationalized because each tailoring course now receives orders suitable for the other. "But, more than that, the girls could grow up with boys and learn not to be fooled by the first charmer. Because now they are vulnerable through being too protected." The Diamond Jubilee celebrations of the Guild of Service in 1983 were an encouragement to this end. ("Sixty Sparkling Years," declares the souvenir booklet, dedicated to Mrs. Mary Jadhav, who died of cancer in 1975). More than a thousand graduates from Saligram and the Girls' Home and Training Institute returned for a week of songs and dancing, of shared memories and plans.

The life workers of Bangalore

Bangalore is a proud city sitting on top of the Mysore plateau, the hub of South India's road and railway system. Its center is spacious with an ancient grandeur. Lal Bagh, a botanical garden, was laid out in the eighteenth century, and a plaque records a visit by Edward, Prince of Wales. The Vidhana Saudha legislature building is only thirty years old but has the imposing dimensions of Curzon's India.

There is, of course, another side to any industrial city of 2 million. Bangalore had quite humble origins to judge from its name that means, in the Kannada language, "village of boiled beans." In 1930 a small group of Gandhi's disciples vowed to do what they could about that other side. They formed the Deena Seva Sangha ("Association for the Service to the Poor") and began working in the Srirampuram slum, carrying drinking water to the "untouchables" as they sweltered on the construction sites, helping to build shelters for their families, and starting a school for their children. They so impressed the municipal council that it gave the group some land — which had formerly been a burial ground for executed convicts. There, Mr. S. Sadanand, the group's leader, built a center from which a whole range of services – feeding programs, a dispensary, adult literacy classes, schooling, social services – was offered to a population in Srirampuram that by the 1960s had grown to more than 50,000.

Dr. Lotta was introduced to Mr. Sadanand and DSS by Mrs. Sarojini Aiyar, who for seven years had been on the USC staff in New Delhi as supervisor of rural and urban development programs. Mrs. Aiyar was well respected and well connected in Delhi, and indeed knew Mrs. Indira Gandhi as a friend. In 1963 she turned her back on that life, to go to Bangalore and work as a volunteer for Deena Seva Sangha. She came to know the core group of DSS, the twenty men and women teachers who, as Dr. Lotta wrote, "have given their all to serve the neediest." They were like a religious order, and those who wished to join served a five-year probation period. Dr. Lotta was deeply impressed by these "life workers" and wrote in 1965: "You only need to look into their eyes to realize that you stand in front of very extraordinary people. There burns a fire in their looks that I have not encountered anywhere else in India."[5]

Every life worker did more than double-shift teaching. Some, for example, were in the feeding squad that would tour

---

[5]Circular no. 5, July 1965.

the vegetable sellers and grocers for kilometers around, to beg for the day's supplies. They would bring them back to the tiny kitchen, where six days a week a midday meal was cooked for fifteen hundred children.

Over the next ten years the USC helped DSS considerably; in monetary terms, USC aid amounted to $142,000. Much of the assistance went to improving the skills of the life workers, to produce a multiplier effect. Additional teacher training, training in leadership, sensitivity, and group dynamics, language courses, and two degree courses were all funded by USC grants. It also paid for their medical relief and for ten-year premiums into a small social security fund – for these teachers had no savings. After Oxfam withdrew in 1965, the USC took over support of the midday feeding program, donating funds for a larger kitchen, and Mrs. Aiyar did a house-to-house survey to identify the neediest. Gradually, numbers were reduced.

Canadian foster parents sponsored 105 children through their years at the Seva Ashram boys' home, which Dr. Lotta several times called the best-run home she knew in India. She equally praised the Srirampuram dispensary, staffed by two doctors, including (for all ten years) Dr. Y.R.N. Murthy who would come in the afternoons after covering his own practice and stay long hours, worrying over his most malnourished babies and later rejoicing over their progress. This dispensary treated as many as 40,000 patients a year, of all ages, at the extraordinarily low cost of twelve cents a patient.

By the early 1970s, conditions were improving for industrial workers in Bangalore. There was steady work in the textile mills, and, consequently, families were eating better. When there was illness, they went to doctors sooner. Patients also began to contribute, by dropping a few coins each visit into the "box collection" at the dispensary, as much as two thousand dollars a year toward its running expenses. Meanwhile, after 1971, the USC shipped to Bangalore some twenty-five thousand dollars worth of milk powder, and Mrs. Aiyar, as the agency's chief representative, supervised its distribution through the boys' home, the dispensary, and DSS itself. Mrs. Aiyar also led the USC to support a rehabilitation project for the physically handicapped, to provide wheelchairs, surgical shoes, and crutches, as well as lunchtime vegetables for 150 trainees in a production unit.

With some hesitation, the USC board also supported the

buying of land and the construction of three community centers by the DSS. The hesitation was due to the experience that there were nearly always cost overruns, which Dr. Lotta refused to meet beyond the pledged amount. But she wrote, in 1970, about her pleasure over the last building effort, whose main contributor had been a local bank during the Gandhi centenary year. The six large and airy classrooms, the meal distribution room, the offices, and the community center itself, were a great stride on from that first building on the convicts' burial ground.

For ten years the USC contributed to a working capital fund for the DSS, making possible, for example, payment of teachers' salaries without having to borrow at high interest rates, at times when government grants arrived late. This reserve fund grew to eleven thousand dollars, and as a parting gift in 1975, the USC added another forty-five hundred dollars and turned it into an endowment fund, whose yearly interest was to be used to cover needs at the boys' home or with the medical or meal programs.

Planting skills in Bihar

The year 1967 will long be remembered as the terrible time of famine in Bihar. In the months when Canadians were joyously celebrating their Centennial and making a summertime trek to the delights of Montreal's Expo, more than 30 million people in this northern Indian state were facing starvation.

Bihar is one of the most rural states (its largest city, Patna, numbered only 474,000 in the 1971 census), and when the monsoon rains failed for three consecutive years, its farming population was in deep trouble. In the northern part of the state, the Ganges and its tributaries provided irrigation for some, but as one climbed to the Chota Nagpur plateau to the south the lack of rain brought desperate conditions. Dr. Lotta drove through drought-stricken villages in April 1967, and in a searing circular she wrote of the haunting sights she saw: the bullock collapsing and dying at sunset as it pulled a hay-cart, the dried-up riverbed where her jeep stuck in the sand, the food distribution center in Kuaikala village where a widow told her she had eaten some bark the day before and nothing that day, the mahua berries spread out to dry in a yard, a last resort for food. She wrote: "Every hour children and adults are dying in Bihar. Hunger and thirst do not kill instantly, as a hand grenade does, or an earthquake. This dying inch by inch is much more cruel."[6]

Her immediate response was to organize carloads of milk powder through the Rama Krishna Mission, to which she was introduced by Jayprakash Narayan, the respected Indian leader who was then organizing drought relief. Wheat was already being sent in vast quantities by the U.S. and Canadian governments. She also thoughtfully organized a distribution of five thousand saris by jeep to women "whose only sari is in such shreds that they can no longer go to the food distribution center to fetch their rations. They must wait until a neighbour returns to lend them her own tattered sari, to cover their nakedness."[7]

The next year brought a bumper crop in Bihar, and the urgent crisis was over. But Dr. Lotta had by then met Swami Yuktananda, a calm and rather frail monk at the Ranchi ashram, who turned out to be a rebel in the midst of the elderly swamis who governed the order's headquarters at Belur Math, near Calcutta. While the old men's interests were in theoretical discussion and old-fashioned styles of education, Swami Yuktananda was a practical man, who kept up with the changing techniques in agriculture and who worried about the future for minority groups. Bihar state had, among its total population of 56 million (1971 census), some 4 million tribal people – Oraon, Munda, Santal, Ho, and others. And in Ranchi district, nearly two-thirds of the people belonged to aboriginal tribes who had survived in forested areas through the centuries of imperial powers, from the Magadha to the British Empire.

The swami talked to Dr. Lotta about the problems, ranging from hunger to drunkenness and outright despair, of the young tribals in the Ranchi area – and then sketched on a piece of paper an outline for an agricultural training center which could turn despair into opportunity. Dr. Lotta spontaneously offered USC's support.

A good deal happened during the five years the Ranchi project had Canadian support. The actual sums from Canada amounted to $87,100 from CIDA, $10,000 from the British

---

[6]Circular no. 4, May 1967.

[7]Circular no. 4, May 1967.

Columbia government, and $134,800 from the USC, so these were a major contribution to getting the center launched. The project made swift progress, despite the doubts of the conservative swamis at headquarters. The training center and hostel, called Divyayan ("The Way of God" in Sanskrit), near the Ranchi ashram were originally built to accommodate twenty tribal farmers doing an intensive six-week course, which showed them what they might achieve with better seeds, fertilizer, and an irrigated second (or third) crop. They were also introduced to beekeeping, fish culture, better forms of animal husbandry with piggeries and poultry, and they were taught the elements of financial management, from bank loans to marketing.

Soon there was such demand for these courses that the capacity was increased to sixty-four, and a four-storey hostel-center was built. The greater numbers, in any case, made better use of staff time and provided continuous labor for the demonstration farm. In the new building, the swami included a "Western apartment" to persuade Dr. Lotta and other visitors to stay, and she used to compare this place to her other favorite retreat in Marathon.

The crux of the project, however, was the Seva Kendra (meaning "Service Organization") which was to provide the follow-up services for the trainees who had returned to their own land after a course. These needed to include the loan of equipment at nominal cost; the obtaining and guaranteeing of bank loans, at about 10 percent a year instead of a moneylender's 100 percent, for buying tools and seeds and pump-sets; and, perhaps most important, the stimulus of regular visits to spur them into action. As Dr. Lotta explained to her board in 1970: "Tribals have been used to a hand-to-mouth existence for so many centuries that regular, hard physical work is a new and difficult assignment."

By 1973 more than five hundred young people had undergone training, and to keep in touch with them in villages spread through Bihar and three or four other states required a complicated network of Seva Kendras. Soon there were fifteen of them in Bihar and West Bengal. They interpreted their mandate of "customer service" broadly. In 1970-71, there were already twenty half-hectare demonstration plots in fifteen villages, and the cooperating farmers did well; one of them earned a net three thousand rupees ($430) from his spring crop of paddy and potato on one hectare. The Ranchi Seva Kendra itself bought a tractor and sprinkler irrigation set on a bank loan and lent them to farmers at nominal charges, and it constructed wells in villages where trainees had returned. In 1972 Dr. Lotta exclaimed at the greenbelt of rotating crops around Ranchi and at the transformation of hundreds of hectares around the village of Bhita where there had been nothing but desert in 1969. Someone replied: "Bhita is the yeast of this whole area." A multiplier effect was at work.

The Ranchi project soon became quite famous. Mrs. Gandhi visited the institute and one of the experimental villages in 1970. The photographer John Buss made a film for the USC that year, *Dormant Land*, following the story of three trainees who put their course lessons into practice with a poultry farm, intensive vegetable farming, and a plot on which the ex-trainee rotated four crops (wheat, rice, vegetables, and maize) in one year. Wealthy Indians, such as a member of the Birla family, toured the center and the demonstration farms and were impressed enough to leave generous donations. Swami Yuktananda received pressing requests to help set up Seva Kendras in other states. And a tea-planter gave the project nearly eighty hectares he said he was not using. After some early difficulties, it has been turned into an efficient modern farm, whose produce has helped cover running expenses of the training center.

Even more important, the Divyayan pilot project was accepted by the Indian Council of Agricultural Research as a model for the whole country, and plans were made to establish similar training centers in all states. Agricultural staff from other state governments were offered training at Ranchi. The Seva Kendra pattern of follow-up services has also spread, particularly in Tripura state and near Darjeeling in north Bengal.

In March 1974, Swami Yuktananda was transferred to headquarters in Calcutta, and a shy, younger monk took on the tough job of fund raising to meet an increasing budget. He worked energetically and raised, in his first year, as much as the older swami had in his last, from Indian industrialists as well as from Delhi. But although the worldwide budget of the Rama Krishna Mission was about $6 million, the headquarters had no funds and left it to individual ashrams to cover their own budget. The cost per student at Ranchi for a six-week course rose from $65 in 1969 to $87.50 in 1975. So Dr. Lotta recommended to her board, that as its farewell gift, the USC should give $50,000 to an endowment fund, whose interest should be used exclusively to cover training costs.

It was not a final farewell because in 1973 Dr. Lotta met with the RKM's governing council at Belur Math as they debated whether to act as a partner agency with the USC in Bangladesh. The old, venerable monks were silent and negative, but she felt "a new wind blowing" among the younger swamis who believed that the two agencies were working to the same principles. She left them still in deep debate, but long after midnight Swami Yuktananda called her at her Calcutta hotel with the news that the council had decided to ask the ten RKM centers in Bangladesh to cooperate. So the rest of the story of that partnership belongs in Chapter 10.

False start in family planning

Another entry-point to the work of helping social and economic development in India has been to take health services into isolated places. In doing so, Dr. Lotta tried whenever possible to link maternal and child welfare with family planning.

The most isolated project was the Kharang Health Center in the Khasi hills of Assam, where a British Unitarian missionary, Dr. Margaret Barr, cared for the tribal people within a thirty-two kilometer radius. Dr. Barr strongly supported the Gandhian principle of training village people to help themselves rather than bringing in educated townspeople who, she wrote in 1953, "seem unable to stand the primitive conditions of village life and the harsh climate."[8] She herself lived in a small house without electricity, but with a variety of animals, and swam daily in a nearby pond.

From 1953 the USC helped her establish a dispensary and maternity health center, and train village girls as midwives. She also set up a children's home, which Canadian foster parents supported. Dr. Lotta made the long journey to see Margaret Barr several times, and in 1969 found herself clambering down jungle paths back to Shillong when rain made the jeep track impassable. In 1972, the last time Dr. Lotta saw her, she was seventy-three years old but eager with plans to build a small

---

[8]Letter to USC Ottawa, 24 March 1953.

hospital (which was eventually financed from the Netherlands). She was treating five thousand patients a year at the medical center, and two of her midwives were touring the villages to advise on family planning. She died in August 1973, but the staff she had trained continued her work, and the USC supported the center and children's home until 1975.

Some other efforts were not so successful. One of the first five Willys-Overland jeep ambulances the USC donated in 1955 went to the Kodai branch of the All India Women's Conference. Its job was to carry medical services to sixteen villages high in the mountains about 480 kilometers south of Madras. Dr. Lotta toured these villages in the ambulance at various times, and after going back to Kodaikanal for a last visit in 1974, concluded that this emergency aid had saved innumerable lives. She had, however, to add: "But because of immense isolation, total disinterest of the government, lack of funds for a massive job in public health — and not only in emergency services — we have made no permanent impact on the area."[9]

A special effort had been made to promote family planning in the villages around Kodai. A second USC-donated van was used for this specific purpose, and in 1969, at Dr. Lotta's insistence, the agency engaged a trained family planning extension educator, Mr. Maruthamutu, to tackle the men. But by 1973 she was forced to conclude that these efforts had been "a dismal failure, because the completely illiterate just do not understand what we are talking about and only agree to an operation if they are bribed into it with amounts of money which only the Government can pay, but no voluntary agency can afford."[10]

On the other hand, she called the Thana project, which the USC underwrote for six years from 1967, a family planning success. This was because it served a literate population. The Thana-Kalyan industrial estate outside Bombay was the largest in India, with some fifty-thousand employees in textile, engineering, and other plants. Through the Family Planning Association of India, the USC paid for six staff to hold general meetings, group talks, and individual counseling among workers and their wives, and to train worker-leaders. The FPAI held vasectomy and tubectomy camps and clinics, operating on 794

---

[9]Report to the USC board, 17 April 1974.

[10]Report to the USC board, 27 April 1973.

men and 436 women in the first four years. The USC support, amounting to about five thousand dollars a year, which included CIDA matching funds and a special donation from Calgary's Miles for Millions, ended in 1973, because by then the FPAI was receiving sufficient funding from the International Planned Parenthood Federation.

Dr. Lotta wrote then that this pilot project had been "very useful to demonstrate one vital point; that family planning in India is acceptable only to those who are sufficiently educated to understand the need." She recorded the statistic that an estimated 14 percent of the 100 million couples in India in the reproductive age group (i.e., between fifteen and forty-four) were then practicing some kind of family planning method, "but this figure should be 50 percent to be truly successful." By 1973 the figure in the Thana region was more than 20 percent.

Karnatak and the Gandhian heritage

The proudest acheivement in the health care field in India was certainly the twenty-year collaboration between USC and the Karnatak Health Institute. The story of KHI, of Dr. Narayan Hardiker and the amazing Vaidya family, deserves a book in itself. What follows is no more than a sketch, or a prologue[11].

KHI dates from 1929, when Dr. G.R. Kokatnur returned from Minnesota and soon afterwards started building a rural dispensary and later a sanatorium on a seventy-nine hectare site near the Ghataprabha river, four hundred kilometers south of Bombay. It has a dry, breezy climate suitable for treatment of TB and chest diseases. But the land around is arid until one gets at least halfway to Belgaum, and the villagers then in these barren lands were desperately poor and backward. Dr. Kokatnur struggled for thirteen years to serve the area with his forty-bed sanatorium but he was getting old and irritable, and as soon as he had found a likely successor and tried him out for a year, he retired.

He obviously could not have chosen better. Dr. M.K. Vaidya was then a young bachelor who had studied in Bombay and

---

[11]Moira Farrow, a staff reporter for the *Vancouver Sun*, wrote four good descriptive articles about KHI after visiting there in 1965. They were featured on the front page, 23-26 November 1965, in support of the paper's Cup of Milk Fund that Christmas season.

worked in his native Goa. There is probably no other family in India today more engaged in the practice of medicine. In the previous generation, there were five brothers who all practiced herbal or Ayurvedic medicine. One of them, Dada Vaidya, was honored with a bronze statue by the Portuguese governor-general of Goa for saving the life of his newborn son. Today there are no fewer than eighteen medical doctors – thirteen men and five women – among the first and second cousins of two generations in the Vaidya family. All his own four children are medical graduates, and Dr. Kiran, an orthopedic surgeon, Dr. Ghanashyam, a general surgeon, and Dr. Alaka, a gynaecologist, all work with him at KHI.

Today the institute is a wondrous place to find in this barren region. There is a chest hospital of 160 beds; by Dr. Vaidya's own figuring, nearly 8 million people in India have TB, and some 600,000 die of the disease every year. There is a general hospital of 166 beds, so well equipped that he occasionally does brain surgery (and charges only 500 rupees). There is a 55-bed maternity hospital, a large training school for nurses, and a dental department, largely equipped with USC support. There is a medical museum with some extraordinary exhibits, a primary school, and a craft school.

But to list only the facilities is to dismiss the spirit of the place. A visitor will, if he rises at dawn, be astounded to find the trainee nurses already outside, their saris tucked up, as they scamper around on the grass playing quoit games and doing physical exercises. Dr. Vaidya himself will have been up for two hours, thinking and writing, for by 7:00 A.M. he has started to perform operations. In those predawn hours, he has written a half-dozen booklets. Some are strictly medical, like the alarmingly illustrated *Scourge of Humanity – WORM*. In others, he merges philosophic and religious thought in his marveling at the wonders of the human body (each containing 60 trillion cells, "administrations working most harmoniously") and the vision this microscopic view offers to the quarrelsome world.

KHI is a place of discipline, thoughtfulness, asceticism, and vision. In the words of its 1983 annual report, KHI "is not a Hospital Complex alone...It is basically an educational institution meant for spreading the gospel of healthy life – individual, family, community and nation." It is a Gandhian heritage. Part of this is due to Dr. Hardiker, the founder of the Hindustani Seva Dal, the disciplined youth movement which Jawaharlal

Nehru described as "the iron frame on which Congress fought the war of freedom." For he lived his final years at KHI and is called its architect. Today it is the quiet, courteous figure of Dr. Vaidya, in a white jacket with stethoscope always around his throat, twinkling eyes hidden behind sunglasses, who is the soul of the place.

Dr. Vaidya has made KHI into much more than a rural hospital with many modern techniques that has spread its benefits inexpensively to surrounding villages. Rather, it is a hospital with its roots deep in the local rural life, and many aspects of its management — from recruitment of employees to methods of treatment — have a rural bias. Health and education merge, for example, in the eye-camps, for while one family member is having an operation for cataract, the patient's relatives standing nearby are being instructed in some basic knowledge of health and sanitation. Through the leadership conferences for women and holiday camps for children, a spirit of cooperation and self-sacrifice has permeated villages. Mr. M.S. Kirloskar, president of KHI, has written: "It is this very local, very Indian character that makes KHI a unique hospital complex, as compared to dozens of hospitals spread all over India."[12]

The USC involvement began in a somewhat indirect way. A force of eight hundred workers was building a canal from the Ghataprabha river, and nearly half of them succumbed to a high fever, which Dr. Vaidya managed to control with Mepacrine. The director of public health in Poona would not accept that it had been malaria but, years later, asked a government adviser on maternal and child health to make a special journey to KHI by train. Dr. Vaidya thought this "an unnecessary botheration," but Dr. S. Bhatia turned out to be an amiable person who studied every aspect of KHI and said, rather mysteriously, that she had never seen an institution like it before. She recommended that Dr. Vaidya start training village girls as nurses and that he replace the old bullock cart with a modern ambulance in order to meet village emergencies swiftly.

She met Dr. Lotta in Delhi and heard that the USC had been providing jeep ambulances elsewhere, so she made her pitch for another. She also introduced her to Dr. Hardiker, who was in Delhi as a member of parliament (the Rajya Sabha), and on

[12]Letter to the author, 12 September 1984.

126

the strength of these two interviews, Dr. Lotta recommended that the USC spend thirty-five hundred dollars to provide an ambulance. The USC board was not too pleased that she had done so without first visiting KHI, but Dr. Vaidya saw the touch of destiny. He wrote a reminiscence, "The Unknown Hand Works," for Dr. Lotta in 1975 recalling this first contact.

She did, however, reach Ghataprabha in time for the handing over of the ambulance in June 1955 and recorded it as one of the happiest days in her life. "There they both stood – the van and the bullock cart – gaily garlanded with red flowers and light green leaves, somehow reminding me of the old India and the new..." After the breaking of coconuts and offering of rice, she took a ride in the bullock cart (at five kilometers an hour) round the hospital grounds, and then rode out in the white ambulance to Mamadapur village to announce the regular medical visits being planned with a doctor and nurse.

The ambulance medical work went through two stages. For a dozen years there was constant touring, six days a week, by two USC ambulances equipped with examination table and medicine around the eighty-four villages within a fifty-mile radius. There were deep suspicions to be overcome, but changes came relatively fast. Several young doctors who came to KHI as interns and did the village rounds stayed on. So, in 1968 this free service was suspended. In its place KHI sent out specialists – gynaecologists, dentists, eye doctors, enterologists – who charged a small fee (for people tended to distrust what was entirely free), which was put into a fund for community improvements. Special campaigns and camps were run to vaccinate children against polio, whooping cough, and diphtheria.

In fifteen years, in fact, a silent revolution took place in the villages, as the figures for 1969 prove. In that year, 12,187 patients were treated at the paying dispensaries, and telephones having meanwhile been installed, KHI received 1,924 calls to fetch patients ill in the villages and requiring hospital treatment. It had become second nature to call for a trained doctor instead of turning to a local quack.

The extent of this revolution is well illustrated by Dr. Vaidya's description to me of a typical village childbirth in the early 1950s, and of how difficult it was to begin maternity work at KHI:

The belief was that, if a woman gave birth horizontally, the baby

127

could reach up and grab her heart. So they made the woman stand up and tied her hair to the ceiling of the hut; and women sat round to make sure she didn't collapse. The men sat outside beating pans and burning incense, to drive away the demons. Instead, it smothered all those inside. Then when she was in labor, they tied a rope around her diaphragm. Birthgiving was horrors.

But I had one persistent midwife, and I told her to live in a village for one year and make friends — and finally she will be able to bring me a case. At last there was a woman who had lost three or four babies whom she convinced. But the men said "Don't take her" and fought her to the last minute; but she was insistent. I made a caesarean operation; and, when she and baby went back, it was a miracle — the baby had come this new way. But still in the first year, after building a special maternity compound, only seven women came. I sat with every one, telling her this way is better than the rope and tied hair. The next year there were 50, then 100. Last year [1983] we delivered 1,500 at the hospital.

In addition, maternity clinics have been built in several villages, usually a couple of rooms alongside the community center, and ten to twenty babies are born in these every month.

Dr. Lotta was quite puzzled by what she thought was Dr. Vaidya's resistance to the government's all-out drive on family planning from 1966. She put it down to the fact that he and Mrs. Vaidya are deeply orthodox Hindus. It is equally likely that the Vaidyas accurately estimated how quickly they could introduce changes in the area. In 1970 he accepted government funds to set aside beds in the maternity hospital for tubectomy cases, and in 1972 the USC paid the transportation cost of ninety-six hundred kilometers motoring to bring three hundred women into KHI for free tubal ligations.

When Dr. Vaidya showed me round the maternity hospital in February 1984, we also went to the ward where some mothers, after giving birth, were waiting for, or resting after, tubectomies. Did he and his doctors preach family planning to these mothers? I asked. They didn't need to, he replied; the women talked it up among themselves.

From the back of the bus

Welfare work among the village women did not start very

long before Dr. Lotta's first trip to Ghataprabha. Mrs. Vatsalabai Vaidya remembers a visit in 1954 from the chairman of the Central Social Welfare Board in Delhi, Mrs. Durgabai Deshamukh, which aroused her own enthusiasm for rural welfare. Mrs. Vaidya herself comes of a patrician family. Her father was the Sardar of Satara, ruling over, and caring for, some twenty-one villages south of Poona. He was also on the Governor-General's Advisory Council. In one generation of her family there was a leap from feudal supervision to more neighborly concern.

In the second Five-Year Plan (in the early 1960s), the CSWB delegated the work of rural welfare to the Mahila Mandals, or women's clubs, while providing much of the early funding. It was at this stage that the USC was trying to stimulate community development through regular conferences of village leaders. Every two months ten people (five men and five women) from each participating village were to meet for two days, either at KHI or in one of the villages, to discuss what they had done since they last met and what they would plan for the next two months. It was an idea that Dr. Lotta transplanted from her experience in Macedonia and from the work of Tony Trimis.

These joint conferences with both men and women helped the creation of schools, dispensaries, bus stops, temples, and so on. But they were only a qualified success. The women tended to keep quiet in the men's presence, and men began to lose enthusiasm as party politics became their preoccupation. After nearly eight years and thirty-six of these conferences, the experiment seemed about to collapse in 1968.

At this point Dr. Lotta gave some firm advice: Forget the men, let the village women leaders hold conferences by themselves. Mrs. Vaidya toured the villages and won assent for the change. This turned out to be the breath of life for them. But in her challenging way, Dr. Lotta put them to the test when she visited in 1970. She announced that it was time to stop these conferences. Spontaneously, the fifty women there (who had taken time off from harvesting) said no and gave at least eight good reasons why they wanted them to continue. These included: "We meet you and get new ideas...We move between villages and see new things...We used to follow the men at joint conferences, as at bus stops; here we assert ourselves, and confidently carry out plans...The men, who ignored us before, are now jealous, they even ask our advice...We have confidence to demand our rights from government officers...We are wiser, more alert; we've developed the power to think."[13]

So the leadership conferences continued (how could they not?), supported by USC until 1975. For a tiny investment of about five hundred dollars a year, these conferences with women from thirteen villages stimulated, in seven years, an almost exhausting number of activities: educational trips to Goa and other states; weekly discussion centers in the villages with government-donated transistor radios; many health activities, from polio vaccinations and specialist camps to baby shows and family planning propaganda; picnics, festivals, and agricultural camps including tree-planting; and such fund-raising moves as selling cloth, soap, and neem-tree seedlings. They organized yearly medical checkups for all Balwaddi preschool children, and they sent other women to KHI to attend Better Living Weeks, and they chose girls and boys, ten to 14 years old, for a three-week Holiday Home there.

Mr. Kirloskar attended his first women leaders' conference in 1975 and recorded these impressions in *The Golden Leaf:* "What I saw today was fantastic: these village women conducting a meeting so systematically, one after the other giving their work reports and then assuring Dr. Hitschmanova she could go away confident they will raise funds and carry on all the activities... Dr. Hitschmanova has not just given these uneducated women bread to eat, but has gifted them with a power to make their own bread. It is a great achievement."

The Better Living Weeks ended when a network of village health workers was set up. During my visit, the health worker in Nabapur village acted out for me the nutrition lecture that she gives as she goes from house to house. As she talks, she flourishes a series of big cards with grains, foods, and vegetables drawn on them, colored in the green, white, and red of the national flag. She receives a monthly salary of fifty rupees ($6.50) from KHI. It is no princely sum, but she gains prestige among her neighbors and has a satisfying job.

The Mahila Mandals have grown in strength, and twenty-four villages now have thriving women's centers. It took twenty years to develop eight of them; then all suspicions vanished and the

---

[13]From *A Golden Leaf*, a book of testimonial essays written by KHI staff and villagers, compiled by Miss Muktamala, and presented to Dr. Hitschmanova on her last visit in 1975.

number tripled in two years. Their leaders have remembered the part Dr. Lotta played in their launching. When, in 1977, she stopped briefly in Bombay (on her way to Bangladesh and Indonesia), the Vaidyas journeyed by train to see her and carried letters from the villages with some memorable compliments: "We are standing and stepping on the footprints shown by you to us" (Phulgaddi) and "Eighteen years back our village was as a thorn forest, but now with your help and guidance by Mrs. Vaidya it has become a flower garden" (Musuguppi).

Awamma Mulla's drinking well

The village that may have most reason to remember the USC is Maldinni. The tale of Dr. Lotta's visit there in 1962 has become a legend. Maldinni had a bad reputation, a place of drunkenness and murders, where women stayed indoors after dusk. When Dr. Lotta arrived, she was offered the customary gift, a coconut and a piece of cloth. According to Mrs. Vaidya, the response was an angry outburst, unexpected of an ordinary visitor: "No, no. I cannot accept these things...I have never seen children so dirty – I cannot accept anything in this village with such children. Tell me why you cannot wash them and comb their hair?"

The crowd realized this was not going to be the usual kind of visitation. The headman of the village explained: "It's not their fault. There is no water for washing."

"But did you try to get it?"

"We have tried, but the government does not help, and the underground water is salty."

"Why do you wait for government? Why cannot you dig a well? You women can forego a sari or some sweets and collect funds to get the water."

In the somewhat electric silence, an elderly Moslem woman, Awamma Mulla, stood up and promised in shaky words that she would work to organize the women.

"Do you promise that, when I come next time, I shall see water in your village?"

"Yes, I do promise" – this said, with a coconut held in her hand for a vow.

By Awamma Mulla's own description in *The Golden Leaf*, the work began well. Some funds were raised, and on Republic Day

131

the wife of a rich landlord started the digging with great vigor – five baskets of earth before she stopped! But then people began to say that women should not leave their homes to do such work. She ignored this criticism and also turned the damage of a big storm to her advantage, for the village Panchayat committee auctioned off some uprooted trees and gave a hundred rupees of the proceeds to her fund.

The digging continued, and six meters down, sweet-tasting water was found. Awamma Mulla filled a bottle with it and hurried to KHI – in Mrs. Vaidya's account, to annouce the joy of success, and in her own account "to get it blessed by Rev. Dr. Hardiker and our dear Mrs. Vaidya."

The government technician still had to be persuaded that the water was not salty before a construction grant was made. And fortunately, two members of the village Panchayat committee who tried to use the money for other purposes were arrested in a murder case. Awamma Mulla's son happened to be a stone-mason and he completed the construction "working day and night in fifteen days, and he also finished it very finely and with affection," just in time for Dr. Lotta's next visit, when she was made to enter the village in a triumphal procession on a decorated bullock cart.

The Mahila Mandal in Maldinni subsequently overcame another crisis, when all the chickens in its poultry farm died in an epidemic. The members recouped by buying cloth in bulk and organizing a retail sale each year to raise funds for the club. Wrote Awamma Mulla in 1975: "I have full faith that God helps those that have good purpose in their mind."

I was taken to Maldinni village in February 1984 by Dr. Kiran, and we shone the car's headlights on the famous well that even serves people from surrounding villages. Suddenly, out of the starry darkness, came a bent old woman of more than eighty, to hold my hand. "When I heard someone was here who knew Lotabai," said Awamma Mulla, "I came running!"

KHI and the surrounding region are still subject to disasters. There was a three-year drought in the 1970s, during which trees died, people fled from villages, and a good deal of community activity lapsed. Dr. Hardiker, who was then eighty-five, announced that he was giving up wearing a shirt until the rains came again. And in June 1982, a wild hailstorm and gales did heavy damage to buildings.

But progress continues. A popular new rural dairy scheme

involves giving buffalo cows to poor women, paid for from a fifty-thousand rupee ($6,500) revolving fund. Each woman pays back what amounts to a two thousand rupee loan by providing half the daily milk (about seven liters, in all) to KHI, the local Mahila Mandala or some government collection point; the rest she keeps for her family or sells. Its popularity was so clear that the nearby Gokak Mills added sixty thousand rupees to the fund to bring into the scheme villages from which it draws many of its employees. A group in Seattle contributed almost as much.

As well, KHI's increasing needs in water supply were secured in 1984 when the regional commissioner sanctioned a government grant to dig a well beside the Ghataprabha River and pump water up a four thousand meter pipe to a two hundred thousand liter tank. The work began during my visit, and with Dr. Vaidya I joined the construction gang at the riverside in a short ceremony of blessing the pickaxes and splitting a coconut before the ground was first dug. Dr. Vaidya relies as little as possible on government assistance, and a large bequest from a New York couple was recently added to the endowment fund to which USC had contributed ten thousand dollars.

Is KHI unique because of some special circumstances and the remarkable character of the Vaidya family? Or can its achievements be replicated elsewhere in India? Oxfam has obviously hoped for replication. Having helped launch the village health worker network around Ghataprabha, that agency arranged that social workers, priests, and medical staff from different parts of South India should visit KHI and learn from it. Let us trust that some of this seed takes root elsewhere.

CHAPTER 7

Building the Canadian Constituency

A memorable address

"OH, THE USC has nothing to worry about over its support in Canada," said the head of another voluntary agency recently, with perhaps a touch of envy. "There are only two addresses in Ottawa that every Canadian knows. One is 24 Sussex Drive. The other is 56 Sparks Street."

Certainly, Dr. Lotta did everything she could to make the address of the USC headquarters as well known as that of the prime minister's residence. Those short urgent messages or "spots" about critical situations overseas, broadcast first on radio and later on television, in that accented voice which had depths of compassion, are remembered years afterward. Neill McKee, who went with CUSO to Malaysia and then joined the International Development Research Centre as its film-maker, says: "That voice was part of my growing up in Elmira, Ontario. I first learnt anything about the Third World from her."

The same was true of Margaret Catley-Carlson, president of the Canadian International Development Agency. She grew up in Nelson, British Columbia and says: "I used to get taken to Sunday school to hear her."

Dr. Lotta clearly knew the importance of the well-remembered address for an organization that relied on many thousands of small donations. The agency has worked out of five different premises in forty years: briefly, at the outset, from her apartment at 668 Cooper Street, and then from 48 Sparks Street, 78 Sparks, and two different floors of 56 Sparks. When a search began in the mid-1950s for less cramped quarters, everyone realized it could mean not only more rent but the loss of a memorable address. The obvious solution was found; to move along the street that was named after Ottawa's first landowner-farmer (Nicholas Sparks), but whose name also happily gave an image of briskness and self-starting energy.

As well, every advantage was squeezed out of the personal approach. Dr. Lotta used to call the USC "the agency with a heart"; everyone else recognized that she was the heart of it. Bower Carty, whose involvement began as national treasurer in 1949 and who has been chairman during two periods since then, says: "For many years Lotta Hitschmanova *was* the USC. Board members acted as a sounding board and asked questions, but rarely if ever imposed decisions. The only decision we made in the early years over her protests was to increase her salary."

This picture began to change in the 1970s, and indeed, one theme of this book is the restructuring of a personal organization. But for the first thirty years the USC grew, spread its name into and drew support from many corners of Canada through the extraordinary energy and dramatic singlemindedness of one woman. If a hundred women in St. John's, Newfoundland, were knitting sweaters, or if Rita Huddlestone in Nanaimo was making a hundred flannelette pants between Christmas and New Year's, it was because Dr. Lotta had recently been to their city and told them, in the most human terms, about the needs in the Middle East or Korea. Lorna Henderson, who was an army wife at Camp Borden when Dr. Lotta came there in 1952 straight from her first trip to Korea, says: "There was not a dry eye in the place when she'd finished with us."

Her skills in communication were many-sided. She could talk to young children as effectively as she did to elderly farmers, who offered her boxcars of wheat and remembered the USC in their wills. The children sent what they could. In 1962 there arrived in Ottawa a cardboard poster with a train drawn on it – "The Banff Trail School Clothing Express" – together with twenty cartons of blankets, towels, and baby clothing which those primary school students had collected. And Stephen Hussey of Clinton, Ontario sent his tooth-money – enough, he was assured in a thank-you letter, to feed a hungry child for a month. The only audiences she seems not to have conquered were the more sophisticated teenagers. One graduate of the posh Havergal School for Girls remembers how Dr. Lotta's annual appearance, in uniform, at the lectern was occasion for the school's best mimics to polish up their imitations of the visitor for later performance. (But this woman ended up working in CUSO and CIDA, as have other Havergal girls.)

She put to excellent account her experience as a newspaper reporter. She could make a reader of her circular letters and jottings feel he was alongside her, solving problems in Hanoi or Madras, when he was actually a railway accountant in the

Maritimes or bedridden at ninety in St. Catharines. She could also mix this vivid style with the solid, detailed accounts of overseas projects or Canadian branches she had visited that were needed for her reports to the USC board.

As well, Dr. Lotta made good use of film from the earliest days. From 1948 until 1972, the USC produced an annual film based on her overseas tour, which was shown to strong effect during her fund-raising trips. She shot her own film for the first few years but began hiring a photographer so that she could concentrate on gathering facts. She narrated all these films, which had titles that were either cautionary (*Tomorrow is Too Late*) or inspirational (*Paving Stones, Hand in Hand, Bridge of Love*). John Buss, a longtime CBC cameraman, traveled with her for several years and somehow managed to juggle three cameras. At other times Andy Clark, David Maltby, and Eric Bremner went with her. Back in Ottawa, Pamela MacRae edited the film and wrote the scripts for many productions, notably *The USC Story*, a composite film summing up twenty-five years' activity.

Pamela Lee MacRae vividly remembers the hectic conditions under which these films were scripted and edited. When she first joined the USC in 1966, she had to write scripts for two films during her first three months. One film focussed on the story of an Indian boy, and Pamela had no background knowledge of life in India. She says:

> I did the only thing possible: read up fast everything I could. And the promos for the films had to be ready for her return to Canada, as well. The work was exhausting, with four of us in a small, airless room. I remember late one summer afternoon, collapsing face down on my desk. You either walked right out of the agency then, or you pulled yourself together and worked till midnight.

Perhaps an even rarer gift for a writer was Dr. Lotta's ability to produce a good story for other reporters, columnists, and radio interview hosts. She made lifelong friends with publishers like Stuart Keate and columnists like Mamey Maloney Boggs. Ida Clarkson, who first met Dr. Lotta in 1948 when interviewing her on CJVI, then Victoria's only radio station, and later invited her to appear regularly on her CHEK television show, describes her appeal in these words:

> Her smallness helped. She seemed vulnerable and you wanted to

protect her. She also was always humble and never demanding. She would never talk about herself. She told stories about the people in the photographs – and the camera would come in tight, as she laid them on the table... And her humility always had dignity, there was no wheedling. Oh, I adore her!

She would, of course, use the media for USC purposes, but she would make it their purpose, also. For example, CHAB radio in Moose Jaw sponsored twelve foster children for years after 1956. Stuart Keate began a Christmas Appeal when he was publisher of the *Victoria Daily Times* and instituted the Cup of Milk fund on the *Vancouver Sun*. In 1966, the third Christmas appeal for *Sun* readers, things did not go as well as before, so the publisher wrote a front-page editorial: "...This year our campaign is lagging, and we are ashamed." It had moved on from being her fund-raising campaign to being their chosen task.

In the same way, Mrs. N. Willard wrote in 1964 from Eyebrow, Saskatchewan, that she was knitting her 209th birthday shirt (for a baby's layette): "It is an easy pick-up pastime ...Sorry I cannot do more." And Marjorie Woods, who was blind and deaf, knitted 1000 sweaters. She was awarded the Order of Canada – and knitted three more on the return flight from Ottawa to Vancouver! It was Dr. Lotta's dedication, symbolized partly by her uniform, that inspired knitters and newspaper people alike.

Not everyone was inspired, or admired her. One business teacher at a technical school she visited several times in Regina speaks somewhat mockingly about the uniform and says, "I thought she came on a little too strong." And the former head of another national agency is franker: "She was a martinet. She wore that uniform for a purpose. The only thing lacking was the general's insignia on the shoulders."

That criticism comes closest to truth in her relations with her own office staff. She brought a form of Central European authoritarianism to the office, and the annual turnover of staff was heavy for many years. Certainly, there were good times. Birthday cakes on 29 August to mark another landmark for the agency, genuine friendships, and strong links of affection. But it was an earnest, industrious atmosphere. Her demand for perfect performance, to match her own standards, led to frequent disappointment, most particularly in what an associate calls "her eternal search for a twin, a clone, to act as her assistant," and perhaps, one day, to take her place. This search for an assistant failed time and again, until Raymond ven der Buhs settled into this position in the 1970s.

Branching out

Every voluntary agency in Canada has faced the question of what sort of organizational structure is appropriate in this huge country with dispersed communities and limited travel funds. Almost inevitably, an agency decides to have an executive whose members live close to headquarters, usually Ottawa, Toronto, or Montreal, and a national board that meets once a year. The branches, or local committees, have a lot of autonomy in local affairs but little practical say in the workings of the national organization. How one eases any strains between the center and the branches, how one keeps all the little parts turning independently; these are the secrets of running anything bigger than a parochial business in the Canadian confederation.

In general, Dr. Lotta took the usual organizational path in setting up the USC but she added some characteristic touches of her own. For the first $3^{1}/2$ years the Ottawa branch simply acted as the executive committee. Then, in March 1949 an outline constitution was drafted, and a national board was formally established, with an executive committee which was basically drawn from the Ottawa branch but was occasionally attended by visiting representatives from the other branches. Approvingly, Mrs. E.J. Ransom wrote from Winnipeg that year: "It [the constitution] seems to be putting into words practically what we have been doing in the past three years."

Links with the branches were created and maintained almost entirely by Dr. Lotta alone, except when supporters moved between branches, as Dr. Wickenden did from Ottawa to Calgary. She did the traveling between cities, and when a branch collapsed or needed reorganizing (as, for example, Winnipeg and Vancouver branches did in 1950), she undertook the job of finding new enthusiasts during her next speaking tour. In between such crises, she kept up a busy correspondence with the branches through her circular letters; by March 1954 she had written no fewer than 182 of them, or one nearly every two weeks. She also wrote the minutes of the executive committee and annual meetings, so that nearly all the material received by branches, except for routine letters, came from her pen. The annual meetings were normally attended by no more than a dozen people — at least, until the twentieth anniversary in 1965 – because everyone agreed that it would be a misuse of USC funds to spend a thousand dollars or more to subsidize travel to Ottawa of a representative from each branch. So it was the thread of Dr. Lotta's spoken words and writings that held the USC together across Canada year after year.

She did more than just keep the branches informed. She tried to involve them in the decision-making. In those days, when mail delivery was inexpensive and speedy, and a reply to a letter posted in Ottawa on Tuesday could be expected back from Vancouver on Friday, this involvement was feasible even for a cost-cutting agency. It was written into Article 11 of the USC's first constitution in 1949 that "resolutions passed by the Executive Committee of the National Board have to be communicated as promptly as possible to the local Branch executives for their approval." An amendment from the Winnipeg branch sensibly modified this in 1951, so that branch approval was only needed on "matters of policy and major expenditure." The branches did express opinions on whether the USC should start working in particular countries, although they never combined in sufficient strength to change any proposal made in Ottawa.

Another element in the USC organization was the advisory committees set up in the capitals of countries where the USC was working. They were a useful combination of Canadian embassy staff with host nationals, and the wives of Canadian diplomats were often pressed into service: among many others, Mrs. George Magann in Athens, Mrs. Escott Reid in Delhi, and Mrs. John Small in Hong Kong.

Unitarians and the USC

The relationship of the Unitarian Service Committee with the Unitarian Church in Canada had to be resolved at some stage. But it proved to be an awkward process that stretched over many years. It led to a three-year-long constitutional review in the late 1950s, and even after that Dr. Lotta and others were frequently asked at public meetings or in letters whether the agency was controlled by the Unitarian Church. The registration of USC Canada as an alternate name in June

1979, and its increasing use, has not completely ended such questions, even today.

In 1945, the agency was launched through six branches of the Unitarian Church in Canada which were themselves linked to the American Unitarian Association, with its headquarters in Boston, until the Canadian Unitarian Council was formed in 1961.[1] But, more fundamentally, USC Canada began when USC Boston authorized Dr. Hitschmanova to set up a committee, and it was registered as a charity under Canadian law. The links were close for a few years; Dr. Lotta's salary originally came from Boston, as did some ten thousand copies of an initial brochure.

The dissolving of ties with USC Boston by 1948 was accomplished without rancor. The two committees had already begun to go their separate ways. USC Boston had decided to concentrate its resources on sending medical teaching missions to countries that had been cut off from Western medical advances by the War. They recruited first-rate staff; for example, Dr. Paul Dudley White, a heart specialist from Harvard Medical School who later attended President Eisenhower, led the two-month mission to Czechoslovakia. Howard Brooks, who acted as administrative officer for some of the eleven medical missions says, "they were the best thing we did." For a time, after the National War Fund money was exhausted, and a fund-raising campaign in the United States had a poor response, the medical missions were its main overseas activity.

Dr. Lotta, meanwhile, was building up her own program with Canadian funds and local branches. She was also starting to appoint her own field representatives from among host nationals, a point of difference with Boston, which had always wanted to have American supervisors of their overseas programs.

When USC Canada made its independence clear, and Dr. Lotta's visits to Boston ceased, there were no hard feelings there, says Howard Brooks, "only a grudging admiration for Lotta – grudging because she did some things so much better than we could do. Her journalistic sense left our people way behind, and we never got anyone of a calibre approaching the prime minister level to support our campaigns, as she did."

So the problem of relationships was contained within Canada

---

[1]A 1961 census recorded an increase to 15,062 in the number of people in Canada giving their religion as Unitarian, from only 3,517 in the 1951 census.

and came to a head in 1954. The Winnipeg branch of USC Canada, which had some Icelandic Unitarian communities affiliated with it, met ahead of the annual meeting of the national executive committee that January and expressed the feeling that the current (1949) constitution did not define clearly enough the relationship between the USC, the churches, and the local branches. A resolution, moved by the Reverend Philip Petursson, stirred matters up because it assumed the USC was then, and would remain, under the control of the Unitarian churches. It asked the executive committee

> to canvass the various Canadian Unitarian Churches and Fellow-ships as to their opinion of the desirability of the continuation of Unitarian Service Committee work – whether in Canada, or abroad – as a recognized long-term denomination activity for the future, and that, if the decision is favorable, a more comprehensive and definite constitution than the present one be drafted in consulta-tion with the member churches.[2]

The main response at the annual meeting was given by the USC's honorary solicitor, Richard Barber. He pointed out that the USC of Canada had not been founded by the Unitarian churches in Canada but established by the USC in the United States, and it might best be described as "an independent affiliate" of USC Boston.[3] While the USC was really grateful for Unitarian leadership, especially for handling most of the clothes-packing and shipping efforts, "only a very small part of the funds received are contributed by Unitarians across Canada." If the USC had not established its nondenominational character, he said, its fund-raising efforts could never have been endorsed in 1952 and 1953 by the Prime Minister, Louis St. Laurent.

The annual meeting unanimously supported a resolution declaring that "it is advisable that the USC of Canada remain essentially independent of the Unitarian Church as a denomi-nation." Fred Scott, the national treasurer and a born peace-

---

[2]Letter from Mr. W.F. Oldham, chairman of the USC Winnipeg branch, 16 January 1954.

[3]In December 1948, by becoming incorporated as USC Inc. under the Massachusetts Charitable Act, USC Boston had itself become a nonsectarian, voluntary agency and thus independent of the AUA for fund raising, al-though most of its funds came from Unitarian churches.

maker, offered a motion inviting all nine branches to offer concrete proposals for clarifying the 1949 constitution.

The Vancouver branch, which to this day has required that its chairman should be a member of the Unitarian church, soon replied at length. Its reply went into historical origins and drew on the words of the original Boston-produced brochure – "When we are asked what Unitarianism means, we tell about...the Unitarian Service Committee, our faith in action" – to show that "in its formative period the USCC was essentially an expression of Unitarianism and the Unitarian Churches." The branch also argued that, in November 1948, Dr. Hitschmanova had encouraged them to establish clearly that the USC in Vancouver was under the control of the church. And it proposed an amendment to the constitution which would put all full-fledged branches effectively under the control of the local church or fellowship.

From Winnipeg, Mr. Petursson pointed out that, after nine years, only two branches – Moose Jaw and Brandon – had no direct Unitarian church affiliation. But he said he was more concerned about the permanency of USC Canada. In his earlier resolution, he said, "all I was seeking to know was whether the USCC was now, or was to be, on a permanent basis; and, if so, the whole constitution should be re-drawn."[4] He did not offer any amendments, but the Winnipeg chairman, Mr. W.F. Oldham, suggested a two-tier organization: a national board of persons appointed by the boards of each participating Unitarian Church to act simply as a watchdog, and a national executive as administrative body including delegates "from all the branches, whether church branches or otherwise."[5]

Mr. Petursson had made an important point. The permanency of the USC had been several times questioned, not least by Dr. Lotta herself. In an executive committee meeting in November 1949, when the Canadian Appeal for Children was siphoning off possible funds, she thought the next six months after the CAC ended would be crucial: "either the USC will have raised a lot of money...or we will have to disband altogether." The uncertainty lasted, for in April 1950, Howard Brooks wrote from Boston that he would be "terribly disappointed if

[4]Letter to the USC executive committee, 25 March 1954.

[5]Letter to Bower Carty, chairman of the USC national executive, 11 April 1954.

the Canadian USC liquidates...You should still continue even if you should have to limit the scope of your program to one or two countries."[6] And at the 1951 annual meeting, Dr. Lotta said the future of the USC depended on the continued cooperation of branches to pack and ship clothing. If the volume of shipments fell, she said, the committee would not be justified in asking for continued public support.

The period 1951-52 was a critical period for the USC. Although the needs in Greece were stirring a large public response, USC workers were tired and somewhat dispirited. In February 1951, Dr. Lotta acknowledged this in a circular to branches: "Some of our most devoted workers are tired from long and exhausting packing hours, especially in Winnipeg." Indeed, the Winnipeg branch dissolved in September 1951 for lack of volunteers. As well, Ottawa and Vancouver branches were having to find new packing quarters, and there was doubt about the Vancouver branch continuing after a new minister arrived in mid-1951. The Montreal branch had discussed the issue of continuing that January, and though its members voted in favor, its chairman, Mrs. Macdonald, felt compelled to write to Ottawa about the "somewhat unsatisfactory relationships" between the branches and the national executive: "It appeared that on no occasion had a matter been brought up for considera-tion by the branches, but that it had already been definitely decided on by the National Executive."

Dr. Lotta herself was feeling the strain. During 1951, she certainly contemplated leaving the USC, for she filled in an application form for the job of director of information in the department of National Health and Welfare. And at the 1952 annual meeting, she asked for the early appointment of an assistant director, who could undertake most of the traveling and fund raising for at least a year. "After doing the job of at least two full-time people for $6^{1}/_{2}$ years, my physical strength and resistance have diminished to the point where I feel I must spend at least one year mostly in Ottawa..."

The question of permanency still hung in the air in 1954, when under prodding from Winnipeg, a constitutional review committee was set up. Milton Dewey, from Toronto, was its chairman, and its work continued until 1958. Although there

---

[6]Letter to Dr. Hitschmanova, 3 April 1950.

were questions to settle about the size of the board and the procedure for elections, the issue throughout the patiently conducted negotiations was always whether the USC should be under the control of the Unitarian church. If not, should the name "Unitarian" be dropped? Finally, in September 1957, Mr. Dewey reported that he had nearly unanimous approval for a clause saying that, if a majority of the Unitarian churches disapproved of the USC, the agency would relinquish the name Unitarian if requested to do so after explaining the reasons for any acts to which the churches had objected. It was a convoluted and rather adversarial formula, and the thought was clarified in the constitution ratified in April 1958, where Article 1 stated the organization's name and added: "The name 'Unitarian' shall be contingent on the continued approval of a majority of Unitarian congregations in Canada."

There is total silence in this constitution on the issue of Unitarian church control of the USC, and, by implication, it is entirely independent. A branch can be formed by five people banding together "for the sustained promotion of the purposes of the organization," and the national board is the body to approve the establishment of new branches. In June 1959, the clarification was added that branch status should depend on "sustained interest and activity for a year...and reasonable prospects for continuance." There is no mention of church affiliation.

In addition to branches, work groups were set up in serveral cities from about 1957. Some were in smaller centers such as Kelowna and Vernon; others were in larger places like Victoria, Charlottetown, Lethbridge, and Regina, and for years have had active groups. They chose not to become full-scale branches because, as a former chairman in Victoria, Mrs. Hazel Woodward explains, "nobody wanted the formality of electing a treasurer and producing an annual report. They just wanted to do a job." But under the 1983 bylaws, branches and groups combine to choose the regional representatives on the board.

David B. Smith took over from Bower Carty as USC chairman during the years of constitutional review, and in a paper written in 1963, he summarizes the situation:

> Though the agency has now no formal connection with the Unitarian Churches and at present less than half the branches are connected with these, a close liaison continues to exist...Unitarians predominate

in the management of the Committee. However, the present independent position of the Committee is of great advantage in its primary role of serving as an efficient channel for aid from concerned Canadians to people in need overseas.

Nevertheless, the questioning continued and the board stood its ground. In 1959 and 1962, it did consider the possibility of changing the organization's name and decided against it. When the chairman of the Moncton work group resigned in September 1960 after asking the religious affiliation of Dr. Lotta and board members, she replied: "Members are chosen according to their devotion to our cause and their ability, and not according to religious affiliation. This in our eyes is an essentially personal matter and we would find it improper to investigate. I believe, however, that nearly half the present Directors are not Unitarians." And in January 1964, in answer to an inquiry from Alberta, the phrase was coined by Bower Carty that was used widely later: "The Unitarian Service Committee as such is not associated with any specific doctrine of theology." In 1969 Harry Bolster, then the national chairman, wrote to the Unitarian Universalist Alliance and the Canadian Unitarian Council, asking them to remove the USC Canada from their directory, as it had no affiliation with religious bodies.

Finally in 1979, after registering the new alternate name, the board of directors issued *What's in a name?*, a single-page explanation of the significance of the word Unitarian in the agency's name:

The name "Unitarian" in its fullest sense signifies "a united world community" or "the fellowship of all mankind" ... [In 1945] the USC was born with a great deal of help from Unitarian churches. The following year the government permitted the agency to appeal to Canadians at large and two years later, in 1948, formal links with Unitarian churches were dissolved, making the agency non-sectarian and non-denominational. The USC maintains strong, informal relationships with members of all churches and religious groups in Canada, and its humanitarian objectives are endorsed by people of all faiths.

The veteran campaigners

When members of USC branches and work groups talk today

of their work in collecting and packing relief supplies, it is rather like listening to veterans describing wartime experiences. There is the camaraderie that overcomes drudgery, the satisfaction of having accomplished a lengthy and precise task compounded by having done it as part of a long-standing team, the learning of extra levels of character in a colleague. It was the way in which several of the most active board members – among them Harry Bolster, Gordon Merrill, and Jack Todd – first became heavily involved with the agency. There is an inevitable comparison with the bonds shared by old campaigners.

The tales from various cities bear a resemblance to each other, like soldierly reminiscences. There are occasional horror stories about working conditions, or life in the trenches, as in Victoria where, as Hazel Woodward explains, the packing at one stage was done in an ex-winery: "The smell was enough to give you DTs. There wasn't water laid on, but it came through the skylights and ran down the middle of the floor. We wore rubber boots and stood on the pallets. We laughed at it. You have to have a sense of humor, like a teacher or a parson, or you're dead."

Dr. Lotta bullied the mayor of Victoria into providing better quarters, and then the group found a welcome in a firehall. The Winnipeg packers overflowed their church basement, and firemen came to their rescue, too. Conditions were often awkward. Margaret Donald in Vancouver remembers packing in the old church basement, where steps went round right angles up to the street, and the plywood cases left her bruised from leaning over and into them. In Winnipeg the firemen helped carry boxes, and more recently the stronger boys from a high school have come, lured by Euphemia Tainsh's cookies. Frances Nicholson, the Nanaimo chairman, has packed in her own basement since the mid-1970s (some 269 boxes in 1981!) and says gamely: "There is no challenge in receiving one bag of clothing, but what a grand feeling it is to get twenty or more plastic garbage bags stuffed to the top!"[7]

There was friendly competition. Christine Appleton, who used to be the wool convenor in Moose Jaw (which around 1960 had a population of thirty-three thousand), talks about their packing depot running neck and neck with Calgary and

---

[7]Letter to the author, 12 January 1984.

shipping twenty thousand kilograms of clothing in a peak year. But Dr. Lotta resisted the idea of stimulating competition between cities and provinces. Some branches had certain advantages, like the Truro branch which was just down the road from Stanfield's Ltd., the family woollen and textile firm that has never looked back since the Klondike Gold Rush spread the fame of its unshrinkable underwear across North America. Dorothy Legge, who started the Truro group in 1957, used to get lots of high quality seconds from the factory and also wool at a dollar a pound (about two dollars a kilogram) from the "sweepings." Her friends would knit them into shawls for Greek women after the earthquakes or into sweaters for Korean children. On one March day in 1958, Miss Legge organized a clothing drive for Korea around Truro and collected over three hundred kilograms. She also kept in touch with dry cleaners, who let her have garments that had not been claimed for two years. "Better clothes then, all wool", she says.

The camaraderie of packing groups had a democratic effect. Rita McConkey, who was a founding member of the Ottawa branch and the national executive, and who, with Anne Dewar, used to supervise the workroom where clothes were sorted and mended, remembers Gordon Merrill saying, "You all wanted to be Indians and no one to be chiefs." Certainly, when I interviewed Dr. David B. Smith, a research biochemist who was USC national chairman from 1956 to 1965, his first inclination was to recall the 1950s when he was in charge of the contingent of packing crews. With all the technical relish of a captain of engineers describing how his company threw a Bailey bridge across the Rhine, David Smith explains how his crews of four men worked the baling machine which the Ottawa Board of Education had used for wastepaper before selling it to the USC: two of them cranking down a piston with a two-meter lever, the others crimping the steel tapes round the jute sacking with metal clips... Three times a month, from a list of seventy volunteers who included Doug Fullerton, the future chairman of the National Capital Commission, Smith had to find a captain and crew.

How did Dr. Lotta manage to recruit such people to do these tough jobs for years on end? David Smith says: "Once you were thanked by Dr. Hitschmanova, you came back to do more." Christine Appleton, who had been housebound for months with a new baby when she first heard Dr. Lotta speak in Moose

Jaw in 1958, says: "That night I was glad I didn't have fifty dollars in my pocket. It would all have gone to her. She made you grateful you had a roof and three meals a day." Lorraine Cameron, who was a summer volunteer before becoming projects officer in 1978, remembers that "as the tour organizer in Hamilton in 1977, I was downcast when only a dozen people came to public meetings. But she was never upset. If she got to a few new people, or reinforced the faithful a bit, that was enough." Hazel Woodward has a similar explanation: "A great thing about her was that she never looked down on anyone's effort. She was always enthusiastic and the immediate person's effort was the most important to her. Our first meeting [in Victoria] raised only $80 from 25 people, but she was delighted."

Efficiency and personal organization were important elements in Dr. Lotta's success in keeping branches going. Jack Jefferson, an investment broker who is chairman of the Vancouver branch, remembers how she "always got people's names to send thank-you notes, and wrote her letters in the mornings on her little typewriter before meetings." And Dorothy Legge describes how she and Eva Munroe in Truro first got hooked by the agency in 1957. After deciding that a list of baby garments for UNRWA layettes was incomplete, as given in the *Family Herald*, "we wrote to the USC to say so. We got a letter back, explaining it all. That was the start. Once you're on their list, they never let you be!"

Dr. Lotta had her way with hotel managements, also. She used to stay at the Royal Alex in Winnipeg and once left a gold watch that had belonged to her grandmother in the pocket of a blouse when it was sent to the nearby laundry. The hotel got the laundry to shut down until the watch was found, unharmed. Dr. Lotta vowed never to stay anywhere else in Winnipeg (nor did she, until the hotel was demolished). In Victoria, the manager of the Empress Hotel once put on an exasperated air with Dr. Lotta because she insisted on staying at a minor hotel. "I can't afford more than thirty dollars a day," she replied. The following year the Empress offered her a section of the vice-regal suite – at thirty dollars a day – and the arrangement ran for years. The manager, Ted Balderson, says: "We might as well change the sheets there as elsewhere."

The legendary Empress Hotel, with its Edwardian flavor and its gallery of Canada's "First Ladies," from Lady Durham to

Lily Schreyer, was an unlikely place for the ascetic Dr. Lotta to hole up while writing her reports on Asian projects or resting at the end of the fund-raising tour. She seems to have preferred a carton of cottage cheese in her room to buttered crumpets and cream teas in the lounge.

The stories of Dr. Lotta's concern for economizing are legion. Iona Pilowski remembers how critical she was about any apparent extravagance, asking "Why so many cookies here?" at a reception in Winnipeg. When Ottawa's oppressive summer heat in 1957 made it hard for the office staff at 78 Sparks Street to work efficiently, Fred Scott was asked to hunt for a reconditioned fan. (He got one for $63.96.) It was equally important to recycle materials. Sales staff at Shirley Leishman's bookstore, which lay on the route between Dr. Lotta's apartment and the office, told of her coming in to collect old padded envelopes for reuse. And the collecting by hotel staff of small bars of soap that have hardly been touched has been a routine activity for some USC volunteers ever since Dr. Lotta broadcast in the 1950s about Asian children suffering from diseases due to lack of cleanliness and hygiene. Alex Pilowski makes the rounds of Winnipeg hotels to collect soap every Saturday, and the Duncan group collected 140 kilograms of soap in 1983, mainly the work of eighty-year-old Mrs. J.S. Lang and the local chairman, Arthur Mann, who keeps plastic pails in his car for this purpose.

The matter of office overheads greatly concerned Dr. Lotta. In 1949-50, Bower Carty, as national treasurer, did a comparison which showed the USC at just over 7 percent, considerably lower than the two other main agencies in the same field of relief work with children. In 1953, when cash receipts and the value of clothing shipped abroad had both doubled, Dr. Lotta was able to report that overheads were down to 5.75 percent at a time of public criticism that relief organizations had extravagantly high salaries and administrative costs. (Dr. Lotta's own salary for that year was $3,840.) By 1956 it had crept up to nearly 8 percent, but some board members told her the increase should be seen as investment; for example, the mailing list had been expanded to thirty-five thousand people.

So tight was the control on expenditure that the USC did not take out any fire and theft insurance before 1958. A Christmas-time break-in and a run of mail losses put a premium on prudence; over a three-year period thieves in the post office removed a total of $4,413 from 171 letters, but more than half this amount was paid over again by donors. In the 1980s, with a larger staff, the administrative and fund-raising costs of USC have stayed at about 11 percent of total receipts, still low by comparison with other voluntary agencies.

One reason for Dr. Lotta to wear her unique uniform was to emphasize the USC concern for economy, both to Canadian donors and to poor people abroad. She has given several other reasons to inquirers over the years. Its origin is in the requirement by the United Nations in the late 1940s that relief workers from any voluntary agency should wear a distinctive uniform while in the field. Dr. Lotta explained to reporters that hers was modeled on an American Army nurse's uniform. Theresa Potter wore a similar uniform while in Korea for the USC in 1953. In later years, Dr. Lotta has talked about how convenient it was to have one set of clothing that you could wear all day long and which could withstand months of travel, packed in a small space of a suitcase to leave room for files. She also talked about − probably an increasingly important reason − how she was instantly recognizable in her uniform when she arrived in a Canadian city for fund raising, or somewhere overseas to look at projects.

Dr. Lotta's sense of humor made her collect stories of misunderstandings about her uniform: the RCAF veteran who congratulated her on still being in the air force; the waitress in Winnipeg who wanted her to baby-sit when she had explained that her agency looked after children; the guest in a Korean hotel who exclaimed "Telegrams!" on seeing her in the elevator; and the Japanese tourist who tried to buy a bus ticket from her to Niagara Falls. She also recounted episodes when her uniform helped save the situation. Once she was disturbed in the middle of the night on a 480-kilometer train journey in Korea, when two strange men pulled aside the curtain of her sleeping bunk and shook her awake. "Under such circumstances, a uniform like mine is the only thing to travel in," she said later.[8]

Her bridge of words

To analyze her writings, in order to bring out her skill in

---

[8]Interview with Pat Dufour, *Victoria Times,* 27 November 1964.

communicating with Canadian donors, is an irresistible temptation. But it can leave the impression that the emotive phrases in her branch circulars, and later in her *Jottings*, were contrived, that she coolly chose from an armory of English words those most likely to penetrate her target group of readers, rather like Cupid selecting particular arrows.

Certainly, she used all her reportorial and advocate's skills to put over, in a hundred different contexts, her basic message: that there were enormous needs in Europe (and then Asia and Africa) which fortunate Canadians should be happy to help meet, and that past successes should spur greater efforts now. And she made it the more palatable through neighbourly chat that assumed the reader was a close companion who happened to have stayed behind on this trip. The very name *Jottings* suggests off-the-cuff comments, almost gossip. But there was no contrivance or trickery or distortion. She spared the general reader the organizational and personnel problems she faced, but she described scenes in exactly the vivid way she saw them. And her writings were widely distributed. Euphemia Tainsh writes: "The *Jottings* were a wonderful success in holding people's interest. We in Winnipeg mailed copies with our thank-you letters to clothing donors. Copies were always on hand at public meetings."

One might identify five main elements in her success in communicating. She used remarkable phrases to describe how needs were fulfilled and lives transformed. She had a neat set of adjectives to assure donors that the projects were cost-effective and the partner agencies trustworthy. She always remembered to make an identification with Canada. She was never afraid to express her own moods. Finally, she threw in just enough reference to the arduous conditions overcome on her journeys to make readers realize that she was no part of any international jet set, but always with the workers.

Examples can be drawn from her writings about any country, although most that follow come from India. In expressive phrases about relief supplies, barley in Korea is "this precious bowl of gruel," milk powder in India is called "white gold" or "miraculous powder," blankets and sweaters are "instant warmth" (and often "Canadian warmth"), and funds donated to projects are expressed as "Friendship dollars," and sometimes, to emphasize how far money can go, "miracle dollars." The transformation of young people's lives is often described,

151

and here is an early example about the beggar boys of Madras taken into the Seva Samajam boys' home:

> You would never guess the tragic backgrounds from which these youngsters come, when you look at them, because after only a few days of adaptation and regret for the lost freedom of the streets, they start loving their new surroundings. To be given regular meals every day, to go to school – which in itself is a great privilege – to be dressed in clothing which is not in rags, but is in good condition and smells clean and fresh; to have the company of other happy children, and to be surrounded by a staff of teachers and volunteers who really care – these are new and moving experiences which no boy can long resist.[9]

Assurance that projects are cost-effective is achieved with phrases such as "immensely necessary work" that is "infinitely worthwhile." And, almost like ancient Homer, she adorns partner agencies and their directors with a stock of impressive adjectives. The Agricultural Bank of Greece, which looked after housing loans in Macedonia, was "trusted and efficient," while Bruce Lansdale was "the gifted director" of the American Farm School. The Rama Krishna Mission was "beloved for its integrity and efficiency." The Karnatak Health Institute could count on "an exceptionally devoted and capable staff" and had "an enviable record of medical service." A friendly CIDA officer in Saigon is introduced as "the trusted André Gingras," while her first project officer is called "gifted, meticulous Charles Gray." The former chairman of the Victoria group is described as "dynamic, witty Hazel Woodward."

The identification with Canada is sometimes made directly, as when she describes the "dream – come – true" of a thirteen-year-old girl meeting, for a few minutes at an Indian railway station, the Pointe Claire couple who were her foster parents and were visiting on a business trip to Delhi; or her own "pure bliss" watching someone in southernmost India opening a twenty-three kilogram bag of milk "marked 'Canada' in big, green letters." At other times it is indirect, conveyed through her own mind: "My thoughts very quickly crossed two oceans and flashed to you back home who make this effort possible. How I wished you could have been at my side! ..." And sometimes she transposes her thoughts to, say, Tamil villagers

---

[9]Circular no. 4, 26 March 1957.

walking six miles to a food distribution center: "Not a single one would miss this rendezvous with Canada for anything!"

Her own moods she describes dramatically. She was often "ecstatic" and experiencing "utter bliss" when a project made progress. But the scene of famine "rends my heart"; and, when a Vietnamese official in 1978 was obdurate, "I was stunned, deeply unhappy and completely silent...tears would have been the only release."

The description of modest expenditures and arduous conditions of travel is usually inserted as an aside. When Dr. Margaret Barr took her up into the Assam hills in 1957, she records that the jeep held five others "...and myself, including my fortunately very scanty luggage." In Bangladesh in 1976 the Dacca hotel management put her in "a skimpy room." Often, she refers to "the beating sun" and returning from seeing a project "utterly exhausted from the heat." Occasionally, she explicitly underlines the hardship. Her 1957 report to the board on her visit to Greece was "drafted under difficult circumstances: partly in the earliest possible hours of the morning, but most of it in the drafty and noisy airport of Milan, where we were kept waiting for nine hours, due to a broken door on the aircraft."

To extract, as I have done, these sweetmeats is to make the whole mixture seem cloying to the taste. As any cook knows, the balance is all important. And you have to read through whole pages of circulars, *Jottings*, and reports to realize how often she did strike the right balance of fact and emotions, of information and purple passage.

Back at Sparks Street

Dr. Lotta expected the same high standards of work from her staff and had ways of keeping them up to the mark even when she was absent from Ottawa. Twice a week when she was abroad, three times a week when she was touring Canada, a letter was sent to her detailing the latest office news. Each of the "desks" (Canadian, Publicity, and Foster Parents) took their turn at adding to the current letter that was set up in a typewriter. Theresa Flower, a Londoner who had worked in radio stations in the Maritimes and at the Indian High Commission, and who looked after publicity for a time, says this discipline "served so many useful purposes." Dr. Lotta was kept fully informed, and the staff were conscientious in meeting all their personal deadlines. So conscientious, in fact, that Mrs. Flower, who had three children under ten, used regularly to take home piles of letters, to be got ready for the midnight pickup at the local mailbox.

Shirley Plowman, who was in charge of publicity from 1960 to 1965, had to send all the scripts she wrote for radio spots and news releases to Dr. Lotta while on her cross-Canada fund-raising tour. "And she used to grade them Excellent, Very Good, Good, and so on down." Shirley said that when in Ottawa Dr. Lotta sometimes liked to show off her staff's skill to visitors. Once, when a visitor from British Columbia came in, Dr. Lotta called her up the length of the room and told her to write a "brilliant" thirty-second radio spot within one minute – and got out a stopwatch. Shirley went back to her desk with sweaty palms but managed to get the completed script back to Dr. Lotta while the watch was still running. She recalled mildly: "I was impressed that she thought I could do it. She brought out the excellence in everyone..."

She checked work thoroughly. As a summertime volunteer, Lorraine Cameron had the tedious job of typing envelopes for four months. Dr. Lotta refused to have machine plates for addresses and insisted that each envelope containing the appeal letter be individually typed and the stamps stuck on it. Says Lorraine: "It made sense when the doctor explained that for many donors the appeal letter was the only one they received, so it had to be individual. But she spent weekends checking through the boxes of envelopes for any errors, and on Mondays a pile would come back with paper clips on the ones to be corrected."[10]

She took the business of economizing to great lengths, saying "Nothing is wasted in the USC." But time was still spent unproductively. Deborah Mason, who looked after the administration of overseas projects in the early 1960s, remembers that, when the branch circulars and *Jottings* arrived in rough-typed form from Dr. Lotta's latest point abroad, her secretary would have to spend almost a week deciphering and fitting these writings onto two pages "and no margins were allowed."

There was something of a strict convent atmosphere in the USC office at 78 Sparks Street. "I remember there were twelve women all in one room, and you had a tiny room at the end

---

[10]Conversation with the author, Vancouver, December 1983.

with the door open," Theresa Flower wrote in a reminiscing letter in April 1983. Dr. Lotta did not employ any men for more than twenty years, until Raymond ven der Buhs, who had been a priest, joined the staff in June 1969 as her personal assistant. She did, however, employ (if sometimes briefly) some outstanding women. Among them were Wendy Dobson, who for a time looked after Foster Parents and who is now executive director of the C.D. Howe Institute; Debbie Mason, who went on to work with UNRWA, write regularly for *Reader's Digest* and edit *Canada Weekly* for External Affairs; Pamela Lee MacRae, who in between spells at USC has edited *Canadian Consumer*; and Lorraine Cameron who has since worked for UNICEF in Asia and for Katimavik as a field officer.

But the dedication required of the staff made heavy demands, not only on themselves but also on their families and friends. Lorraine Cameron says that, when she left USC in December 1979, "my parents were relieved as though I was rescued from a cult." And Shirley Plowman, who went on to work in External Affairs, has said: "It was the most 'fun' job I ever had [but] I had to leave − to rediscover men! I was encased in Lotta's world."

The golden media

The newspaper appeals became a major source of funds for the USC. Stuart Keate, who launched them when he was publisher of the *Victoria Times*, estimates that together the FP papers raised more than $1 million. He wrote recently:

> I remember very well my first interview with Lotta. Who could forget her, in the olive-green uniform and ribbons? She told me about her campaign. I was looking for a worthy Christmas project and told Lotta we would support her campaign, via the news columns, listing the names of all donors and taking care of all the operational expenses, so that the money raised was guaranteed to the fund, down to the last cent...
>
> Our campaign was so successful, other publishers and editors began to express interest. I think Cleo Mowers of the *Lethbridge Herald* was the next to sponsor an appeal. Our owner Max Bell was very supportive and brought in the *Calgary Albertan*. In due course Dick Malone of the *Winnipeg Free Press*, Norman Smith and John Grace of the *Ottawa Journal* came in. When the *Globe and Mail* joined

the FP group, chairman Howard Webster, and later the publisher, James Cooper, lent its considerable prestige.[11]

The scheme spread beyond the eight important papers in the FP group, and in a peak year as many as nineteen Canadian dailies were running a Christmas appeal for the USC. In general, Dr. Lotta's relations with the media were excellent. In an interview she was able, with her reporter's eye, to give another journalist the sort of graphic details that light up a story. For example, she described the conditions in schools in northern Greece in 1964 this way: "[They are] so poor that children break their chalk in many pieces to go round, and pencils are so small that an adult can't hold them."[12] And in 1950, the Hamilton branch recorded that Dr. Lotta produced, at their annual meeting, the patched and tattered shirt she had taken from a Greek boy in exchange for a garment from Canada. The *Hamilton Spectator* and other newspapers could make a good story of that.

Dr. Lotta did not necessarily use kidgloves in this relationship. Stuart Keate writes: "We referred to her as 'The Atomic Mosquito'. She cut a dashing figure in newsrooms and rode herd on her newspaper friends. She examined copy closely — both editorial and art — and did not hesitate to chastise editors if her beloved USC was consigned to the inside pages of the paper."[13]

She was also skillful in using the artistic talents of supporters. Eva Prager, a Berlin-born portrait and landscape painter who has made her home in Montreal and has painted many famous Canadians including the Trudeau family, has for many years contributed an appealing drawing featuring children for the USC Christmastime gift card donations. Bruce Cockburn, the folk singer, has helped in recent years with television and radio promos. And Vera Johnson, a composer and singer who lived in Vancouver, wrote a number of songs specially for the USC; one song, written in 1972, was called "What can a dollar buy?" and neatly brings out in three verses the conditions of life of a Swazi girl, a Bangladesh boy, and a Korean mother.

---

[11]Letter to the author, 9 January 1984.

[12]Interview with Pat Dufour, *Victoria Times*, 27 November 1964.

[13]Letter to the author, 9 January 1984.

A decade to decide

The issue of whether or not to give direct support to family planning activities took ten years to decide; rather, it was ten years after the issue was first raised by the Toronto branch in 1955 that the agency as a whole accepted such projects without question.

Dr. Marian Hall, a Methodist missionary, spoke to Toronto USC members that year about her work in Indian villages as an obstetrician and gynaecologist. They were so impressed by what she said about Indian women being eager for information about contraception that they asked her to speak again at a meeting which Dr. Hitschmanova would also attend. Dr. Lotta took a negative line during the discussion afterwards and warned that adding a family planning project might seriously harm fund raising in Canada, where opinions were deeply divided.

Undeterred, the Toronto branch, under Jack Tracy, pushed for a vote on the issue by all branches. He wrote a letter in October 1955 for circulation via Ottawa, expressing Toronto's concern that the USC "should direct some of its efforts towards solving some of the fundamental problems of [India] rather than providing temporary relief. Overpopulation is one of the biggest difficulties in India, and it will be getting worse..."[14] He wanted the USC, as a first step, to buy Dr. Hall a jeep and trailer unit.

The USC chairman, David B. Smith, played for time, asking for a six-week delay before circulating Toronto's letter. (This meant it would probably not reach branches before Christmas, when the annual fund-raising campaign had almost ended.) Smith took exception to the suggestion that the USC had not been tackling basic problems in India and said the larger investment in medical vans and community centers helped "responsible people...in their efforts towards population control." But the colossal population problem in India could not be solved in isolation. He argued, that if the problem were ever solved, it would have come about because of a general lifting of standards of life.

Dr. Lotta did send out the Toronto branch's letter on 20 December, together with her own, still negative comments. She thought it could hurt the USC in the eyes of the Indian govern-

---

[14]Letter from Jack M. Tracy to Dr. Hitschmanova, 18 October 1955. The reply was written by Dr. David Smith on 3 November 1955.

ment to be supporting a missionary's project. "It has taken considerable time and effort to convince Indian authorities that ours is no missionary effort, and that our help is given with no strings attached." But she worried more about the effect on fund raising: "I recognize that a few groups may become very interested in such a project and generously support it, but I am much afraid that their contributions could never make up for the loss in donations from regular sources which I anticipate."[15]

The branches broadly supported her. Those with the strongest Unitarian affiliations were sympathetic to Toronto's desire, but even the Vancouver branch called it "a very complex matter." Montreal members unanimously felt it might "greatly interfere with donations"; they saw the USC's work primarily as relief to the hungry, and education and training of orphans. So Toronto's initiative died for a time, but the episode provides a revealing set of snapshots of the differing shades of opinion within the USC in the mid-1950s, ten years after the agency was launched. Toronto stood at one end, Montreal at the other.

Attitudes shifted in the 1960s. In 1965 the USC began giving direct grants to the Family Planning Association in Hong Kong and then, two years later, to its counterpart in India. By 1969 Dr. Lotta was writing to her Canadian donors that "the USC passionately believes in family planning, since the eradication of hunger, the attainment of a higher standard of living and a smoothly working family planning program go hand in hand."[16]

And the USC has gone on to sponsor other family planning programs in Bangladesh, Indonesia, and southern Africa.

Bilingual by-and-by

A curious fact is that Dr. Lotta made little sustained attempt to build up a constituency for the USC in the French-speaking parts of Canada. It is all the more surprising since her four years as a student in Paris had been some of her happiest days, her French was originally better than her English, she had good friends such as Marius Barbeau from Quebec, and had loved the province from the first, when she enjoyed an idyllic holiday in Ile d'Orléans. Also, the first USC projects were in France.

---

[15]Circular no. 30, 20 December 1955.
[16]Circular no. 3, May 1969.

The explanation for this neglect seems to be that the USC was at first built around the framework of the Unitarian churches in Canada, and in Montreal the Church of the Messiah, under the Reverend Angus Cameron, was an anglophone congregation. The Montreal USC branch remained an English-speaking organization, and although Dr. Lotta, on her early speaking tours, made several good contacts in other Quebec cities and communities, she had no time to cultivate them further. In the 1970s she tried a few visits and speeches, but with no lasting effect.

There was also no stock of USC publicity material in French because she made no provision in the budget for translation and printing, being always concerned about overhead costs. The very useful article, "Dr. Hitschmanova, Canada," which Carroll Holland wrote for *Reader's Digest* in March 1973, was translated for its French edition, and offprints of this six-page article became one of the few pieces of publicity material in French the agency had during most of the 1970s.

Towards the end of that decade, however, the heroic Madame Marie-Jeanne Musiol began offering free translation services of USC material for the Quebec media, and when she and her husband left for Upper Volta on posting, her brother Richard Ranger took over. By 1981 most of the USC material was available in French, and an active publicity campaign began in Quebec and New Brunswick's francophone communities: radio spots went to 29 stations, short fillers or snippets of USC news (rather than the harder-to-place feature articles) went to 140 weekly newspapers, and libraries began receiving background material. With the coming of Gilles Latour as head of the Projects Section, speaking tours were extended to several cities in Quebec, and a francophone constituency is growing steadily. The use of the shortened name USC Canada has obviously eased the acceptance of the agency as a bilingual organization.

Another criticism of the USC until recent years was that it kept its distance from other nongovernmental agencies in Canada, that it was not prepared to spend time in coordination and collaborative efforts.

It is certainly the case that Dr. Lotta considered this very much a secondary concern, ranking far below the need to raise funds to keep her own agency alive, and the interwoven need to give a full account to USC donors of the progress of projects overseas. Among those donors, of course, were some voluntary organizations, notably the women's institutes and teachers' associations, the Kinsmen Clubs and Kinettes; and to these Dr. Lotta paid plenty of attention. But for NGOs that were doing work similar to the USC and were likely to be raising funds from the same general sources, she did not spare much time.

In her defence, it should be said that the years 1948-50 had been disillusioning for anyone attempting such collaboration. In 1948 an official Canadian Appeal for Children was launched, which preempted the field for fund raising. On her speaking tour, she properly included a passage urging her audiences to contribute. In recompense, however, the USC only received $25,000 from the appeal. Then in 1949-50, the government's support was given to a large-scale ten-month appeal for the fledgling United Nations Children's Emergency Fund (UNICEF), which netted more than $435,000; in consequence, the USC just failed to reach its own target of $50,000 for 1949. By 1950 she was beginning to doubt whether the USC could survive another year. It was the public response to her appeals later that year for relief shipments to Greece that lifted the USC to a more secure level of activity and funding.

Again in 1959, she was worried that the World Refugee Year campaign would cut into USC fund raising. Her own small staff was too busy to take part in WRY activities, and crop failures that summer made it a difficult year for raising money. The drama of whether she would reach her target by 31 December was particularly intense that year. In fact, World Refugee Year helped the USC in certain places because it was known that the USC helped refugees, so that WRY publicity benefitted the agency.

When the umbrella organization, the Canadian Council for International Cooperation, was set up in the 1960s, the USC was slow to join it and then played a minor part in its work for many years. But recently, it has been much more active in the CCIC and in collaborating with other Canadian NGOs in development projects. Raymond ven der Buhs has taken a different approach since becoming managing director and has played, in particular, a leading role in fostering the South Asia Partnership organization, which will be described in Chapter 12. The pattern, therefore, has been one of increasing cooperation as the expansion of staff in the USC has allowed time for this work.

CHAPTER 8

Population and Progress

Hong Kong

THE 1960s were called, by the wishful thought of the United Nations, the First Development Decade, and the decade was almost over when the Pearson Report was published. Lester Pearson, at the invitation of World Bank President Robert S. McNamara, had asked seven other men, including reputable economists from Brazil and Jamaica, to join him on his Commission on International Development. Their report packed some punches for its time. For when, after a chapter dealing soberly with recent achievements, it reaches "The Problems Ahead," it bursts out with sentences of frustration and warning:

> *The Population Dilemma*: No other phenomenon casts a darker shadow over the prospects for international development than the staggering growth of population. It is evident that it is a major cause of the large discrepancy between rates of economic improvement in rich and poor countries...
>
> Twenty years ago, it was not expected that population growth would become such a major problem in low-income countries. As late as 1951 a U.N. projection assumed that between 1950 and 1980 the populations of Africa and Asia would grow at an annual rate of 0.7-1.3 per cent. The remarkable and largely unexpected success in reducing mortality brought a sharp change. The rate of population growth in developing countries increased steadily in the 1950s. By the mid-1960s, it settled down at an average level of 2.5 per cent.[1]

The Pearson commissioners listed the difficulties of rapid population growth: sharply increased expenditures for education, health, housing, and water supplies; the quality of the next generation ("There is a strong inverse correlation between child health and family size"); severe urban problems, particu-

---

[1]*Partners in Development*, Report of the Commission on International Development, Praeger, New York: 1969, p. 55.

larly over housing, compounded by migration from country areas. They concluded:

> We are well aware of the controversial nature of the matter which, until very recently, placed family planning behind a wall of silence in the industrialized countries themselves. But it is clear that there can be no serious social and economic planning unless the ominous implications of uncontrolled population growth are understood and acted upon.[2]

How does an agency like USC face these more puzzling aspects of development? By the mid-1960s, it had twenty years' experience in many countries in doing the basic lifesaving acts for a child, of clothing and feeding and healing. But does a large number of children represent security for a family – or poverty? When and how does a change in perceptions come? And how can projects help improve the position of women and recognize their crucial role in development?

This chapter will describe some of the ways the USC began to find answers to these questions in its programs in Hong Kong, and later in Indonesia. It will show how the population issue was inevitably dominant in Hong Kong, and how a number of remarkable medical doctors in Indonesia have defined health in the broadest terms and led communities in imaginative experiments of development.

Resilient refugees

The population of Hong Kong passed the 5 million mark in 1979. It is difficult to imagine that it was virtually uninhabited when a British fleet forced the cession of Hong Kong island in 1841 during the so-called first Opium War with China. Lord Palmerston, the British foreign secretary at the time, was not too pleased with the acquisition; he called it "a barren island, with hardly a house upon it."

By 1939 there were 1.5 million people living on the island or across Victoria Harbor on the flat Kowloon Peninsula, the prize from another Anglo-Chinese war in 1859-60. Trade, built around this great harbor, and successive waves of refugees from the mainland had swelled the population. The largest influx

---

[2]*Partners in Development*, p. 58.

came after the Japanese invasion of China and the capture of Canton, and at the height of the invasion about half a million refugees were sleeping in the streets of Hong Kong.

The population dropped to about 600,000 during the Japanese occupation of Hong Kong after 1941, as families flowed back into rural China for safety. But then it soared. In five years, as the Chinese Communists defeated and drove out the Nationalists, Hong Kong became a main refuge for city dwellers fleeing from Canton and Shanghai. By December 1950 it had grown to 2.3 million people, and by 1960, when Dr. Lotta began looking for projects there, it had risen above 3 million. Thereafter, the largest part of the population increase resulted from births to couples already settled there, rather than from immigration. In 1956 the birthrate was 39.7 per thousand of the total population.

The authorities, in collaboration with voluntary agencies, have for many years worked to bring this birthrate down. For the colony's prime problem, as Dr. Lotta observed at once, has been lack of space. The overall density is about 5,000 people per square kilometer. But the New Territories, on lease from China since 1898 until 1997, make up 90 per cent of the area and, until recently when six new towns began to be built, remained comparatively undeveloped. These hilly territories comprise some 650 villages of fisherfolk and vegetable farmers. So the metropolitan areas on Hong Kong island and on the mainland coast from Kowloon to Tsuen Wan are among the most densely populated places in the world. There the population density is 25,400 per square kilometer. For comparison, the most densely populated province in Canada – Prince Edward Island – has 20 people per square kilometer.

As usual, Dr. Lotta saw and described this lack of space in individual human terms. She wrote about eight-year-old Che Wong Fai, who survived a sampan capsizing on a winter's night, to escape with his carpenter father from China. She found father and son one evening in Tung Wong School, where Wong Fai was a student: "They both sleep right on top of the desks at night, covered with a blanket, for there is no other space in that flat, where teaching is done in two sessions each morning and afternoon to a different group of children numbering 752 altogether."[3]

For anyone visiting Hong Kong today, it is surprising to learn

---

[3]Circular no. 2, 8 March 1965.

that the very first public housing estate was built only in 1954, after fifty thousand squatters lost their homes in a Christmas Day fire that swept through part of Kowloon. Once started, however, the housing authorities and construction workers moved at phenomenal speed. In 1968 Dr. Lotta recorded that "the one millionth resettled person – a handicapped girl – entered her new abode." Today nearly half the total population live in government-subsidized housing on sixty-four resettlement estates.

What, then, in the early 1960s was the best response an agency like USC could make to help economic and social development in Hong Kong?

It settled on three projects, two of which were in line with work it supported in other countries to free both parents for wage-earning jobs. One consisted in helping meet the running expenses of two day nurseries in Kowloon, and the other to help cover the expenses of the St. Nicholas' Day Centre in the resettlement city of Tsun Wan. The third project, however, broke new ground. For over a fifteen-year period from 1965, the USC provided nearly three hundred thousand dollars in grants to the Family Planning Association of Hong Kong.

The two day nurseries were run by a Chinese organization of small businessmen originally from Canton, the Five Districts Business Welfare Association (FDBWA), on two government resettlement estates near the airport. They each were planned for 180 children of working parents, and the USC grant, which tapered off from a peak of $16,500 in one year, allowed some of the poorest families on the estates to place their children there for free. Officials of the Department of Social Welfare several times said, in Dr. Lotta's hearing, that these nurseries were the best run in the colony, and the cosponsoring relationship with the FDBWA worked out well. The superintendent of the first nursery for all these years, Miss Poon Lee-Kai, prompted many superlatives in USC reports, while Dr. Lotta wrote of the connection with the FDBWA, that

> We were the first agency to undertake the daring step of choosing a Chinese partner agency and I still vividly recall that there were many Westerners who were extremely skeptical...We were the winners, and the USC added one more telling example to our longstanding record that indigenous agencies, if properly chosen, are ever so much better and more efficient partners than those who stem from

overseas and do not have the knowledge of local cultures and customs that are a prerequisite for success.[4]

The experience with the St. Nicholas' Day Centre at Tsun Wan was not so happy. It was intended as a broadly based community program by the Anglican Bishop Hall, who in his thirty-five years in Hong Kong had been a leading spirit behind many progressive moves. The day center was to help working parents of some four hundred children from five to seven years, in the gap between nursery and primary school. Dr. Lotta was shocked during her visit in 1966 that the prayers and hymns each morning were purely Protestant and, despite her urging that Buddhist and other readings be included, changes were only temporary.

The final break came in 1968, when Dr. Lotta found the accounts in disorder and the latest USC funds practically untouched because most children were coming on a full paying basis. Also, the government had by then lowered the primary school admission age to six. So the USC cut any further support in 1968.

Relations with the Family Planning Association, on the other hand, went smoothly from the start. When the first USC grant of five thousand dollars was made in 1965, the FPA had been in existence for fifteen years, with the broad and constructive aim to promote a happy family life through sound family planning and to help improve living standards. "A planned family is a happy family" and "Quality is better than quantity" were two of its slogans. Assistance was given to those whose marriage had been infertile, to help them produce healthy children. Basic family planning services were seen in the wider context of social welfare. And, another broad approach, the FPA tried to impress on people the problems of population in general. It is easy to see why the FPA's approach appealed to the USC directors.

In return its executive secretary, Mrs. Peggy Lam, appreciated that the USC did not want to build monuments but was prepared to see its funds earmarked for the running expenses of existing clinics. At that stage the clinics concentrated on IUD insertions (later the demand grew for pills), and Dr. Lotta cal-

---

[4]Report to the USC board, 11 May 1975, p. 3.

culated that, in seven months of 1965-66, the USC grant helped four thousand patients, for the cost per patient to the FPA, including all overhead expenses, amounted to no more than $1.25, while the client herself paid the equivalent of twenty cents.

The birthrate, which had been 39.7 per thousand in 1956, dropped to 27 by 1965 and continued to fall during the fifteen years' association of the USC with the FPA, to 16.9 per thousand in 1979. With the death rate remaining stable throughout the 1970s at about 5 per thousand, population growth dropped to below 12 per thousand — or less than half the average rate of increase in Africa and Asia that had so alarmed the Pearson Commission.

The reasons given for the impressive drop are various. In the early 1970s, there were fewer women in the prime childbearing ages of twenty-five to thirty-four, but women were also starting to have fewer children. "In recent years, later marriages also have contributed to this trend, along with improvements in education and job opportunities."[5]

Gordon Merrill, who visited Hong Kong with Dr. Hitschmanova in 1976 and described it as giving "the appearance of a human beehive, crowded, swarming and productive," wrote of the success story of family planning there:

> Such accomplishments involving the acceptance of new ways of living by a very large number of people do not simply happen, but rather they are made to happen through the persistent and intelligent efforts of a corps of dedicated people.
> Very few opportunities to promote family escape the attention of the Family Planning Association of Hong Kong, which now has 31 family planning clinics. There are 18 field workers on the staff...and they do motivational work. There is a family planning field worker at the desk of the marriage registry, in order to offer advice to couples intent on matrimony; another field worker is present at the registry for births; the field workers frequent the maternity wards of the hospitals in order to motivate the new mothers to practise family planning.[6]

The USC contributed heavily to the FPA's educational programs. During 1976-78 it made grants totaling $105,000 to the cost of developing programs for young people, from lectures in

[5]*Hong Kong 1980*, Government Yearbook, p. 206.
[6]Report to the USC board, 4 June 1976, p. 2.

the first years of high school to counseling couples about to marry. All sorts of educational materials were involved: a comic book that was also published in weekly instalments in the Chinese press, posters, a film library, exhibitions, a referral system for young couples, a "no sex-preference" campaign aimed at changing the traditional Chinese belief that boys are better than girls. The campaign included TV spots, mobile shows in resettlement estates, and interviews with model families that were written for magazines and newspapers. These programs got off to a good start; in 1976-77 the school programs reached some thirty-eight thousand students, and another seventy-nine hundred out-of-school youths attended FPA programs specially designed for them.

But it was not all successful. The Tsuen Wan family planning clinic, with a modest-sized neon-lit sign, had done well in attracting males to special sessions for vasectomies. The response led the FPA to experiment in introducing family planning in factories. But, as Dr. Merrill reported in 1976,

> the experiment has not been a success, and it has been discontinued. The factory workers want to maintain their privacy on such delicate matters, particularly from their associates at work, and so they do not attend the clinic despite the convenience of location. Factory owners do not generally wish to cooperate, particularly in schemes that involve time off work to attend the clinic.[7]

By 1978 the FPA had moved to concentrate more on the New Territories, among the rural population and the fisherfolk "whose normal family up to now consisted of seven to eight children," as Dr. Lotta noted. Earlier, with a bequest from the Brine family in Edmonton, the USC had equipped and furnished a family planning center at Yuen Long, a new industrial city some forty-five kilometers from the heart of Hong Kong. The hope was that it could serve some two hundred thousand people, most of them farming families in surrounding areas. The Yuen Long center was soon full of townspeople, but rural women, it was discovered, would not take half a day to travel there to renew their supply of contraceptives, even after a fieldwork team had toured villages to motivate them. So fieldworkers switched to selling villagers a packet of supplies on the spot and

---

[7]Report to the USC board, 4 June 1976, p. 4.

giving a set of purchasing coupons to exchange at the village shop for pills or condoms at the same price. The shopkeeper was offered an honorarium equivalent to thirty-five dollars a year to act as distributor, and a bonus if he distributed more than fifty packets a month.

This "doorstep" approach was not immediately successful, either. In the first year, the acceptance rate among rural women in the reproductive age group was only 8.4 percent, and the overhead costs amounted to about eight dollars per acceptor. So the USC shifted its support from this experiment to educational programs.

Dr. Lotta had a running battle at home over the family planning program in Hong Kong, not with hesitant USC supporters but with the Canadian Broadcasting Corporation. The CBC, in 1972, refused to broadcast USC promos that dealt with this project, and in 1974, when John Buss made a short film about the Yuen Long center, she wrote that it "will of course not be acceptable to the CBC, which still maintains that family planning is the domain of public affairs and not that of voluntary agencies – the approach could not be more backward."[8]

But Dr. Lotta had nothing except praise for the FPA, and in particular for its most senior staff: Peggy Lam, the director; Professor Daphne Chun, and the chairperson, Professor Ma Chung Ho-Kei, "a very remarkable person indeed." She had complete confidence in these three women, when in 1980 she visited Hong Kong to say goodbye to the project. The FPA is, she wrote, "recognized as the best on the continent. They do not need our assistance any more, and thus we have worked ourselves out of a job which, fifteen years ago, was absolutely essential."[9]

Indonesia: women in charge

In 1975, when its programs in India and Korea were coming to an end, the USC was exploring possible programs in other Asian countries. Several people with long experience in Asia, including the photographer John Buss, recommended a survey

[8]Report to the USC board, 12 April 1974, p. 4.
[9]Report on Hong Kong to the USC board, 1980.

of Indonesia. When Dr. Lotta visited there that year, she was struck by something different from other Asian countries where the USC had worked. She wrote home: "In Indonesia, it was not the children who impressed me most; it was the women, because they so obviously play a decisive role in the present shaping of their country's destiny. I discovered remarkable women in key positions in and outside of government..."[10]

This was surprising to find in a country where 94 percent of the people are Muslim. But it is certainly true that Indonesian women are in charge of many social welfare programs at every level. Two of the first people Dr. Lotta met were Mrs. Roesiah Sarjono, secretary-general of the Department of Social Welfare, and Mrs. A.H. Nasution, chairperson of the Indonesian National Council on Social Welfare (DNIKS), which coordinates all the nongovernmental activities in social welfare. DNIKS has units in nearly all the twenty-nine provinces in Indonesia, and the wife of the provincial governor is *ex officio* head of the unit. And all the way down the structure, the wives of the heads of the district, subdistrict, and village (Bupati, Chamat, and Lurah) are made responsible for supervision at their level.

Some governor's wives, like Mrs. Soepardjo in Central Java and Mrs. Nafsiah Mboi in Nusa Tangarra Timur (NTT), came to play active parts in several USC-supported projects. Elsewhere, an energetic woman in the number two position might become the USC contact, as in West Kalimantan where Mrs. H. Soedarso, the widow of a prominent doctor, had a particular interest in health services and child welfare. Another woman in this circle of government wives was Mrs. C. Utaryo, a trained social worker who formed her own family welfare organization (Yayasan Syap Ibu) in Jogjakarta in Central Java. Her particular approach to development was to start with nutrition programs for mothers and children, and then to move on from these to income-generating projects for women.

This group of women had a ready-made network around this huge country of 150 million people and some 3,000 inhabited islands, because they moved out from and back to the capital, Jakarta, as their husbands or they themselves were promoted. And they spanned the never-very-wide gap between governmental and nongovernmental structures. Mrs. Nasution and her assistant, Mrs. Maryono, acted, in effect, as the unofficial

---

[10]*Jottings*, April 1975, p. 2.

USC representatives until Mr. Sofiyandi Wangsamihardja was hired as the official representative in 1983, and the earlier projects supported by USC were ones with which they were familiar.

Among these were a number of children's homes. The phase-out from Indian projects in June 1975 left 130 Canadian sponsors without foster children, so it was sensible to ask as many as possible to transfer future contributions to children in Jakarta and elsewhere in Java. Other early projects of child welfare included support of a rehabilitation center for cerebral palsy children at Solo, of a crippled children's center run by Dutch-speaking nuns at Palembang, and of a training center for deaf and dumb children at Surabaya.

It was not long before the USC found more venturesome projects to support on the island of Java. These were headed by two medical doctors of very different backgrounds, Dr. Hadji Kusnadi and Dr. Lukas Hendrata. What they shared was a concern to broaden the concept of health care from treatment to training and education, and a belief that ordinary villagers possessed the capacity to improve their own lot.

Dr. Kusnadi, a man of warm personality, moved in very senior circles in Indonesia. He was one of twenty-two members of President Suharto's Supreme Advisory Board. He was also director of the social welfare branch of Muhammadiyah, a social organization formed by Muslims in 1912, which had spread through Indonesia with some four thousand branches. It had built a university and some seven thousand schools, as well as hospitals, maternity homes, and clinics. It also ran many orphanages and was eager to expand vocational training in them.

One evening Dr. Kusnadi took Dr. Lotta and Gordon Merrill about twenty-five kilometers out of Jakarta to the site of a small training center. He wanted USC support to expand it greatly. Within a few years, the Ciputat project had become the first national training center for trainers, some of whom would go back as instructors in the orphanages, while others would train artisans — tailors, welders, printers, carpenters, mechanics among men, beauty care experts and seamstresses among women — in towns and villages. Not all became trainers but they received a good start in a job.

By 1984 the USC had invested some $150,000 in the center, and it had expanded with a brick-pressing factory, a chicken farm, and a service station and auto repair shop. Gilles Latour paid tribute to "the efficiency of the Muhammadiyah operation and how it benefits a large number of young people who otherwise would probably be...unemployed." Dr. Kusnadi hired managers for the center, but kept a close personal interest in it. He once said: "I am mentally present always."

The Klampok experiment

Dr. Hendrata, in contrast, was a younger man, a Christian of Chinese descent. He practiced medicine for five years in Indonesia and had become Coordinator for Health for the Council of Churches in Indonesia, when he decided to set up his own nonprofit organization, Yayasan Indonesia Sejahtera (YIS), translated as "Foundation for a Prosperous Indonesia." Its primary objective was to train village leaders as paramedical staff.

Dr. Hendrata had concluded that there was a basic injustice in the health service in Indonesia. About 10 percent of the people (mainly in cities) could afford – and received – good care, while the rest received little, if any, care. Since there would never be enough money to extend the present services, the solution lay in training health cadres to treat the most common diseases.

A system of "barefoot doctors," or village health workers, is now common across the globe, from China to Panama. What was special to YIS, and was shared by some like-minded doctors such as Dr. Zafrullah Chowdhury in Bangladesh, was a fundamental faith in a drive for self-improvement among village people. This faith was hardheaded and not sentimental. Like Dr. Chowdhury, Dr. Hendrata demanded a good deal from villagers. For example, both of them developed a health insurance scheme that required villagers to contribute money that could be used for others who fell sick in the community.

YIS began a program of primary health care combined with community development in 1972, in two large villages in Central Java, Klampok and Sirkandi. The first health cadres were taught a range of subjects, by medical staff, on a problem-solving rather than academic basis: under-five care, family planning, environmental sanitation, first aid, minor diagnostic procedures, plus thirty-two hours of instruction in locally prevalent diseases. Later groups were taught by the health cadres, and these second and third generations are said to be more

171

effective and practical-minded, as they escaped all the "academic bias" unconsciously imparted by the medical staff! Meanwhile, the villagers were being motivated to improve their agriculture by better irrigation, upgrading the roads, and so on.

By 1975, Klampok alone had eighty-four trained health workers, and any of them could consult the medical doctor at the nearby health center during one hour every day; this personal contact was seen as crucial to an effective system. USC was asked to help extend this successful pilot project to six nearby villages with a total population of thirty thousand, and over the next four years it contributed fifty-six thousand dollars, mainly for a training center and a village development fund. This fund first supported the health insurance scheme until it had enough members (contributing fifty rupiahs, or twelve cents, a month) to pay for the medical services themselves, and then it financed community development projects.

Another health insurance scheme started by YIS on the same basis was at Semarang, a city of 1 million people on Java's north coast. It began in the particularly poor community of Rejosari. USC contributed $18,500 to cover the running expenses of the medical clinic at its core, and within three years the insurance scheme became self-supporting.

In 1978 the scheme entered a much more ambitious stage, because the leadership of North Semarang had been so impressed by changes in Rejosari that they wanted to extend it to all their sixteen villages and 177,000 people. Actually, North Semarang was by then an urban slum rather than a collection of villages. USC contributed $51,500 over three years to this urban counterpart of the Klampok primary health scheme. But it was not so speedily successful. There was less mutual trust and help, less acceptance of new ideas in the diverse population. Many were fishermen and factory workers, rather than farmers. Priorities were different in an urban slum; environmental sanitation took precedence over nutrition.

Out of the experience at Klampok and Semarang grew the Central Java nutrition program. Dr. Hendrata proposed an immense scheme that might cover 810 villages and more than 2 million people, but it was scaled down to 27 villages in Boyalali regency. The main objective was to reduce by half the cases of malnutrition over four years. At that time, out of the 22 million children in Indonesia under the age of five, 7 million were suffering from varying degrees of malnutrition, and another

800,000 had vitamin A deficiency. The results were sadly predictable; half the deaths in Indonesia were of children under five. Dr. Hendrata maintained that half the cases of malnutrition were due to "mal-education." If villagers could be mobilized actively into health programs, the mortality figures would drop dramatically.

The four-year program was managed by three agencies: YIS, the Women's Welfare Movement (PKK) headed by Mrs. Soepardjo, the governor's wife, and the doctors from the medical faculty of the University of Diponegoro. It was a good example of collaboration between governmental, nongovernmental, and university organizations. The USC put nearly a hundred thousand dollars into the program, with matching funds from CIDA.

The project was built around the basic activity of a weighing program, or Operation Timbang. By 1984, some four thousand mothers were involved in bringing their young children regularly to weighing stations and in doing so became part of a broad educational program, covering many subjects from vaccinations and family planning to planting a vegetable garden. In the third year, a Gizi Plus (or nonnutritional) element was added. This included donations of chickens, and sometimes cows and goats, to generate income, and it also involved financial support in the digging of latrines and wells. The agencies encouraged the women to be active participants, not just in a mother-child context but in improving the whole community; the villagers were to draw up a "nutrition profile," to give them a sense of direction of what they wanted to achieve together.

Success on such a broad front is difficult to measure. The university team did an evaluation based on a questionnaire bringing out knowledge, attitudes, and practice of mothers in the first and third years of the program. They went to fourteen villages involved in the program and eight "control" villages outside it. Disappointingly, the evaluation showed there was hardly any reduction in the incidence of diarrhea. Mothers apparently still considered it a normal part of childhood and did not report the sickness to doctors. As well, the level of knowledge and practice was higher in the villages that had joined the scheme halfway through than in those involved for all four years, which suggests that people lose interest after a time and slip back into old ways.

On the other hand, the health and nutritional state of children and pregnant women had improved; there were about 11 percent more well-nourished babies in program villages than outside, five times as many mothers were using Vitamin A as before the program, and nearly twice as many (57 percent) were using some form of contraceptive.

Lighting lamps with water!

The other major project that the USC supported in Java was the rural development work of a group of university graduates who had, in 1967, formed their own organization, called Dian Desa or "Lamp of the Village." In contrast to other partner agencies, it was not headed by doctors. Its original dozen members had graduated in such subjects as animal husbandry, agriculture, food technology, engineering, and environmental studies. Its leader from the start was a lively character, Anton Soedjarwo, an engineer of Chinese background. He likes to wear bright batik shirts, and finds fascination (as a good engineer might) in exploring ways to make technology serve the people. He is also a student of psychology, skillful both in building trust among villagers and involving them in the work, and also in dealing with businessmen. Under this type of leadership, Dian Desa quickly became widely known for its achievements, its staff grew to 140, of whom 42 were engineers, and the World Bank began adopting some of its techniques.

By staying in villages in Central Java where they were invited, and by studying the villagers' needs, the Dian Desa staff often found that water and energy came at the top of the list. Since the ground-water table was as deep as three hundred meters in some areas, Dian Desa engineers designed, in their workshop in Jogjakarta, an inexpensive rainwater tank with a capacity to serve two households. They also designed a fuel-efficient cooking stove that could be made from local clay and sand.

A few figures can indicate the savings the engineers effected. The tanks, measuring ten cubic meters and holding twenty-five hundred gallons, were made of bamboo woven, in a traditional way, into a highly durable mesh and then plastered with cement. Villagers could be taught to build their own tanks. Lorraine Cameron wrote that the ones she saw in Ngestirego in 1979 took only three days to make, and construction costs amounted to about one-twentieth that of the chicken-wire concrete tank that was commercially available. As for the clay-and-sand stove, the single cost was a three-dollar bamboo pipe to draw off the smoke. Compared with the ordinary stove, it used one-quarter of the fuelwood and could cook four dishes at once instead of one. In areas where the forests were fast disappearing for firewood and the land was being eroded, this stove was a general boon.

The USC was asked to support a two-year project in a mountainous area, called Gunnung Sewa, where it was impossible to dig wells. Women and children had to walk long distances in the dry season for water. Dian Desa staff went about the problem with their usual thoroughness. They got meteorological reports on the average precipitation at various times, and aerial photographs to show distances to water sources. Social scientists looked at housing conditions and the nutritional status of families, to identify the poorest six thousand people in the forty-two villages of the area. They gave 380 local cadres a month's technical training (and at least a week of motivational training) and organized them into 95 groups under professional field staff. These cadres taught the villagers to build their own bamboo-cement tanks, and six thousand were constructed in two years; USC funds paid for about sixteen hundred of them, and some six hundred clay stoves.

Anton Soedjarwo does not stop there. He looks at development in three stages. First comes some work of "social infrastructure," like the rainwater tanks and clay ovens. Then, villagers are sufficiently stirred up to try some new or enlarged income-generating activity, such as keeping livestock. The third stage is cooperative action in some processing work. Following this pattern, he turned to USC in 1981 for support in the two further stages. He wanted credit to lend in the form of goats to villagers for breeding. He also wanted equipment for a cassava drying and processing unit: a storehouse, a solar dryer, and diesel engine choppers. He had already made deals with Chinese merchants to supply the processed cassava as cattlefeed. By 1982, more than a thousand families had joined the processing cooperative. The calculation was that, by cutting out the middleman, the cassava producer would net an extra $25 on average per harvest — no mean addition where the average annual income per family was $125.

The following year Dian Desa took its first step out of Java. It was typically well prepared. Two field staff went to live for two years in the hilly Sikka district of East Flores, a long island in NTT province, to get to know the people and their problems. Again, water was the primary problem; very low rainfall and porous soils. During the dry season, people walked up to ten kilometers to fetch water and chopped at banana trees to squeeze some moisture from the stalks. Dian Desa decided the best solution was to build one thousand ferro-cement tanks, made of chickenwire and Portland cement, in five villages. They had trained twenty-two local people as builders but they took the bold step of bringing thirty trained men from Gunnung Sewu because there was only a short period with enough rain to mix the cement. USC was asked to pay for the equipment and for the transport and stay of the Javanese cadres — a total of $296,500.

This large sum proved worth spending. As Anton described it, "The people's enthusiasm has exploded." Everyone – older women and young boys included – joined in carrying the chicken-wire mesh and cement (fourteen bags to each tank) up the hills to their villages. The thousand tanks were completed easily within the year's deadline. The momentum of this work, and the spirit of self-help which it engendered, had to be maintained if any real advance was to be made from a subsistence economy based on a single maize crop. So in 1984, Dian Desa proposed a scheme for processing coconut shells into flour for a dozen industrial uses in Jakarta or Surabaya – it is used as a filler in adhesives and PVC compounds or as a dilutant in insecticides. The proposal made sense because those districts of East Flores are major producers of copra (coconut oil), and some seven thousand metric tons of coconut shells are wasted every year.

"Our goal," Anton has said, "is to help people make the transition from a subsistence economy to a commercial economy. We begin by making a bridge with a project to meet a basic need." So far, Dian Desa has been very successful in helping villagers cross this bridge at surprising speed.

Transmigration of doctors

The population problem for Indonesia is a peculiar one. Its population soared from 60 million people to 140 million between

1930 and 1980, and by the year 2000 it may well reach 210 million. Nevertheless, Indonesia has had one of the developing world's most succesful programs of family planning, and the annual growth rate had been reduced to 2.2 percent by 1981.[11]

Although it is the fifth most populous country in the world, the real problem is the fact that two-thirds of the people live on Java and two smaller islands just to its east, Madura and Bali. These islands have the higher levels of development and receive most assistance, while coping with the highest density of population. As Minister of Manpower and Transmigration, Mr. Harun Zain had the job, during the second Five-Year Plan (1980-84), of resettling five hundred thousand families from these three islands in Sumatra and Sulawesi, which are large and sparsely populated, and of providing them with fundamental amenities.

Among other measures to speed up development in the outer islands of the archipelago is the regulation that medical doctors must serve from three to five years in rural areas. In many cases, this means that city-bred Javanese doctors find themselves on distant and neglected islands. And many of them, after a little culture shock, roll up their sleeves and get to work to improve their adopted community.

The USC came into contact with several of these doctors who were spearheading community development projects, after the agency began to shift the emphasis of its work from Java in 1980. Two years earlier, Dr. Lotta had recorded a conversation with Mrs. Sarjono of the Department of Social Affairs: "She was very appreciative of our USC aid and urged us to move into the faraway islands to help, since the need there is naturally the greatest." By 1982 the shift had taken place. In that year, USC was supporting fifteen projects in Java with $240,000 in funds, and twenty-one projects in the provinces of NTT and West Kalimantan (still known to some people as Borneo) with funds totaling $462,000; nearly two-thirds of USC funds were by then being spent off Java. And the agency found that it was operating in regions so different from Java that they seemed like separate countries. One link was the flow of doctors between regions.

---

[11]This achievement is marred by a continuing high rate of infant mortality. According to *UNICEF: The State of the World's Children 1984*, 100 babies in every 1,000 die before their first birthday. However, the crude birth rate has fallen in ten years from 46 to 35 per 1,000 of total population and the crude death rate (all ages) from 22 to 13.

Regreening of Sabu

One of the most remote islands in the southernmost curve of the whole Indonesian archipelago is called Sabu. It is about 150 kilometers southwest of Kupang, the capital of NTT province on Timor. Its people have always been fiercely independent, and the Dutch colonizers never conquered the island. Not that there was much temptation to do so, for life is hard, and no rain falls during eight months of the year. The crops − rice, maize, and greengram, a kind of pulse − often fail for lack of rain, and in times of famine the children among the island's sixty thousand people are sent to the forest or to the seashore to forage for small fruits, seaweed, and even grasshoppers.

Wryly, Dr. Frans Radja Haba, the executive director of Sabu Ie Rai (the Sabu Development Committee) says: "The only crop that has never failed on Sabu is the Borassus palm." This is why people depend on its juice, especially in the dry months from March to November, as a main source of food. Twice daily, lots of sturdy men and boys scale the spiky trunks of as many as twenty trees, which are often thirty meters tall, to collect enough juice from the trees' flowers to feed a family. The juice is either consumed fresh or boiled to make a liquid much like maple syrup. It has some nutritional value, but it is gained at a heavy cost for many Sabunese men and boys suffer severe injuries, and some are killed, from falling from the tops of palm trees.

Dr. Radja Haba, as district medical officer in Kupang, had responsibility for the people of Sabu among the other 2 million people in his district. He also came from one of the island's royal houses (*Radja* means "king") and had left Sabu at the age of thirteen to work his way through high school and six years of medical school on Java. When he returned to the district as medical officer, he found that little had changed − at least, for the better − on the island. For people still do not use a plough to prepare the land for seeding; instead, young men spend days in mud up to their knees driving herds of water buffalo around the rice paddies to break up and churn the soil. The rice crop often fails for want of better farming methods, just as it does for lack of rain.

In his time away, some things, like the shortage of trees and increasing erosion, had actually worsened. Because there is so little wood, people cannot build boats large enough to fish for

Dr. Lotta meeting Prime Minister Indira Gandhi. Mrs. Sarojini Aiyar in middle.

Dr. Lotta with Mrs. Jadhav in Madras.

After the Bihar famine:a farmer under training at Ranchi.

*Awamma
Mulla with
Dr. Lotta near
drinking well
built at Maldinni.*

Dr. Lotta in a sari near Delhi (1950s).

Dr. Vaidya, of the Karnatak Health Institute, on a tour of nearby villages.

Dr. Lotta distributing layettes to refugee mothers and hardship cases from Dikwani camp, one of the Palestine refugee camps in Lebanon (1966).

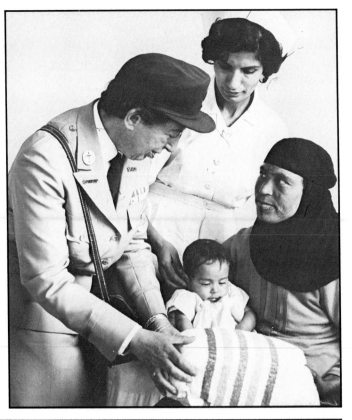

Hong Kong (1950s and 1960s): Overcrowding—even twenty to a room—was a major problem.

Central Java program "Operation Timbang" (weighing program) in which four thousand mothers enrolled their children.

Disabled children at a post-polio center in Saigon (early 1970s).

Lesotho woman collecting eggs for one of "egg circles" (cooperatives) organized with USC funds.

Mrs. Malatele Khadikane, USC representative in Lesotho.

In Swaziland, Ntombgiesa Ngozo, a twelve-year-old student at St. Theresa's High School, Manzini.

Gilles Latour, chief program officer, 1984.

Dr. Lotta and Raymond ven der Buhs, USC managing director, on her last visit to Bangladesh (1981).

Dr. Lotta with a Bangladesh doctor.

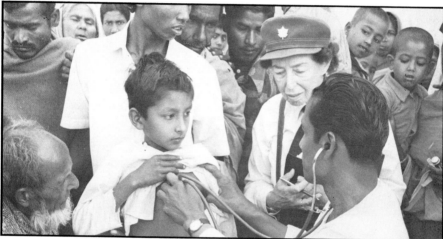

Humayun Reza talking to women in Bangladesh enrolled in the Rural Development Program.

In Victoria, packing clothes for shipment overseas (1982). Foreground: Hazel Woodward (then chairman) and Ida Weisse (chairman now). Background: Joe Barber-Starkey, Augusta Schwartz, Bill Hawker, Joyce Gaddes and Julie Moores.

In Korea, trying them on for size!

the plentiful stocks some distance offshore. One improvement had been the building, in 1974, of the first high school, constructed and staffed by the islanders themselves. Before then, many of the brightest Sabunese left for school in Kupang and then migrated throughout Indonesia, although they kept ties with home through the clan system.

Dr. Radja Haba gathered a number of other Sabunese migrants who were living on Timor and formed Sabu Ie Rai in 1980. Within three years, both by using their family links and by proposing programs in an acceptable way, its founders had formed eighty Ie Rai groups all over the island. Earlier attempts by government officials to carry out social and agricultural programs had collapsed. In the words of Jeff Ramin, "Sabu is like a fortress whose walls consist of an extremely complex culture and set of traditions. Previous attempts to scale those walls...have failed mainly because these outsiders have not understood or acknowledged Sabunese culture. For Ie Rai, however, penetrating these protective layers of tradition has been much easier."[12]

He was not simply concerned about health services, although the first project USC supported in 1981, with a $42,000 grant, was a ten-bed health center and surgery ward. "We deal in death, we don't deal in life," he once said among doctors. The need for a health center was urgent, however, because islanders previously had to travel twenty hours by small motorboat (or sail for several days) across the Sabu Sea to the nearest hospital and surgery facilities in Kupang.

Ie Rai went on to tackle what one might call the health of the island, not simply that of the islanders. The first goal, as Dr. Radja Haba told Jeff Ramin, was to save the island from further erosion and to improve the soil. "Other natural re-sources are not available and, if we lose the land, there will be nothing left. Regreening is the key." But the government had failed in a lengthy effort to promote reforestation. They had failed, Dr. Radja Haba believed, because the officials had not managed to explain to farmers and others why new methods should be tried, why improved seeds and fertilizer should be used. "You have to put knowledge in place first."

His organization concentrated on the planting of lomtoro trees throughout the island. Lomtoro is a species of leucaena, a

---

[12]Report to the USC board, 1 April 1983, p. 33.

tree of the mimosa group, with its origins in Central America, which has spread widely because of its remarkable range of uses. It is sometimes even called a miracle tree, although it has some shortcomings. It grows quickly and can be used for firewood and charcoal, and more significantly for Sabu, for terracing slopes, holding the soil, and providing shade above other crops. Its leaves and seeds are harvested as feed for cattle and poultry, and it is also valuable as fertilizer because it is able to fix atmospheric nitrogen. Research on selecting and improving leucaena species has been done in Australia and Hawaii, and more recently in the Philippines, with funds from the International Development Research Centre. It is clearly a tree of great potential benefit to many developing countries.[13] Don Flickinger, a young American who was the Oxfam representative in Kupang, was the first to give some of this background to Ie Rai and to fire Dr. Radja Haba's enthusiasm for a regreening program with this remarkable tree.

Despite all this promise, Ie Rai had difficulty in persuading the Sabunese to take part in a regreening effort until about eighty farmers came together in 1982 for a two-week course in dry land farming, given with USC's financial support by an agricultural expert based in Kupang who came originally from Sabu. He taught them about erosion and conservation, regreening, terracing and composting, and the use of fertilizers on crops. He also charged them to organize other farmers in their villages and to share their knowledge. They did so, and Dr. Radja Haba says this was the spark that ignited interest in Ie Rai's plans to develop Sabu. Within a year, nearly 3 million lomtoro seeds had been planted on mainly eroded land, and the eighty farmers who took the course became group leaders and the nucleus of Ie Rai's organization for a broader effort at development.

By the end of 1983, all forty villages on the island had joined in the regreening program, and the islanders were not only producing leucaena seedlings for their own use but sending one hundred kilograms of seed to nearby Semau Island to start a USC-supported program of regreening there also. As well as planting lomtoro trees, farmers on Sabu were planting coconut

---

[13]See Clyde Sanger, *Trees for People,* an account of the forestry research program supported by the International Development Research Centre, IDRC-094e Ottawa: 1977, p. 27.

palms and banana trees. In 1983 a Sabunese businessman from Kupang stirred interest through a competition to plant more than a thousand coconut palms on terraces or hillsides; the prizes were stereo cassette players.

Other advances followed. Jeff Ramin records a day when he walked through the village of Daieko, overlooking the turquoise sea. The villagers had built a protective stone fence around ten hectares of rocky land which they had planted with lomtoro trees, and he watched Dr. Radja Haba "carefully clearing away grass and stones from the trees, doting on each like a new delivery." The doctor talked to the villagers about growing maize and cashew trees between the rows of lomtoro, and planting coconut palms and onions — all to reduce their dependency on the Borassus palm. One villager said they would need more water for these crops in the dry season — and this led to a study of whether to build a catchment dam or dig more wells.

Water was a major problem for the island has only one river that runs all year. The USC gave eighteen thousand dollars for an irrigation scheme, to pump water from this river along a three-kilometer concrete canal to storage tanks from which eighty families would carry it in buckets to fields they had planted with maize. A clan leader complained that irrigating these thirty hectares would reduce the river's flow to the sixty hectares of rice paddy his clan members farmed on lower ground. But he was also an Ie Rai volunteer and saw the point that the river should benefit everyone, not just his clan. So he and Dr. Radja Haba got down to technical details of reducing water loss, in order to satisfy both groups.

Many agricultural developments on Sabu will take years. More than five hundred small catchment dams are needed for irrigation in all areas, and in 1984 there was only one Ie Rai worker with training in water resources. So Ie Rai, supported by USC, was pushing other ways of earning immediate income. One was to provide larger boats and better nets for fishermen in seven coastal villages to go further out to sea. Another was to excavate salt beds and produce some 120 tons of salt a year. A third way was to build and equip permanent classrooms at the high school, for the government had said it would take over the financing of this "private school" if it was upgraded. This provided work for artisan groups that Ie Rai had helped organize: for example, a group of four young men were taught by Johnny, the island's only welder, how to make 160 chairs for the school, and Ie Rai, with USC funds, donated the welding equipment to the group for further use. Carpenters, blacksmiths, and shoe-makers were also organized in small groups.

By 1984 Ie Rai had developed a structure that went far beyond the one-man operation that the critics of Dr. Radja Haba – and he had several adversaries in Kupang – suggested it had been. There was a three-man board working almost full time on Ie Rai activities. Below it were four sections dealing with agriculture, cooperatives, women, and technical subjects. Oxfam was funding an agricultural staff member, and USC was asked to pay seven other staff salaries (amounting to less than eight thousand dollars). As well, there were five village boards to coordinate work and motivate the people. Spreading out from there were some fifty active volunteers and eighty group leaders among farmers. But Ie Rai is very much a self-help organization, with the main effort coming from the villagers themselves.

Sampans, wells, and fishponds

Several other projects in NTT and West Kalimantan are partially funded by USC and directed by medical doctors who take a broad view of their domain of work. Dr. Radja Pono, working out of Kupang, was supervising the provision of engines and nets to fishermen on three small islands near Sabu, and the training of the fishermen on the use of their new equipment. He was also spurring on teams of Sabunese diggers who had to use the crudest tools – sledgehammers, chisels, and crowbars – to dig thirty meters down through solid rock to provide six wells for a village on Timor. He called it "traditional technology," none other being available.

Dr. M. Toyibi arrived in Sei Jagan, in West Kalimantan, in 1983 to take over a group fishing project started by his predecessor. Forty families, who had made a bare subsistence from working on other people's boats or wading into the sea to fish, were provided with sampans, oars, and nets on an interest-free loan. They doubled their previous income, and by asking lower prices they broke the monopoly of a businessman for whom many of them had worked. The businessman retaliated by equipping his boats with outboard motors, to seek the larger schools of fish and still return to market ahead of the group's boats. Dr.

Toyibi, a quiet but determined man, found himself acting as the group's negotiator, placating the businessman by buying some equipment from him and bargaining for standardized prices.

Another group project, in Belu district of NTT, involved establishing 180 families in fixed farming of peanuts and vegetables. These families suffered from degrees of malnutrition because, previously, their only form of agriculture was growing maize on a shifting basis. Dr. Felix, the medical director whose health workers supervised the project, was able to record improved nutrition levels after they harvested (and ate) their first beans and onions. Five other young doctors, all from Java, were working in Belu district in 1984 and were inspired by Dr. Felix ("a natural leader," in Ramin's words) to start similar activities in their own subdistricts.

More remarkable, perhaps, was the initiative of a paramedic, Jusef Otgan, at the Ngabang health center in West Kalimantan. He came to realize that the major health problem of his patients – and, indeed, of all the local villagers – stemmed from their reliance on slash-and-burn agriculture, which yielded them too little food. A former farmer himself, he persuaded the Catholic church to give him four hectares of land for a demonstration farm at Jelimpo, and he began to run one-week courses for local farmers in paddy cultivation, cattle and poultry raising, and fishpond operations – everything to encourage fixed farming. The farmers he has trained go back to their villages, some of them fifty kilometers away, and form groups to pass on their knowledge.

In 1984 the USC began supporting this unique effort by a local man. It provided $19,400 to add a dormitory to his training center, to pay a small stipend to trainees and salaries for two staff, and, as well, to provide inputs for the ricefields and fishponds. The courses are necessarily short, and it is not yet clear how much impact they will have. (The example of the Ranchi training center in India suggests that follow-up is an essential part of changing practices.) But his move is surely a start in the right direction.

Finally, a project which began in 1981 within a strict definition of primary health care, was broadened in 1983-84 to become a community development program involving two villages in Nagapanda subdistrict on Flores island. Nagapanda is two hours' drive from the city of Ende, along a winding and picturesque road, but a set of statistics – of illiteracy, of lack of latrines, of child deaths from diarrhea, of per capita income, of cultivated land – indicate (as Ramin's report says) that "Nagapanda is suffering the combined and reinforcing effects of poverty, ignorance, and poor health."

A British Columbia couple, both doctors, donated fifty thousand dollars to USC to support a program of primary health care, and the NTT provincial health planner, Dr. Gatot, laid out a three-year program for Nagapanda district, to provide supplementary feeding and to train village cadres in basic health, nutrition, and family planning. His scheme was at once too confined and too complicated. It was to be managed from far away in Timor, and there is antipathy between the Catholics of Flores and the Protestants of Timor. The NTT governor's wife, Mrs. Nafsiah, with years of experience in community development, contended that it should be widened to encompass vocational training, the provision of clean water, and agricultural support. Only then, she argued, would it tackle the root causes of rural health problems, among them insufficient food and income. The USC team visiting Indonesia that year – Raymond ven der Buhs and Jeff Ramin – agreed with her and also recommended that it should be locally supervised.

In 1984 the changes were being made, and USC has contributed forty-eight thousand dollars to the first year's work in carrying out a more ambitious plan. Once again, it is being built around the formation of groups of about ten villagers, to help them identify their own problems and together find appropriate solutions. That may mean they abandon slash-and-burn farming, or regenerate their coconut forests, or improve the quality of their pigs, chickens, and ducks – or do all three things. Alongside these income-generating activities goes the work of improving health care. Dr. Achmad Chafid, a city-bred Javanese now in charge of the Nagapanda health center, finds himself supervising a broad project. But he has been smart enough to involve, from the outset, all the relevant government officials at subdistrict level.

This is a crucial point. Some of his medical colleagues – Dr. Radja Pono and Dr. Radja Haba, among others – have had difficulties with officialdom. And the USC, like any other agency in Indonesia, has to work inside the framework of maintaining the approval of influential people in government, from governor's wives down to village heads, while adding momentum to the enthusiasm of development workers like these doctors. It is a challenge for all concerned, but at the same time, they share a common goal of human progress, and in Indonesia impressive strides have recently been made towards that goal.

CHAPTER 9

The Art and Science of Aiding People

A rare occasion

DR. HITSCHMANOVA received many honors, as the five rows of ribbons on her uniform have testified. She was especially pleased to be the first to receive the Athena Messolora Gold Medal from the Greek government in 1967 (just before the Colonels' coup) and, much earlier, the Medal of Gratitude from the French government.[1] Most recently, she was awarded the intriguingly named Meritorious Order of Mohlomi by King Moshoeshoe II of Lesotho.[2] The Canadian government gave her its highest honor in 1980, when she was made a Companion of the Order of Canada. And the previous year, she received the Royal Bank of Canada Award — for an outstanding contribution to human welfare and the common good — consisting of a medal and fifty thousand dollars.

What she never accepted, although she was offered one several times, was an honorary doctorate from any university. Why she took one kind of honor and not the other is not entirely clear. Some friends suggest that she was rather scornful of honorary degrees, having worked hard in Paris and Prague to earn her own doctorate. The distinction may perhaps be that she always accepted a medal as an honor bestowed on USC and all its supporters rather than just on herself, whereas an honorary degree was more personal. Another reason may be that she was shy of speaking to university audiences.

There was a single exception in 1973. In that year she agreed to give the Chancellor's Lecture at Brock University in Ontario,

---

[1] Athena Messolora founded the Greek Nursing Corps.

[2] Chief Mohlomi lived in the early 19th century and traveled widely in southern Africa. He was a famous traditional healer as well as a diplomat and administrator, and became tutor and mentor to King Moshoeshoe I. The king founded the Basotho nation and called on Britain to establish a protectorate, writing Queen Victoria to ask her to accept his people as "a flea in your blanket."

although she did not break her rule about degrees. She repeated the lecture a few weeks later in front of the First Unitarian Congregation of Ottawa on 2 December, and most of her board of directors was present. Her lecture, under the title that heads this chapter, was therefore a rare and definitive statement of how the USC approached its relations with partner agencies and its work overseas.

This chapter is straightforwardly cast in the same framework as the Brock University lecture, although a good deal of the material hung on that framework is of more recent spinning. However, some of the language may sound outdated in the mid-1980s. For example, in 1973 Dr. Lotta spoke of "the art of giving aid," while ten years later, the phrase had been amended (in a USC article sent to an Indian magazine) to "the art of cooperation." But to change all the language can obscure attitudes that informed activities at a certain time and distort historical account. So original phrases are preserved here, without apology.

The art of giving aid

Dr. Lotta identified three basic principles in the field of the art of giving aid. She put them in these words: "to come as an open-minded friend and good listener, when offering help; to say goodbye to a project when it can continue on its own; to serve with a personal touch, because a relationship of confidence must lift your aid beyond the realm of a simple business proposition and prove that you really care."

I shall enlarge on each of these principles in turn.

As Dr. Lotta acknowledged, to offer assistance is not an easy assignment. Most people shy away from accepting help if they cannot reciprocate, and therefore, she insisted, from the very beginning a partnership must be established which places responsibility on the shoulders of both the donor and recipient.

In terms of coming "as an open-minded friend and good listener," Dr. Lotta told her audience that the most important attitude was a concern for fellow human beings.

> You have come to help [them], and you want to help altruistically, not for reasons of personal gain. In listening there must be no preconceived ideas, no prejudices as to religion or color or origin –

for it must be your conviction that mankind is one, made up of many faces.

You must love people, and have the sensitivity to be interested in their problems; to be able to settle down and listen, for hours if necessary, in order to learn all you can about their problems before you start offering advice and help.

As an example of this kind of listening, she told of her meeting in Delhi with Dr. S. Bhatia, who told her of the needs at the Karnatak Health Institute and pointed the way to twenty years of cooperation there.

Anyone who has seen Dr. Lotta in action, with her thick notebook and her scribbling pen, will know what a tireless listener and persistent questioner she was. Of course, there is a danger in listening to too many peoples' accounts of need; an assistance program can go off in all directions, lack coherence, and be spread too thinly. She deals with that concern in a later maxim under "The Science of Aid."

The second important aspect in the art of giving, in Dr. Lotta's book, was "not to overstay your own usefulness." She said, in her Brock University lecture: "Just as vital as to extend the right kind of help when it is needed, is to phase-out when your partner is ready to manage his responsibilities on his own. To overstay one's usefulness is a serious mistake, because it dwarfs the sense of responsibility and independence of the recipient. The phasing-out process from a project is just as important as the phase-in."

There are different ways of phrasing this principle. Dr. Lotta qualified it by giving the example of the Karnatak Health Institute (India was much on her mind in 1973) and its achievement in spreading health services around villages in a fifty-kilometer radius: "We are no longer needed, because doctors and services are available in case of need. This is the most beautiful victory that we can think of." And she added later: "Because the USC does not overstay its welcome, we do not crush precious human initiative." Today, Raymond ven der Buhs would phrase the principle slightly differently: "to free people to be on their own." He worries about the danger of doing too much for a community during the lifetime of a project, of its building up too much dependence upon the donor.

What has been the record of USC in phasing out of projects and countries? Some situations have already been described.

The ending of the program in South Korea in 1978 was carefully planned, years in advance, on the initiative of the USC board. Korean government officials were persuaded of the reasons for phasing-out and took steps to continue the funding of projects they thought important. The one mistake was an overgenerous endowment of the Han Kuk Social Service Committee, which was registered as the body to continue various programs. These funds were not properly administered, and the government has been investigating their use.

In contrast, the end of the Vietnam program came abruptly, partly under Canadian government pressure (after Vietnamese troops had invaded Kampuchea), and partly because Dr. Lotta had to cancel her inspection trip to Hanoi in 1979 and could not check on the progress of projects. The decision over Hong Kong in 1980 was a simple one; progress was evident, and in fifteen years of assistance, the USC had indeed worked itself out of a job.

Question marks hang over some other countries. There is, perhaps, little doubt that the programs in France and Greece continued long after they were really needed, even if they were greatly reduced in size. The reason for their continuance at all was the particular love Dr. Lotta had for these countries, and her resistance to discreet suggestions by her board members that she cut the links entirely. She loved visiting Mme Hagnauer at the Maison d'Enfants de Sèvres, both because they were good friends and because Sèvres in the 1970s was pleasantly free of problems. She also looked forward to retreating to write reports, at the end of a long trip, in the small apartment which the Hellenic Red Cross kept for her above the clinic at Marathon. She could at least argue that the residual programs in these two countries involved only a minimal amount of money that might have gone elsewhere, and that they certainly did not smother local initiatives.

The phasing out from India in 1975 falls into a much more grey area. Some threads in this decision can be traced back to a sharp complaint in February 1970 from the Indian high commissioner to Canada. He asked Dr. Lotta to his office and said that he was angry at some of the USC television promos that showed emaciated Indian children. He was also upset by the Milk for India campaign being run in the *Ottawa Journal,* which played up the needs of India without describing any of the achievements since independence. Dr. Lotta agreed that the publicity tended to be one-sided, but pointed out that television commercials only allowed a few seconds to make an appeal. He was not satisfied and said he would refer the matter to Delhi.

During her trip to India in February-March 1970, Dr. Lotta asked the health minister and the minister of Social Welfare if they wanted USC feeding programs to continue. She finally decided to draft a letter to the prime minister herself. In the meantime, Dr. Lotta had been told by the partner agencies in Calcutta and Bangalore that the midday meal and milk distribution programs would collapse without USC support.

Back in Canada, the Indian High Commission, acting presumably on Mrs. Gandhi's instructions, asked the USC not to publish any more photographs of Indian children with empty bowls waiting for Canadian milk. There were also some protests from Indian students at Canadian universities. As well, the high commissioner asked John Buss to remove a section about tribal farmers in Bihar from his film *The Dormant Land*, which described the Ranchi agricultural training center. In consequence, the USC decided to discontinue its Christmas Cup of Milk appeals in newspapers in Ottawa, Lethbridge, Calgary, and Victoria. This hurt the general fund-raising campaign considerably; in September-December 1970, Ottawans contributed less than half their usual amount.

At the same time, the USC board reviewed the whole program and decided to phase out of India in June 1975. So, in 1971 Dr. Lotta was busy explaining the decision to partner agencies and found that the news was received with regret and almost protest, particularly from Mrs. Jadhav in Madras. Dr. Lotta gave them four reasons for the step:

> that we were literally working ourselves out of jobs in India; the reluctance we feel exists in Indian Government circles to admit that foreign aid continues to be needed; the request by the Indian High Commission in Ottawa not to publish photographs of needy children ...But there was still another reason which was decisive in our minds: the recognition that some of our partner agencies were relying too heavily on our outside help and that, in spite of all my pleading and warning, they would never assume their full financial responsibilities for common programs unless we withdrew altogether ...I strongly believe that one of the greatest contributions we can make is to show our partners how they can become self-sufficient, and this must be our major task in India during the next four years.[3]

---

[3]Report to the USC board, 3 April 1971, p. 2.

In any event, the phasing-out process went surprisingly smoothly. By 1974 adequate local funds were assured for all but two of the forty-seven projects that were still being supported by the USC, and in June the board confirmed a complete withdrawal for the following June. The USC's final act was a grant totalling $82,900 to endowment funds for the four programs described at some length in Chapter 6: Saligram, Deena Seva Sangha, Ranchi, and KHI.

Adding the personal touch

The third ingredient that Dr. Lotta identified as essential in the art of aiding others was the personal touch. She used to call the USC "the agency with a heart," which irritated the heads of some other Canadian agencies who did not think of themselves as especially heartless. What she meant was, that in its work overseas, an agency had to be sensitive in offering aid – "partners must be on the same level, otherwise the relationship is degrading both to the donor and to the recipient." Meanwhile, at home it needed to maintain a warm relationship with its branch members, its volunteers, and the people who wrote in for information.

She honored this principle, even at the expense of much extra physical effort. As she acknowledged:

> in many ways our USC is very old-fashioned. To maintain our personal touch we shy away from using an addressograph, because it is so impersonal...I sign hundreds of campaign letters night after night, because a stamped or stencilled signature would be inadmissible in my eyes. During weekends when I am alone at the office, I love to dictate dozens of letters...because I believe that a warm relationship is basic to the kind of agency which I dreamed about 28 years ago, when I founded the USC."[5]

When abroad, she went to great lengths to maintain a personal touch, noting down the names and addresses of many workers, and writing appreciative letters the next morning on her portable typewriter before starting the day's round of visits. She also tried to respond to elaborate and long-planned welcomes.

---

[4]Report to the USC board, 9 May 1975, p. 14.

[5]Speech to the First Unitarian Congregation of Ottawa, 2 December 1973, p. 3.

Lotta

In 1972 she and John Buss made a special five-hour trip to Tanjore in southern India to see some girls from a children's home who were getting married and wanted her to bless them on behalf of their Canadian foster parents. She recorded, with perhaps unconscious humor: "The welcome – including a huge, tame elephant which garlanded us – was very touching."

But she found it difficult to enjoy any of the special foods and national dishes to which she was treated, and she refused to take any time away from work to see places of which her hosts were proud – a museum in Greece, a waterfall in India – because she thought it was indulging in tourism. Others would say she was ignoring a country's culture, and so failing to broaden a relationship with her partners. John Buss refutes this in part. He says he used to persuade her to visit theaters: "she loved music and dancing, and we'd go to see Indian dancing." But certainly she was never confronted with a cultural encounter like the one faced by Jeff Ramin in Indonesia in 1982, when he was the first white person to visit a remote Dyak village in West Kalimantan, where the USC was to finance a piped water supply: "To mark the occasion, an elaborate celebration was held in which I was required to enter a sacred area, to dance with the village elders in traditional dress around a human skull, with the entire village loudly voicing their approval."[6]

The science of aid

Under this second heading of her Brock University lecture, Dr. Lotta listed five rules: (1) be businesslike and practical, (2) be sure to identify felt needs, (3) help develop local leadership, (4) make a real impact in a few well-chosen areas, and (5) practice the strictest economy when spending precious dollars.

Again, we will go through these five points in turn.

Being businesslike and practical sounds like an obvious and simple rule, but Dr. Lotta added these cautionary words: "Don't be encumbered by preconceived ideas. Go to the area where you wish to establish an aid program, and make a survey to gather as many facts as you can – and THEN draw up a plan of action, but not a second earlier!"

This suggests some skill in improvisation and in adapting to

---

[6]*Confidential Survey of Indonesia*, 1982, p. 68.

circumstances. She told the story of how Canadian pearled barley came to be accepted for feeding programs in Korea. She had gone there in 1953, carrying a sample of pearled barley from the federal Department of Trade and Commerce. When Korean officials, faced with a bad crop failure, asked her if Canada could send shipments of rice, she explained that rice wasn't grown in Canada and then asked if they would help her with an experiment; turn the sample grains she had into a gruel and give it to a few children to eat.

Next day they watched three small orphans enjoying it, and one of them, to her delight, looked up to say in Korean, "Please, more tomorrow." Dr. Lotta got her interpreter to ask them what they thought they were eating, and they all replied "rice." So she had won an important battle; children would accept Canadian precooked barley as though it were rice, their staple food. For the next twenty years, the USC shipped pearled barley to Korea, to be used as staple food for the poorest people and also on food-for-work projects in the country's development program.

A challenge to the practical-mindedness of anyone in a donor agency is to try to transplant ideas, approaches, and solutions from one geographic area to another. The International Development Research Centre (with its headquarters only a few paces from 56 Sparks Street) has helped establish many networks among scientists, to spread and transplant results of successful research. In a more modest way, the USC has tried to take good ideas (and good results) from earlier projects to see if they might be copied or adapted elsewhere. The most striking success so far has been to use some of the experience in community development that Tony Trimis built up in Macedonian villages in the late 1950s in order to improve conditions in the Indian state then called Mysore. The idea of village leaders' conferences, to encourage cooperation and to confront them with pledged commitments of actions they had to carry out within a promised period, did transplant itself successfully, even if Dr. Lotta decided after some years to restrict the conferences to women.

Another attempt at transplanting ideas was made by financing two study tours of South Vietnamese officials from the Ministry of Social Welfare to see techniques of physical rehabilitation in Korea, as well as the Mokpo TB hospital. But some other attempts have palpably failed. Dr. Lotta records that the Korean women at the Echon Social Service Centre, which covered a rural area, did not seem interested at all when she told them in 1975 about the experiments at KHI and the village leaders' conference in Mysore, although the credit union members questioned her closely about the "Egg Circles" in Lesotho.[7]

How far can the exciting experiments in integrated rural development in Bangladesh (which will be described in the next chapter) be transplanted to other countries? The feeling at USC is that they would not work in Indonesia, where conditions vary so much between provinces, but that these lessons should be applied in Swaziland and Lesotho, small countries with a homogeneous population. But the practical-minded will always be prepared for setbacks and have ideas ready for adapting the original design.

Local people know their needs

On the importance of identifying felt needs — her second rule in this section — Dr. Lotta used to tell a story against herself. As she warned her Brock University audience: "Never must you make the mistake which I committed in my very early days in India, almost twenty years ago!" She had driven up into the mountains south of Madras, to a village called Villpatti where conditions deeply distressed her: pitiful malnutrition among the babies, dirty children everywhere, the *harijans* confined to the village outskirts, and no place where village meetings could be held. She asked to talk to the village elders, and a meeting was quickly arranged — in a pitch-dark room, the only light coming from the door where the family cow was stretched out to catch as much air as possible on a stiflingly hot day.

As Dr. Lotta recalls the scene, there were thousands of flies, and she listened and listened to words she could not understand. Finally, through her interpreter, she asked to speak. She explained that she had come from far away, as a friend, to help their village and that, to her mind, what they needed most was a community center, with a social worker and a midwife based there. If the village was interested in cooperating, she would go back to Canada and try to raise the necessary funds.

---

[7]Dr. Lotta took some consolation from a literal transplant at Echon, though. The USC had sent twenty-two maple tree seedlings out from Ottawa, and she saw them just appearing above ground and wrote "Hopefully they will grow and become big, beautiful Canadian trees."

There was absolute silence. Not a single question was asked, because the idea was so absolutely foreign to the village headman and the other elders. I knew I had made a terrible mistake, that the request, of course, had to come from the village and not from me. It took three years before the USC was approached to establish a community with the necessary staff; but then we were confronted with a felt need and everyone in the village was ready to do his share.

One pitfall that Dr. Lotta always avoided, according to one of her early friends from USC Boston, Howard Brooks, was that of practicing what he called "chateau philanthropy." (He took this image from the French grande dame descending to distribute charity to the peasants.) There was never any air of condescension on her part, he told me in 1984, only one of compassion.

Just as needs have to be recognized and articulated by the community, rather than by outsiders, so local leadership has to develop if a project is to have lasting benefit. Dr. Lotta was adamant on the subject of local leadership. "It is *their* country," she would say, "which they passionately want to develop themselves. When the foreign agency moves out, the indigenous agency must be able to take over. If this is not the case, then the project is unsuccessful."

She believed in local leadership from the start of any project, and this was her rule from the earliest days of her involvement with development work. One of her main criticisms of UNRRA in 1944, and also of USC Boston in the postwar years, was that they were sending Americans to run programs in Europe, who had neither the grasp of culture nor the knowledge of language to understand a situation in their bones. And she applied this rule of local leadership in every country in which USC Canada came to work, from Greece to Korea to Indonesia. The few exceptions where a project director was of a different nationality − cases like Dr. Margaret Barr in Assam, or Bruce Lansdale in Thessaloniki − were people who had given their life-work to India or Greece and could hardly be seen by anyone as outsiders. All the country representatives, starting with Mr. Cho in Korea, have been nationals of the host country.

Recently, some USC staff have raised the question of whether there should not be a Canadian staff person posted to, say, Indonesia as the agency's field representative for a limited period. The arguments in favor of this are that such a person's presence would underline the serious intentions of the agency in that country; that it would be better to have someone continuously there rather than that a project officer from Ottawa should visit for a few weeks' hasty inspection once a year; and, that in certain circumstances, an expatriate can achieve things no local representative can because he is outside the traditional system or can, if necessary, be replaced without anyone losing status. But the USC board has no intention of taking such a step. As Raymond ven der Buhs says, "It would be going against the whole historical tradition of USC."

Developing local leadership is a task that, of course, should go deeper than the top layer of project directing. That is why Dr. Lotta always insisted on shifting, as soon as possible, from purely relief measures and children's homes to incorporating training programs, however humble the jobs might be for which the boys and girls were trained. Further up the scale came village leadership training and other scholarships; a most coherent program of training is now being undertaken in the Bangladesh rural development program, where the training center built at Thakargaon is giving intensive three-month courses to development officers.

Making a real impact

To her Brock University audience, Dr. Lotta elaborated on the issue of the size of projects. A voluntary agency, she said, must not spread its activities too thinly over too great a territory, because close supervision every year and direct contact with partner agencies is a basic condition for success. "It is much healthier to make a real impact in a few well-chosen areas than to dissipate ones efforts."

She thought a voluntary agency should be a laboratory for larger agencies, to discover and develop ways of solving problems, and then turn over its successful methods to a larger body for wider implementation. She gave two examples of the USC acting this role with United Nations agencies: passing on a milk feeding program in the primary schools of Seoul to UNICEF in 1953, and twenty years later, developing a midday meal program for one-tenth of Swaziland's schoolchildren, before handing it on to the World Food Program.

196

Although she spoke about the size of individual projects, she did not mention the broader issue of the number of countries an agency can most effectively work in at any one time. In 1973 the USC, by her count, was operating in thirteen countries on three continents (Europe, Africa, and Asia), and she was undertaking all the overseas travel to check up on projects. Today the agency is operating in only six countries: Bangladesh, Indonesia and Nepal in Asia, and the three independent states of southern Africa – Botswana, Lesotho, and Swaziland. Four staff members pay regular visits overseas. The Brock speech, in fact, marked a watershed; from then on, USC resources flowed in fewer directions. This consolidation may have been begun for personal reasons; Dr. Lotta found that she could not control such a widespread program, especially when her health began to fail. But consolidation made good sense in general terms.

There was still debate about the number of countries the USC should be working in, both among staff members and in the Projects Advisory Committee (PAC). Raymond ven der Buhs, for one, used to think it should operate in more, rather than in fewer countries. He reasoned that some countries might have little appeal to ordinary Canadians during the annual fund-raising campaigns, or else that some might have to be abandoned because of conflicts in the area. John Buss had returned from one visit to southern Africa to tell the PAC that the area was "a powder keg." But Raymond was converted to the idea of concentrating on six (or even fewer) countries by the experience in Bangladesh with the rural development program.

He believes that an agency the size of USC should not be afraid to take on large-scale projects, but that it should balance that commitment by keeping the number of countries to a short list. Some agencies – for example, the Canadian Hunger Foundation – keep numbers down but move to new countries when a worthwhile project is identified there. Raymond argues for a longer-term commitment in particular countries, to build up trust and knowledge, including knowledge by Canadian project officers of local languages.

This is an appropriate point at which to describe the role of the Projects Advisory Committee, which has changed considerably since it first met in July 1956 under Dr. James Gibson. Dr. Gibson, a Rhodes Scholar and educationalist, was the first Dean of Arts and Science at Carleton University in Ottawa and then the first president of Brock University. As originally planned, the PAC would watch over the long-range interests of the USC, reviewing current projects and studying possible future ones. This would spread responsibility for USC activities, leaving the executive committee free, at its meetings, to deal with more immediate business matters. It was also seen as a way to bring people with overseas experience into the USC circle. Elizabeth MacCallum, then with the Middle East division of External Affairs, was one of the PAC's original seven members.

The PAC had a mixed record over its first twenty years of existence. In its task of looking ahead, it seems to have acted mainly as a restraining influence. In 1956, for example, it suggested that Dr. Lotta should not take extra weeks on her overseas tour to survey Pakistan and visit four countries of sub Sahara Africa (including Dr. Schweitzer's hospital at Lambarene). The following year, it advised a year's delay in starting the Macedonian community development project and felt justified in doing so when Tony Trimis was later hired and put it into shape.

But for a long period it was not a really effective body. It met with Dr. Lotta before she left on her annual overseas tour, and again when she returned. These meetings tended to be occasions for hearing her immediate plans and then her impressions from the recent trip. Norma Walmsley, a PAC member for many years, says she often felt frustrated that there never seemed to be time for a worthwhile discussion on longer-term objectives or on how to increase the developmental part of a program, as opposed to relief work.

However, towards the end of the 1970s, the PAC began to come into its own. Harry Bolster, who had taken over its chairmanship, set out to strengthen its role in the detailed examination of the USC's programs and to provide the Board with reasoned recommendations for the direction and improvement of USC projects. At the same time, and in consequence of Dr. Lotta's declining health, PAC worked with the Board and the USC staff to strengthen the projects section in numbers and professional capability.

Each spring PAC reviews in detail the reports of the project officers after their winter-time survey of USC projects overseas, and it recommends to the Board's annual meeting a budget and work program for the following year. Throughout the year it continues its examination with USC staff of the need for changes in individual projects and in the general direction of

USC work in each country. The PAC Chairman, being a member of the Executive Committee, keeps that body and the Board aware of the progress of the overseas work.

In 1981, when Dr. Lotta decided to step down and become Founding Director, the Board revived the Executive Committee, consisting of the officers of USC together with the Managing Director and the Founding Director. The Executive Committee holds regular monthly meetings, and is accountable to the full fifteen-member Board of Directors at the latter's four meetings each year.

Stretching the dollar

Finally, there is Dr. Lotta's rule of exercising the strictest economy. She was almost fanatical on this subject, using and re-using every scrap of paper, stopping on her walk home from the Sparks Street office to collect old envelopes from a friendly bookstore. She was, to judge from her reports, miserable when money was spent on entertaining her overseas. When UNRWA officials took her to a quiet Beirut restaurant once, she wrote: "The dinner to which I was treated was a terrible, terrible reproach to my conscience...I would have liked a piece of dry bread and nothing else..." She told her Brock University audience:

> How to stretch Friendship Dollars has been a fine science in the USC ever since we began.... We care for every cent, since less than a nickel provides a glass of Canadian milk for an undernourished child halfway round the world. It is amazing how relatively cheap it still is to help overseas.... It is our moral responsibility to obtain a maximum of needed services free of charge, so that the overhead of the agency be kept to a minimum....

Her example is still followed in many ways. All the USC publicity in newspapers, magazines, radio, and television is donated by the media. Volunteers across Canada provide a remarkable free labor force. The agency has never used a professional fund-raiser, and when USC staff tour Canada in the fall to raise funds, several hotels offer rooms at much reduced rates, as their contribution to the campaign. As a result of such economies, the administration budget has been kept below 13 percent of operating expenses in 1983-84. In figures, that is $532,904 out of total disbursements of $4,345,383, and the largest part of that administration cost went to the salaries of the twenty-one members of the staff.

One should not end this chapter by citing million-dollar figures, since the USC has built up its programs on the loyalty of thousands of people, young and old. Cash donations have been one of the two pillars in the USC structure since 1945, with sources ranging from large bequests to smaller amounts often raised by picturesque means – including renting a thirty-hectare Ontario farm to holiday-makers and selling birdhouses in Vancouver.[7] But when the collection and packing of clothing was phased out in the 1980s, several branches feared that their own groups would fall away. Yet they have nearly all made the transition to fund raising with imagination and success.

Quilts appear to be ideal ways to raise funds, and the idea can presumably last until every Canadian family is supplied, by raffle or sale. (There can be none quite so beautiful, though, as those stitched by Louise Hopkins of Victoria.) But the brains at USC are not resting on quilts alone. In 1984 a four-page list of fund-raising suggestions was compiled, and they descend from the sublimity of carol singing to the barnyard: "money from manure," for farmers to pack in used fertiliser bags and sell to city dwellers for their gardens. Every city has its own ideas: mini-afghans for hospital patients in Brockville, clothing sales in Winnipeg, crafts for London bazaars, thrift shops in Montreal and Ottawa, collection boxes in Oshawa, piggy-banks in Pincher Creek...

"Stretching the dollar," to return to Dr. Lotta's phrase. While many were modest donations, every one of them counted – and Dr. Lotta would make that clear in letters. So let's end the chapter with an exchange that took place in July 1969 between her and two girls in Vancouver, Judy and Janice Irving, then aged eight and six. The sisters wrote:

> We were glad when we knew that the poor children got the money last time we had a Koolaid stand. We thought they might be hungry again, so we had a popcorn stand. 10 cents a bag was the price. Please use the money for the poor children.

---

[7]1972 Year End Review, p. 4.

And Dr. Lotta, with her personal touch, wrote back:

What an absolutely beautiful letter you sent me a few days ago!...With the newest gift of yours – $1.60 – we can provide...a lot of food! It would be lovely if you could be at my side just once to watch with how much eagerness your little friends in India enjoy what you have sent them.

   With a big hug to each one of you for your generosity, I enclose our official receipt. Affectionately yours...

CHAPTER 10

Breaking the Pattern of Poverty

Bangladesh

THE PROGRAM in Bangladesh, with more than thirty projects and a budget, in 1984-85, of $1.16 million, is the largest that the USC is supporting anywhere in the mid-1980s. The rural development program, based in Thakurgaon in northwest Bangladesh under the direction of Humayun Reza, is the biggest and boldest venture that the agency has backed. The first three years of this project have been so successful and exciting that there is hope of spreading its system much more broadly across Bangladesh. In USC eyes, Bangladesh, like its green and red flag, represents hope of a new dawn and a better life for farming families, beyond its own narrow borders.

This was certainly not the view that the USC board and others connected with the agency held in the turbulent days of 1971-72. The storm had broken in March 1971, when Pakistan President Yahya Khan had sided with his foreign minister, Zulfikar Ali Bhutto, and would not acknowledge the recent election results that would have made Sheikh Mujibur Rahman (at the head of the Awami League) prime minister of the whole country, both West and East. The postponing of the National Assembly session, the civil disobedience campaign of all Bengalis, and finally the shelling by West Pakistani troops of Dhaka University on 27 March, were the last steps into a conflict in which 2 million died, nearly 10 million fled across the India border into West Bengal and Assam, and an already poor country was laid waste.

Like everyone else in Canada, the USC was appalled at the reports of slaughter and repression by Pakistani troops and quickly came to admire the efforts of the Indian government to care for the millions of refugees. Unlike others, the USC had links with two partner agencies in India by which Canadian relief aid might reach the refugees. These were the Ramakrishna Mission (RKM), with whom the USC had worked to set up the Ranchi agricultural training center in Bihar and whose headquarters were near Calcutta, the center of relief operations; and the All India Women's Conference (AIWC), also based in Calcutta.

At the USC annual meeting in June 1971, members agreed on a budget target of $125,000 for refugee aid. The response greatly exceeded this figure. By April 1972, the agency had received $323,600; CIDA had contributed $140,000 of this total and the British Columbia government another $40,000. Campaigns in newspapers and the annual fund-raising tour were, in Dr. Lotta's words, "immensely successful," despite a lack of photographs and slides. This was the first time, she noted, that she was appealing for a cause she had not surveyed before the campaign was launched. But people were "yearning for a reliable, humane channel to dispense aid effectively and rapidly to the most needy." Swami Yuktananda and his RKM volunteers were efficient in distributing three carloads of Canadian skim milk powder (16,330 kilograms in each carload) and clothing in the refugee camps, and humane in caring for hundreds of women who had been raped by soldiers. The AIWC was equally effective in looking after refugee children and setting up a special clinic.

By January 1972, however, the situation was transformed. The Pakistani troops had surrendered, Bangladesh had been formally declared an independent nation, and the refugees were trekking home. Should the USC follow the refugees home and help them develop their newly won country? Opinions were divided. In the Projects Advisory Committee, it is recorded that, "a very intense discussion on the advisability of taking on rehabilitation projects took place." At least two influential members cautioned against moves that could spread the USC resources too thinly, require cutbacks of programs in other countries, and involve a long-term commitment in Bangladesh.

But in January, there was still $189,000 to disburse of the amount raised in Canada for refugee relief, the Ramakrishna Mission staff members were returning to the ten centers which some of them had left in what had been East Pakistan, and many Canadians felt that the year ahead would be a crucial period if this brand new country was ever to stand on its feet. The board therefore asked Dr. Lotta, when she visited Bangladesh in March 1972, to study further relief needs, but to make no commitments beyond planning, with RKM staff, the best way to use the outstanding funds. However, those who had urged a cautious approach were soon outflanked. To board members who had said no funds for rehabilitation, only for relief, the subtle Swami produced a compromise of rehabilitation-oriented relief. So began the USC's long-term commitment to development in Bangladesh.

Dr. Lotta's first visit to Bangladesh was a mixture of grandeur and grimness. She, Swami Yuktananda, and the photographer John Buss arrived on the same plane from Calcutta as the Yugoslav foreign minister who was coming on a state visit. There was a crowd of women well-wishers on the tarmac of Dhaka airport ready with garlands, and (she wrote later):

> I guessed correctly that this delegation had come to welcome us and not the official guests from Jugoslavia... Naturally we were deeply embarrassed since we had not yet proven ourselves as friends, and every little flower costs money which was a reproach to me... We were whisked into the VIP room, and then there was a large limousine to take us through the city to the Intercontinental Hotel, the nerve-centre of the nation... I was greatly relieved when a jeep arrived on the scene – a much more useful vehicle for bad country roads.[1]

Grimness was in the destruction to be seen everywhere, from Dhaka University where women students ("so fragile, like slightly wilted flowers") said they lacked books and even a single decent sari, to the village of Kholamora where troops had killed twenty-six people and burned nearly two hundred houses. When she asked the prime minister what his top priority was, Sheikh Mujib replied "shelter," for the monsoon rains were imminent. And as she was talking to the health minister, Zahur Ahmed Chaudhury, in his office, he was handed a long list of villages where cholera had broken out. She heard elsewhere that the hunger was such that in some villages people were driven to eat leaves from the trees. There were, indeed, so many priorities.

On her advice, the USC put its funds into another carload of milk powder and into large shipments of light clothing, as well as some seventy thousand dollars into reconstructing homes, mainly by providing corrugated iron roofs. There was a Stitch a Shirt campaign and a further collection of Distress Dollars to

---

[1]Report to the USC board, 19 April 1972, pp. 5-6.

provide village women (not just the university students) with a sari to replace their rags.

Canadians responded in their different ways. Students at Argyle Secondary School in North Vancouver raised $1,650 in a ten-hour dance marathon, while a more sedately conducted appeal in Prince Edward Island produced enough money for twenty-one houses.[2] The RKM was the channel for milk distribution and the reconstruction of one thousand homes, and when Dr. Lotta went back in April 1973, she saw the results in Kholamora. Reaching the village by barge across the Burigonda River (a special act on her part, for Dr. Lotta used to avoid crossing water, whenever possible), she was led in procession to all the rebuilt houses and to watch people working at traditional crafts, making kettles and cutting spices for the Dhaka market. The words from her 1972 report rang true: "The situation is desperate but not hopeless, for there is one major asset I have not yet talked about − the spirit of the people of Bangladesh. They own the land which produced a Rabindranath Tagore; they are as soft as music and as hard as rock − people with tremendous charm, who are fun-loving and infinitely resilient."[3]

Years of frustration

The next few years of collaboration in Bangladesh had more than their share of frustrations. Two statistics that haunted Dr. Lotta were the scarcity of doctors working outside the cities − only twenty-five hundred, or one doctor to every twenty-eight thousand people − and the population explosion, with a projection of some 140 million people by the year 2000, living in a country only twice the size of New Brunswick. But she was not at all impressed by those who were then officers of the Family Planning Association of Bangladesh and could recommend no projects with them.

Nor were relations entirely smooth with the Ramakrishna Mission. The RKM monks and volunteers had coped magnificently during the refugee period, even dealing cheerfully with

---

[2] *Jottings from Bangladesh*, May 1973.
[3] Report to the USC board, 19 April 1972, p. 14.

the red tape of Indian Customs clearance that required fumiga-
tion by hand of every item of imported clothing.[4] They had
supervised the reconstruction of one thousand homes with
USC funds in 1972-73, and the distribution of milk and saris.
But in 1973, the mission refused to handle the task of
constructing five hundred more houses because it was short of
monks to supervise the work and to account for the thirty-five
thousand dollars involved. And Swami Yuktananda's initiative
in launching a Bangladesh women's auxiliary of the RKM
(Sarada Seva Sangha), which started with plans for a half-dozen
USC-supported projects, soon shrunk to a single day-care
center in Comilla district. The Kolo-Kakoli center, "sweet chatter
of birds," was a pilot project for Bangladesh, but it depended
heavily on a high school teacher, Mrs. Shiria Khatoon, who
after a few years was transferred elsewhere.

Meanwhile the RKM refused, in 1974, to continue with the
free distribution of saris. These distributions were extremely
popular, because a sari in the Dhaka market then cost the
equivalent of $5.50, although RKM was buying them in bulk
for one-third that price. Dr. Lotta had that year taken part in
several distributions and recorded: "I shall never forget the
pathetically torn garments in which the women stood in long,
long lines, under the beating sun, guarded by police to avoid
riots. It was all a terribly humiliating experience − more for me
than for the recipients, I believe."[5] The RKM had been investigating the needs of every recipient before handing out tickets
for free clothing, and this task was becoming both overwhelming
and dangerous, despite police protection during distribution.
So the service ceased, and to this day the smuggling of saris
across the border from India is a major nocturnal business.

The USC continued to support three medical centers established by RKM after a hesitant start because the mission wanted
a three-year commitment, which the agency eventually gave.
The center at Narayanganj, about twenty miles from Dhaka,
opened in March 1974 with three staff: Dr. Amitava Mondal, a
compounder, and a medical assistant. It was the only nonpaying

---

[4]Dr. Lotta indignantly called it "one of those unbelievable, unexplainable
Indian chicaneries that, with cholera and all kinds of other diseases rampant
in the country, they insist that Canadian clothing be fumigated, piece by
piece!" (Report to the board, April 1972).

[5]Report to the USC board, April 1974, p. 5.

dispensary in the area, and hundreds of outpatients would come with prescriptions from the local hospital to claim free drugs, purchased in India with USC funds. Dr. Mondal, like his counterparts at the other centers at Bagerhat and Dinajpur, worked long hours six days a week.

Dr. Lotta described watching him one day in March 1976, when he treated 300 patients. "Most are well known to our doctor. He takes one look at them, listens, prescribes, gives instructions, pats the children on the back, says a few words of encouragement – and the next patient takes his turn."[6] Under his desk he kept a big box of new and half-used tablets of soap that he gave to those most severely afflicted by scabies. The soap had been collected from hotels, motels, and homes across Canada by USC volunteers. Dr. Lotta recorded that in the past eight months Dr. Mondal had attended to no fewer than 38,661 ill adults and children.

It was heroic work; but, as with the RKM milk distribution, the emphasis was on numbers and relief measures. These early projects were treating the surface symptoms of poverty in Bangladesh and not reaching the root causes. Those concerned with development began to look elsewhere for projects to launch or support. Jeff Ramin made this point in his 1983 report on the RKM mobile clinics:

> ...the problems have not changed. Patient after patient was quickly diagnosed to be suffering from a combination of bowel disorders, due to drinking polluted water or poor sanitation, scabies due to poor hygiene and the lack of clean water, or respiratory problems due mainly to an unclean environment – smoke due to cooking fires in a confined area. Again, I could not help but feel we must do something to remove the root causes of these ailments. Fortunately we are now moving in this direction with our Rural Development Program.[7]

A final major frustration during the 1970s was that of finding the right person to be USC representative in Bangladesh. Mrs. Sarojini Aiyar, whose job as USC representative in India would end with the phase-out there in mid-1975, made a survey of Bangladesh projects the year before and suggested that women's groups needed more training before becoming part-

---

[6]*Jottings from my Bangladesh Diary*, April 1976, p. 4.
[7]*Survey of USC Program in Bangladesh*, 17 February 1983, p. 69.

ner agencies. The USC invited her to move to Dhaka in 1975, but she demurred and interested herself in Nepal, where she did become the representative in 1977 for a short time before having to retire to south India from illness. If she had chosen to move to Bangladesh, the USC might have faced an awkward situation. For by 1977, Bangladeshis, who five years earlier had called Indira Gandhi "the mother of our nation" for her part in its liberation, were seized with an anti-Indian sentiment that could have made Mrs. Aiyar feel unwelcome.

Fortunately, Dr. Lotta had by then come to know Mrs. Syeda Jahanara during a trip to Thakurgaon in northwest Bangladesh. Mrs. Jahanara had been running the Munshirat Women's Cooperative, a project for "women's uplift" funded by Lutheran World Service, which provided jobs and income for 150 women who were victims of the 1971 war, either widowed or outcast because of having been raped. It included a sewing section and smaller groups making products from jute and bamboo. She was also running a primary school for children of the workers. She was a social worker by training and had moved into these ventures after being asked to do a survey on poverty after the war – the area had been particularly devastated by troops. But when Dr. Lotta was introduced to her through Swami Yukta-nanda, the Lutheran World Service was about to cut off funding because its global budget had been virtually halved.

Dr. Lotta recognized another determined woman of action, and the USC found a new partner agency in the Munshirat Women's Cooperative. The sewing section had to be disbanded because the withdrawal of LWS support ended a supply of Norwegian materials, but in 1984 there were fifty women in the production units at Thakurgaon and twenty others taking training in various trades. A number of other women's production units in the district; for example, sixty women making garments in Mirzapur, thirty in Panchagarh doing sewing and jute work, were linked in a network she set up, and are now being integrated into the main rural development program.

In 1977 Mrs. Jahanara formally became the USC's representative in Bangladesh. The next few years also saw a growth of support for children's homes and orphanages, and the Bangladesh program proliferated. However, the launching of the Rural Development Program in 1982, to which we should now turn, offered an opportunity to give it a more orderly shape.

Devious route to RDP

Humayun Reza, whose name translates as "Lucky Agreeable," came to design the Rural Development Program (RDP) by a very roundabout route. His family had property in Rajshahi district, just east of the River Ganges about 320 kilometers from its mouth. But after Partition in 1947, his parents stayed on the Indian side, in West Bengal. Like many Bengalis, he grew up studying literature and writing poetry. One of his poems – "Basana" ("The Desire and Ambition") – was inspired by the great river. It was published in a Calcutta weekly around 1960, and this is an extract in translation:

> Let my mind be as clean
> As the vast water in the river.
> Let my heart broaden
> While I sit alone under the open sky
> On the river side.
> Let the broad blue sky
> Be reflected in my heart...
> O, Lord, make my heart
> The reflection of the world, thy creation,
> Make me closer to everyone...
> Let me feel I am of all.

In 1962 some of this cosmic togetherness was shattered by communal strife in West Bengal, in which many Moslems were killed. Humayun, still a student, hid for a time and then, on a winter night, swam a mile across the Ganges, a few clothes tied on his head. He walked to Rajshahi but found he could not recover the family land. So he moved to Thakurgaon and taught school while taking a commerce diploma in night school. When the liberation war began in March 1971, he was working as an insurance agent there. He bicycled down to Dinajpur, where the troops had killed many young men, to search for a younger brother and eventually found him barricaded in a house. They double-rode the bicycle out of town and then walked for thirty-six hours by devious trails to reach Bihar, fleeing from Moslems this time.

Humayun returned to Thakurgaon immediately after the Pakistani surrender and worked with the Lutheran World Service on relief to the homeless. He liked the Norwegian director, he says, but was never keen on relief work. He persuaded his director to put money into sericulture, his brother planted hundreds of mulberry trees, and they set up a silk factory to make cloth. It is now a government-run factory because Humayun decided he did not want to continue in business after joining USC part time in 1975. That was the year the USC took over the funding of Mrs. Jahanara's cooperatives from the Lutherans. Among other things, Humayun began the Jagarani Club, based on land near Thakurgaon, which includes a large fishpond and surrounding wheatland and orchard. Its aim has been to train young people for development projects and also build up some income, through projects and members' savings, to loan to other members.

It was still seven years before the Rural Development Program began with substantial USC funding ($187,275 in 1982). In those years, Humayun was looking at existing schemes and trying his own experiments with two small groups near Kushtia. He decided that the development schemes launched by the government's Rural Social Services unit lacked follow-up and monitoring. He was also sceptical about the strategy of the leaders of the Proshika movement (with which CUSO and later CIDA were deeply involved). He was impressed by their training programs but he could not accept their basic philosophy of a perpetual struggle by the landless people against landowners. Despite the rough times he himself had endured, he clung to a belief in reconciliation, a conviction that the landless and the smaller landowners could work together to everyone's benefit. But he realized that one had to produce swift results to cement such cooperation, and this required close management. He gave the Kushtia agricultural groups some clear guidelines on what he expected them to do and the methods to achieve it, and he used to pay three-day visits to them fairly often.

Focus on 50 million poorest

In January 1984, the Association of Development Agencies in Bangladesh (ADAB) organized, with USC backing, a national seminar in Dhaka under the title "Focus on 50 million: Poverty in Bangladesh." It prompted thoughtful speeches from (among others) the food minister and the agricultural minister, detailed research papers on rural employment and land use, some passionate statements about women and poverty and local power structures, and a great deal of frank conversation between Bangladesh officials, UN advisers, Catholic priests, NGO representatives, and CIDA officers. Many CIDA staff were also in Dhaka for a meeting on the second stage of the World Bank's Rural Poor Program in Bangladesh, to which the Canadian agency is contributing $20 million.

For a visitor like myself it was a treasury of information, and yet profoundly depressing. Humayun Reza was also there but very quiet. I soon realized that cities and seminars were not to his taste; he withdrew into himself and almost wilted. But as soon as it was over, and we set out on the eleven-hour journey by road and ferryboat and bumpier road to Thakurgaon and his beloved project, he blossomed again. It was during the next week of traveling with Humayun that I could put some of the seminar statistics into perspective and contrast the gloomier statements with the positive action being taken by some inspired people.

But first to the statistics, which illustrate what one Bangladesh document inventively termed "horripilating socio-economic conditions." During the 1970s, the population of Bangladesh increased by an average 2.6 percent a year, but food production increased by only 1.9 percent. The vast majority of the country's 95 million people still live in rural areas and depend on agriculture, crop production, and processing for a livelihood. Yet nearly two-thirds of the households are functionally landless; that is, they own less than half a hectare, and the land, which could be extremely productive with all the silt deposited by the great rivers in the flood season and the abundance of water for irrigation, yields a disappointing harvest. The average yield of rice per hectare, at 1.2 metric tons, is less than half that of Malaysia or Sri Lanka, for only about 20 percent of the crop land is sown with high-yielding varieties and even less is irrigated for a second (or third) crop.

The consequence is increasing poverty. Indeed, the title of the seminar was already out-of-date; many more than 50 million people were mired in poverty.

The problem is more easily stated than the solution. The reasons for this good land producing such a poor yield are interwoven. Landholdings, even for the middle-sized land-owner (from 1 to 10 hectares), are badly fragmented as they are divided and passed down generations. Typically, a 1.5-hectare farm would be in ten separate pieces, far too small to irrigate economically. Landowners do not spend money to improve their land when they can get better, or more immediate, returns from trade – or from moneylending at interest rates of up to 100 percent a year. The sharecroppers who lease land by the year (and about one-quarter of the land is cultivated by sharecroppers) rarely have any surplus money to improve their yields with fertilizer or better seed, especially as they have to give half their gross return to the landowner.

Because of the lack of an irrigated second crop, there is significant underemployment in agriculture; on average, a farmer works 185 days a year. Meanwhile landless women, who have derived much, if not most of their income from rice processing (for at least 15 percent of the total household income of landless families has come from traditional hulling and milling operations), are threatened by the increase of automatic rice mills.

So there is a downward spiral as the population increases, the land becomes more fragmented, landlessness spreads, and processing jobs decline. To cap it all, an extra 25 million men and women (equivalent to the total population of Canada) will be added to the country's labor force by the year 2000.

The government's response, to judge from speeches made at the seminar, can hardly be faulted. Dr. Muhiudin Khan Alamgir, joint secretary in the Ministry of Finance and Planning, set out a half-dozen indispensable steps towards lifting the weight of rural poverty. These steps begin with an expansion of irrigation and flood control works, progress through seven stages of land reform for the benefit of sharecroppers, and broaden out to embrace improved educational and health services, the supply of drinking water, and the encouragement of better nutrition and family planning. His steps also include "target-grouping the small farmers, sharecroppers, the landless labor [and] disadvantaged women" in order to mould each interest group into an effective production and marketing unit.

Dr. Alamgir was speaking of plans rather than achievements. Nevertheless, in 1984 the government took a substantial move towards addressing rural problems by decentralizing much of its administration, sending many officials out of Dhaka to work from some four hundred subdistrict offices. His list of government objectives in rural development contained many of the aims of the RDP, which is reassuring since contacts between USC Bangladesh and the government in its decentralized form are bound to increase.

The problem of rural poverty and its causes were not, of course, suddenly discovered during the 1984 seminar. For more than a decade, successive Bangladesh governments and NGOs had tried to tackle them in their different ways. Relief measures had dominated the first year after independence, and total aid commitments to Bangladesh amounted to more than $1.2 billion in 1972-73. Significantly, one-tenth of this came through voluntary organizations. Then the emphasis switched to development of a rather conventional sort, but halfway through the First Five-Year Plan, it was clear that the larger landowners were benefitting much more than the poor and landless.

From 1976, several NGOs began helping poor people to organize themselves into groups of ten to thirty members according to their socio-economic interests − fishermen's cooperatives, for example, or a group of rickshaw pullers. Proshika has helped form more than four thousand village groups and offered them technical training − like maintenance of irrigation equipment and vaccination of poultry − and more general courses in human development. The Mennonite Central Committee has proved, from pilot projects, that rural women with a minimum of capital equipment can market import-substitution products − desiccated coconut, and oil from sunflower seeds. And the Bangladesh Rural Advancement Committee (BRAC) has not only mounted training courses for younger village leaders and launched women's cooperatives but also published two detailed studies from its experiences, under the revealing titles *The Net: Power Structure in Ten Villages* and *Who Gets What and Why: Resource Allocation in a Bangladesh Village.*

Organize and reconcile

A particular USC contribution, under Humayun Reza (who is now deputy director of the whole USC Bangladesh operation under Mrs. Jahanara), has been to bring an expandable structure to these efforts, and to equip the poorest people with the means to work that structure. He insists on the improvement of an entire family, not just of individuals. He has taken ten (and sometimes eleven or twelve) families as the basic unit for a farming group, or a small business or industrial group; and he has picked out that number for several reasons. The primary reason for farming groups is that a household of six people can live off the produce of one well-farmed hectare, and a shallow tube well can provide enough water to irrigate four to five hectares.

Other reasons, applicable also to business and industrial groups, are that a ten-family unit is small enough to work as a team, to interact with each other, and yet large enough to cover a gap left by some member who is sick or temporarily absent. Put negatively, it is also small enough for members to keep an eye on each other, especially on the person responsible for communal loan funds. It is also a small enough group for a field worker to advise and supervise in a personal way, through weekly meetings. Finally, a larger structure can easily be built on this base: ten families in a development group, one hundred in a development block, up through a thousand (comprising a unit) and ten thousand to a peak of a hundred thousand families in a zone. This figure has not been reached yet, of course. In late 1984, a total of some twelve thousand families had become involved in the RDP, but a structure of this sort had been set up in three zones.

Humayun has also put into practice his belief in conciliation rather than confrontation. He says: "We are not creating any class conflicts. We hope to give poor people the opportunity to raise their living standard. And if the rich want to buy more land, we can't prevent it... When they work in agricultural farm, they will give their solvency and will also get the opportunity to buy lands combinedly, for the groups."[8]

The Proshika movement helps to organize groups that have the same socio-economic status – gathering the landless in one group, small landowners in another – because its leaders believe these classes have divergent interests, and the best each group can do is to learn to bargain with the local power elites separately. In contrast, Humayun has been working to bring the landless into the same ten-family groups as the small

---

[8]From the transcript of interviews made with Humayun Reza by Robert Lang, in preparation for the 27-minute film *Moving the Banyan Tree*, which he directed and produced in 1984 for Kensington Communications Inc.

landowners who have up to a hectare of land. In the process of negotiating with various landowners to assemble a four-hectare block from many fragments, a small landowner (or two or three) may be persuaded of the benefits of joining a group. The benefits are unequally shared, and Humayun's system is best explained by taking the example of an eleven-family group who started farming together in 1982 near the Indian border at Garialy.

Before this dry land was consolidated into a 4.5-hectare farm, it used to yield about fifteen maunds (about 550 kilograms) of paddy (rice in the husk) per .5 hectare. The landowners used to receive 50 percent of gross production from sharecroppers but they had to put in the primary investment as well as seeds and manure. Under the new arrangement made by USC field staff, landowners receive only 25 percent of gross production, but they actually receive more in value because their share comes from a greatly increased *aman* crop (rice harvested in December). And, they are not responsible for inputs and have no worries about supervision during the five years the agreement runs. The Garialy group, in 1982-83, planted a high-yielding variety of rice, and their total production, despite drought, was 660 maunds, or four times the previous average.

One member, Mafizuddin Ahmed, who owned one hectare, received income three ways. As a 25 percent share of the gross revenue from one hectare, he received 6,435 taka (24 taka = $1.00). He also earned wages of 1,000 taka as a working member of the group, and a one-twelfth share of the net profit (when wages, irrigation, and other costs had been deducted) which amounted to another 3,146 taka. So, in all he received 10,581 taka, or more than three times what he used to get from his separate hectare. The landless members of his group received their wages and a share of the net profit, amounting to 4,146 taka (or $172), which by Humayun's calculation is four times what they would have got from agricultural laboring. A second crop, of winter wheat, is now becoming popular in the area. Obviously, the group's profits will increase with a second, irrigated crop.

Why divide the net profit into twelve, when there are eleven members? The extra share is for the organization, to go towards running costs.

In January 1984, I walked under the mango trees of Garialy with the group leader and asked him if he would take back his

215

hectare and leave the group when the five-year agreement ended. After all, he would have learned some improved techniques, have built up a cash reserve, and might even have the tube well on his own land.

"Definitely not," said Mafiz.

"Why not?"

His answer surprised as well as reassured me. "Because I can go off, if I have to, to Thakurgaon for a few days' business and know that my land is being cared for." The group approach was definitely taking hold.

Perhaps, though, there may be divisions – and even conflicts – in another direction. Won't the groups want to buy and own the land outright, rather than lease it? And won't the landlords, realizing its enhanced value refuse? John Martin, a Bengali-speaking Canadian who was a priest in an Assam hill-station for years before joining CIDA's NGO division, has a cheering theory on this question. "I don't think land ownership is the issue," he said after touring Garialy and other groups. "It's land *use*. Once people have been farming the land to their mutual benefit, there's no way they will let it go." In other words, the five-year agreements will be (in another colorful phrase of Bengali English) "harmonically renewed."

Literacy first, loans later

Such groups could not operate effectively without members who are literate. Humayun has taken this requirement much further, though, by insisting that every member of a group should be literate and should also have contributed to a savings club for several months before the USC office makes a first loan. Only in that way, he says, can the members show a real commitment to the communal project and later keep a daily account of the group activities. During this preliminary period, his workers do a thorough study of family circumstances, to cope with their problems properly if they join a group. "All families are the laboratories of research," he says.

Humayun and other USC staff certainly showed an encyclo-pedic knowledge of many people I met in Thakurgaon zone in 1984 and they brought out this element of commitment. One morning we climbed a sandbank beside a small river to find fields of winter wheat growing on land that had lain fallow for decades. A Japanese pump was lifting river water to irrigate nine hectares that had been sown with *Sonalika* (golden) wheat from India. Under the roofs of two thatched huts, the heads of the twenty families in the two agricultural groups at Barunagaon were sitting on mats, working at literacy texts. It was surprising to find a ten-year-old boy with a shaven head among the greybearded men. Prafulla was still mourning the death of his father but was determined to take his father's equal place in the group, and he had been accepted.

The agricultural groups are still few in number, partly because it takes time to negotiate with landowners and to assemble blocks of land from fragments. In mid-1984, only 81 hectares were being farmed communally, but the idea of this system was spreading rapidly, and the acreage should increase sharply. There is, at present, a disproportionate number of recipients of business loans, compared with the number of food producers. One example is at Ekterpur in Kushtia zone, where there are two farms totaling 9.3 hectares, but some 250 other families are involved in other activities, including a weaving industry. In 1983 the farms suffered from heavy flooding and produced only half the expected yield. But, according to Gérard Holdrinet, the USC project officer who visited there later, "the setback resulted, if anything, in consolidation of the belief in a group approach to farming, both by the landowners and the group members."[9] The members were compensated with some reserve stocks from the previous harvest; the landowners realized they would have received even less without the groups' efforts.

The industrial and business groups operate under a system of incentives and obligations similar to that of the agricultural groups, whether they are weavers in Ekterpur, or women's groups involved in rice processing who rent drying ground and time on small mills. Like the landowner, the capital investor (in effect the USC-RDP, since it made the loans) receives 25 percent of the profit, and the remaining 75 percent is shared among the workers, with one share to RDP as service charge for supplying expertise and supervision. Holdrinet comments: "The RDP starts with the assumption that, in a production enterprise, human labor is the most important input, and is therefore entitled to the greatest share of profits."

---

[9]*Report on 1984 Survey of USC Program in Bangladesh*, p. 16.

217

There is strong pressure to expand the Rural Development Program rapidly, but there are obvious risks in doing so. A crucial factor in successful expansion will be the recruitment and training of young village leaders as development workers, and also the hiring of good senior staff. While RDP was still small, qualified staff could be found relatively easily. Among them have been Syed Mohammed Rashid, coordinating officer for Thakurgaon zone, with an MA in Social Work. Several others are similarly qualified. And Humayun's skillful leadership – listening, cajoling, inspiring – has been a central factor in persuading villagers to organize themselves. But Gérard Holdrinet strikes a timely warning. As RDP grows, he writes, "the ability of one individual to incite people in villages to change their ways will necessarily diminish, and the program will be faced with the constant challenge of ensuring that the ideas that underlie it are properly transmitted to an ever increasing number of competent field workers and organizers."

To meet this central need, a USC Training Institute was built on the outskirts of Thakurgaon in 1983-84. It is an impressive building, fifty-three meters long, with a second floor to serve as a students' residence and the ground floor housing classrooms and administration offices. An architect, M.A. Mannan, who is on the USC Bangladesh Advisory Committee, designed it using his own form of prestressed concrete, with which he has pioneered the building of several major bridges. The institute, together with the establishment nearby of a four-hectare demonstration farm, is the firmest evidence that USC has moved fully into the role of an implementing agency in Bangladesh.

The first group of 29 trainees, chosen from more than 1,500 applicants, began three months of courses in January 1984. They had twenty subjects in their packed program, ranging from practical subjects like poultry-keeping, sanitation, and family accounting to less tangible topics: moral education, behavioural science, and "The Doctrine of USC Canada/Bangladesh." The center will train up to 120 of these community leaders a year, each of them capable of motivating and organizing a hundred families. What was noticeable with the first group was an imbalance of three men to one woman. It has been difficult to recruit women from the villages where RDP is operating who have the required educational qualifications. It is obviously important to correct this imbalance.

It is difficult to sum up the Rural Development Program at this early stage. Too much could be claimed for it, and yet it has fired the enthusiasm of many people in Bangladesh. Equally, it has attracted support from CIDA of more than $1 million over three years, making a total budget (with local and direct USC contributions) of $2,149,000 from 1983-84 to 1985-86. Let Gérard Holdrinet's careful phrases be my summary, for they emphasize the human element:

> If RDP (as an integrated development program) is to bring about enduring changes in rural Bangladesh, it will be much more as a result of its ability to attract competent and honest staff willing to work with the poor rather than to its capacity to provide tubewells, latrines, high-yield agricultural inputs etc...RDP is, in a very real way, a two-tiered program. One of its functions is to bring about, in a relatively short time, a measurable improvement in the physical quality of life of the poorest...It is also a program of attitude change and of awakening people to their own potential, as individuals and as members of the community.
>
> The program is having a very strong impact upon people's lives wherever it is present, and the example of recent successes...is having repercussions that go far beyond the narrow limits of the relatively small number of villages where the RDP is in action.

Briefly in Cyprus

The Turkish military invasion of Cyprus in July-August 1974, following the abortive coup of Greek Cypriot extremists against Archbishop Makarios, brought a huge refugee crisis to the island. When the Turkish troops occupied 40 percent of the island, two hundred thousand Greek Cypriots lost or left their homes and fled south below the "green line" drawn by UN peacekeeping forces. Displacements of families who had survived in small enclaves in the northern part were still continuing in early 1977. In March 1977, Dr. Lotta witnessed a group of refugees arrive in trucks at the Nicosia headquarters of the Cyprus Red Cross. They had mostly been prosperous farmers or business people before being uprooted in the middle of the night and forced to leave everything behind. She wrote: "For the first time in all my many years of assisting refugees, I firmly believe that those who suffer most on Cyprus are not the children, but the very old...The little ones will forget, adults will adjust, but the old can only cry."[10]

The USC board was extremely cautious about starting any refugee program on Cyprus, for old or young. Dr. Lotta's persuasiveness was such that a small program ran for three years. But by 1979 the board, pressed by the Long Range Planning Group, had asserted its view that the number of countries should be held down to the six in Asia and southern Africa. Dr. Lotta was not pleased and questioned the decision. The program, however, was closed down in 1980.

It had mainly consisted of shipments of clothing (22,680 kilograms in both 1977 and 1978 – "dark colors for the old are a must"), uniforms for refugee children in primary schools', and sponsorship of sixty children at Dassoupolis School. These children's parents were either dead or refugees working at makeshift jobs, and the children were collected by school bus in late morning to go to classes after the regular ones had finished. It was the only time USC used a school, rather than a children's home, as the vehicle for the Foster Parent program.

Dr. Lotta kept returning to the matter of the elderly refugees. In 1978 she launched a "black shawl" project in Montreal and Toronto, and in 1979, after visiting an old people's home in Nicosia built with Rotary funds, she proposed the sponsorship of fifty old men and women at thirty-six dollars a month, more than double the rate for the schoolchildren. The board was not in favor, and the proposal was dropped.

In this short period, however, a good relationship had been forged with the Cyprus Red Cross and its remarkable president, Mrs. Stella Soulioti, a lawyer who had been both justice minister and health minister. When Mrs. Soulioti rebuilt the Sick Children's Hospital in Nicosia, the USC supported her effort with twenty-five thousand dollars for physiotherapy and other equipment. She reminded Dr. Lotta of that powerful lady of Madras, Mrs. Mary Jadhav: "the only difference between these two women is that Mrs. Soulioti is an excellent organizer." Certainly she accepted the USC withdrawal with more equanimity. And indeed, through hard work and good organization, the Cypriot government and people have solved the refugee problem with impressive new housing estates. Nicosia has taken over many of the financial roles once performed by Beirut.

---

[10]*Jottings*, March 1977, p. 3.

Solar heating and direct overseas dialing are the symbols of the Cyprus of today. The USC's place was elsewhere.

Nepal: beyond single-need projects

Nepal is a quite different story. It has its own, unacknowledged, refugees; hill people who have moved south to settle in the *terai*, the flat lowlands of the Gangetic plain, in hopes of a better, less arduous life. But poverty is not so easy to escape. Basic health statistics about Nepal and its population of 14.5 million are appalling. Life expectancy at birth is still only forty-five years, 9 percent of the population has access to safe water, the chances of a baby living to five are not much better than even. To take a typical village, Lubhu, where USC has funded projects: of 1,137 young children who were contacted in a household nutrition survey, only 422 were considered healthy. The rest, 63 percent of the under-fives, were either malnourished or severely malnourished, and the village's drinking water came from unprotected wells and a polluted river.

Education figures are little better. The literacy rate among adults is 20 percent, which is double what it was in 1960. Primary school enrollment has bounded up in the last twenty years − for boys. There are three times as many boys as there are girls in the schools. Lubhu itself has an unusual range of institutions for a village: four primary schools, one middle school, one high school, and a college, built in 1981, for students doing the equivalent of Grades 11 and 12. But − a lesson here, perhaps − there seems to have been no particular improvement of the people's everyday lives from having these establishments amongst them. Rather, the school leavers have tended to head off for Katmandu in the hope of finding a decent job.

When, therefore, the USC made its first survey in Nepal in 1976, looking for a new program to replace the one phased out in India, it was natural that the agency should move towards projects involving the provision of safe drinking water and the training of women for productive jobs other than in agriculture. But, as Dr. Lotta found to her dismay, the business of linking up with partner agencies and agreeing together on certain projects − the way she had worked for twenty years in India − was new to Nepalese authorities.

Until 1977 all aid funds, whether from governmental or nongovernmental organizations, were channeled through the finance ministry. Then the Social Services National Coordination Council (SSNCC) was set up, under the patronage of the Queen and the direction of a retired civil servant with a background in cottage industries. USC and other foreign donors were restricted to supporting projects proposed by local organizations and approved by the council. Moreover, under a formal agreement signed in 1980, it was stipulated that any local representative selected by USC Canada needed to have the approval of the council. In effect, the council and its director, Mr. C.B. Gurung, had far-reaching control over NGO projects and personnel.

It is a system that might work well if there existed in Nepal a few local organizations as imaginative as, say, KHI in India or Dian Desa in Indonesia. But that was too much to expect of Nepal in the 1970s. Small local organizations, understandably, had short horizons and put up requests to the council for projects that addressed a single need – water supply, school construction, a bridge – and usually involved only one year's work. For a donor agency, therefore, there was minimal contact or continuity, and a feeling of some inadequate patchwork being done.

A few figures and examples illustrate this. In 1980 the USC was supporting sixteen projects with total funds of $154,679, and in 1984 the figures had increased to thirty-seven projects with $351,113, but in both cases they were nearly all small projects with an average cost of less than $10,000. The largest projects in 1984-85 consisted of support for two children's homes and 165 children, taking up 18 percent of the total budget.

Sixteen other projects are worthy attempts to generate income for women and young people (and in three cases, the blind or mentally retarded) with schemes for weaving, cap making, candle production, fish cultivation, and other small businesses. They mostly face difficulties that do not exist, or have been overcome, in a country like Bangladesh. In particular, there is not the same network of transportation and markets in Nepal. A Mothers' Club group making sweaters in Katmandu has found big problems in marketing, perhaps because its workshop is in a place remote from tourists or even passers-by. Another Mothers' Club group, at Dang in the *Terai*, has been making honey and selling it over the border in India, but may not find a market in Katmandu because of high transport costs.

Some projects have just plain bad luck. Mrs. Shanti Parajuli, by all accounts a skilled organizer, rented a room in Katmandu and got nine women enthusiastically making two hundred candles a day during three hours' work; as an extra incentive she gave them sewing lessons. She confidently expected a strong market for candles in Katmandu because of the frequency of blackouts, but, as Jeff Ramin noted in 1984, "this project is suffering from a lack of power failures...this year the capital's power supply has been more regular, and the candle business is hurting."[11] Undaunted, Mrs. Parajuli looked elsewhere for more benighted customers, and the USC supported her for a further half-year.

Most of the water supply projects – and there were sixteen of them in 1984-85 – are gravity systems by which water is piped down to a village reservoir from an unpolluted source, and communal taps are installed at several points. At least half the cost is often covered by the local contribution of labor and materials. Some projects are quite complicated, as in Gairi village in the hills outside Katmandu, where three different springs were tapped, six kilometers of pipe laid, and some twenty-four people gained clean water for drinking and for their kitchen gardens. They also organized a small monthly collection from every household to pay a maintenance man.

The next step, which only a few villages have taken, is to use the piped water for community development. One example is Salmitar village, whose four hundred people now get water piped across a deep gorge. Previously, the women had to climb down and then up this steep gorge to get water from the river which was, at that level, polluted. The villagers, who hail from Tibet and are of a low caste that had been consigned to marginal land and subsistence farming, have begun to prosper. For they are also irrigating twenty hectares of village land for rice and wheat and have been able to increase the number of their cows.

Both these projects were steered by Mr. S.S. Thapa of the Sanatan Dharma Sewa Samati, one of the liveliest local organizations in Nepal. The energetic Mr. Thapa has had more ambitious plans with water. In particular, water pumped up from

---

[11]*Report on 1984 Survey of USC Program in Nepal*, 28 March 1984, p. 36.

the Roshi River to the village of Pasthali, forty kilometers east of Katmandu, will irrigate thirty-five hectares of good soil for two annual crops of wheat and rice. Mr. Thapa hopes to organize group farming on this land, following the pattern of the RDP in Bangladesh. It will be a first attempt at applying the RDP system, with interest-free loans following the group's commitment to literacy classes and a savings program.

Whether some of the production groups in Nepal can fit the same system of self-improvement, after being supported by business loans, is another question still to be addressed. Perhaps the best prospects exist for women's groups who gather to make two kinds of popular Nepali snack food, *papad* and *titaura*, from vegetables mixed with lentils. Unlike sweaters or carpets, there is a strong and reliable demand for these foods, and the almost ubiquitous Mothers' Club has a fine distribution network.

To move to integrated community development from single-need projects requires local organizations with imagination. It also requires, at another level, encouragement from someone who can bring in ideas from outside. Mrs. Nirmala Pokharel, who became USC representative in Nepal in 1978, has prevailed on the council to accept that she will travel widely in order to survey local needs and to help put new programs together. This was a substantial advance, but Mrs. Pokharel is a woman of persistence, with a sense of humor that helps in a situation demanding patience. She was secretary of a cooperative that ran the Tara Gaon Hotel where Mrs. Aiyar stayed during the months when she was USC's representative in Nepal, and through her became involved as a USC volunteer. When Mrs. Aiyar had a heart attack and returned to India, Dr. Lotta came to interview her for the job of representative. Nirmala, who was not then married, recalls the scene:

> She asked me: "Do you smoke? Do you like drinking? Do you love your country? Do you plan to marry?" I gave the right answers, and went round projects with her, giving her so many facts she called me "my little book". Later I married my husband, who is a travel agent, and she was very much annoyed. So I invited her to supper, and also my mother-in-law, who was on the king's standing committee... After that, it was all right.

Nirmala Pokharel, tiny figure that she is, has a way of overcoming problems and should never be underestimated. My feeling is that the USC program in Nepal is about to come together in an interesting and productive way.

CHAPTER 11

Southern Africa

Triplets with differences

THERE IS A TEMPTATION to treat the three independent states
in southern Africa — Botswana, Lesotho, and Swaziland — as
though they are some kind of triplets, not identical but with
many of the same characteristics. There are certainly superficial
similarities. Their recent history put them under British
"protection" for nearly a century, until Botswana and Lesotho
became independent in 1966 and Swaziland in 1968. They are
in a customs union with South Africa and economically dominated by that republic in varying degrees. They shared a single
university for a time and still maintain academic and other
links.

But the differences are important, especially for an agency
wanting to help in their development, as the USC did in 1971.
In physical terms, Botswana is large — the size of France — and
there are remote communities and remoter cattle posts towards
the Kalahari Desert and away from "the line of rail" that runs
along its southeast part from Mafikeng to Bulawayo. Lesotho
has its remote communities too, up in the cold Drakensberg
Mountains. The country is no larger than Vancouver Island,
but in 1982 Gilles Latour described a 2½ days' journey by
Landrover and on horseback to reach the village of Malibamatso
and a school construction site — "the most awe-inspiring trip I
have ever taken in the course of my USC work." At the same
time, there is a cohesiveness among Lesotho's 1.5 million
people. For example, in 1984 hundreds of poultry farmers,
even from the far northern villages, crammed into buses to
celebrate the opening of another egg circle, a producers'
cooperative, at Qacha's Nek.

Swaziland is different again. The size of Wales, and described
by Dr. Lotta as "the African Switzerland," it has had a good
system of roads — at least, until Cyclone Damoina devastated
the country in 1984. Sloping down to the Indian Ocean, much
of its land is subtropical, and the people there are vulnerable to

cholera, typhoid and malaria, which the Basotho people, in their mountains, escape.

In human terms, there are striking differences. The women of Lesotho have played a leading role because so many of the males are absent; as boys they are off herding their sheep and miss school, as men they go to work in the mines and farms of South Africa. Botswana has been affected less than Lesotho by the migration to the mines and has had to face the problems of school leavers and youth unemployment sooner. The launching of the brigades system in 1967 was a brave attempt to produce a non-élitist alternative to formal education, combining some further schooling with skills training and production. In 1984 Gérard Holdrinet wrote: "In spite of the many serious problems faced by brigades in all parts of Botswana, these nevertheless remain the most viable village-based, community-owned development organizations in the country."

Swaziland has remained, for outsiders, a much more closed, sometimes almost impenetrable, society. Since the death in 1982 of King Sobhuza, who ruled for sixty years, the political situation has become even more confusing because of a power struggle in the royal family and rivalry between queen regents. Back in 1977, Dr. Lotta was so frustrated by the lack of response from Swazi officials that she urged an immediate phase-out, and was only dissuaded by board members who argued that in a few years Swaziland would recognize a need for the kind of development USC might support. And, in spite of the cloudy politics, this has happened.[1]

These differences, and the difficulties that Dr. Lotta and the USC project officers who visited later found in getting projects going, have pointed up the need to have local USC offices and energetic representatives on the spot in all three countries. By 1984 this had been achieved through the recruitment of three young women with impressive backgrounds: Mrs. Maletele Khalikane in Lesotho, Thabisile Mngadi in Swaziland, and most recently, Thantshi Masitara in Botswana.

---

[1]In 1972 Dr. Lotta canvassed the idea of starting a program in Malawi but was disconcerted to find it was illegal to disseminate information about family planning there. She dropped any idea of a program after Malawi authorities canceled a visit she was planning in 1976. In 1972, also, the PAC suggested a survey of needs in Upper Volta, but a trip was never made.

Lotta

The gum trees of Botswana

The program in Botswana began in a familiar pattern, with USC support for health services, education, and training. Dr. Lotta was struck by the overcrowding and lack of equipment in what schools there were (and there were only eleven secondary schools in 1971). In the yard of a primary school in the capital Gaborone, where classes were on a shift system, she watched children learning the basics of arithmetic by "squatting on the ground, each with two little holes in the sand...lifting little sticks of wood and green tiny apples in unison from one pile to the other, waiting until a classroom would become available to do other lessons such as writing at a much-shared desk..."[2]

So a good deal of early USC funding, in both Botswana and Lesotho, went to the construction and equipping of (mostly rural) schools, and to the provision of secondary school scholarships for the brightest of the needy students. This flow continues, although in smaller proportion to other projects. To the question of how far the provision of formal education contributes to rural development, Holdrinet wrote in 1984 that

> school projects do have some singular advantages over other types of development. First of all, they...can be brought to fruition with a minimum of ongoing supervision. Also, in spite of the doubts regarding the pertinence of formal education to rural people, it remains true that some formal education is better than none... Although the so-called "formal" sector of the economy only employs about 20 percent of the labor force,...nearly every person working in the formal sector will contribute, in the form of remittances within the country, to the upliftment of his or her relatives in a rural Botswana. Secondly, one must assume that...better education means better jobs.[3]

The opposite of this "trickle-down" development is to be found in the brigades system. By 1972 Patrick van Rensburg, the prime mover behind the brigades, had sadly to acknowledge that Swaneng Hill School and others which he had founded with a reformed syllabus to inculcate a spirit of commitment among students, were nevertheless producing young people with a taste for privilege and senior government

---

[2]*Jottings from Africa*, February 1971.

[3]*Report on 1984 Survey of USC-funded Projects in Botswana*, February 1984, p. 7.

posts. So he turned all his inventive energy to the brigades, especially in Serowe. In 1978 there were seventeen different Serowe brigades, from farmers to potters and tanners, and from machinists to dam-builders and bookkeepers. He has written: "The Serowe brigades have demonstrated beyond any doubt the feasibility of creating substantial new resources in the process of training and education... Costs can be recovered almost completely in most of the training activities, and indeed a surplus can be achieved in some, and this has been achieved without necessarily lowering standards."[4]

While Serowe was the model for the brigade system, it has naturally taken different forms in various parts of Botswana. The USC's longest connection has been with the Kweneng Rural Development Association (KRDA), for in 1972 it began supporting an afforestation project. The object was to show that eucalyptus trees could be grown in the semiarid climate of Molepolole, northwest of Gaborone, which has an average annual rainfall of forty-three centimeters. KRDA had begun three years earlier as a discussion group, initiated by the community development officer, David Inger, to present resolutions on community development to the district council. It soon began to take some matters into its own hands, starting a handicrafts center and then a builders' brigade, an engineering works, a dressmakers' workshop, a small hotel – and a forestry unit.

The first eight-hectare plot of eucalyptus, including the tall "Lotta Tree" she had planted, was ready for harvest in 1979. In five years USC contributed $130,000 to what was a pioneering effort in Botswana, for in 1984 the government still did not have a single qualified forester of its own (some were training in Tanzania), and the Forestry Association of Botswana had just been formed by a number of government officials and development group members. By then KRDA had planted more than 250,000 trees in four plantations totaling 240 hectares and had a large nursery of seedlings for other brigades' forestry projects, as well as acting as a resource center for advice and assistance.

Because of KRDA's achievement in forestry and USC's associ-

---

[4]Patrick van Rensburg, *The Serowe Brigades; Alterntive Education in Botswana*, Macmillan, London: 1978. van Rensburg's earlier book, *Report from Swaneng Hill*, published by the Dag Hammarskjöld Foundation, is another important contribution to the subject of education for development.

ation with it (together with several CUSO foresters), the agency was asked to help the projects of other brigades: another eucalyptus woodlot near Mochudi, and other projects in western Kweneng and Kanye districts towards the Kalahari Desert. Sensibly, these schemes have several objects in addition to forestry – among them, beekeeping, gameskin tanning, building-block production – and the USC has helped in many ways, providing vehicles or irrigation equipment, paying for some salaries or storage facilities.

The USC also supported other community groups that had ideas for solving problems. For example, six villages around Pitsani are so close to the Lobatsi abattoir that their land is overgrazed by cattle being driven in and held there. The villagers also find their trees and bushes being taken for firewood by the cattlemen, and the dust area increasing. The six villages grouped together behind a plan to reclaim their land for crops. A first step has been to establish demonstration gardens with crops grown both traditionally and with improved techniques. These techniques include measuring the use of water in planting wind-resistant shrubs and fast-growing trees for fuelwood.

Many problems haunt the brigades and community groups. In Gérard Holdrinet's words,

> From their beginnings in the late 1960s, brigades have been plagued by their double mandate, as many groups have found that training and profit making do not always go hand in hand. If a brigade group is successful as a business enterprise, it can be criticised for its weak training component. Conversely, groups with too much emphasis on training [have constantly to seek] financial assistance to keep the entire operation afloat.

As well, the hasty replacement (known as "localization") of expatriates with Batswana managers has produced some problems of incompetence. One brigade group had the misfortune to hire a coordinator who neglected to tell his trustees that he was about to stand trial on charges of cattle theft. As well, capable managers are soon offered better-paid jobs elsewhere. The USC has for some years supported three-month training courses in cooperative management by covering the salaries of trainees while they are absent from their societies. But of the forty-three trainees who took the course in 1983, nearly half (and probably the best) of them left their cooperatives within a few months for jobs in government or the private sector. The consolation is that they should be better managers, wherever they go. Nonetheless, brigades and cooperatives suffer from a shortage of skilled management.

These are predictable problems in the development of a small nation-state. The Batswana people are resilient enough to overcome such obstacles, just as they may be expected to rebound from the devastating and enervating effects of the long drought they were suffering in the mid-1980s.

Lesotho: erosion and egg circles

Life has never been easy for the Basotho people in recorded history. Since they retreated east of the Caledon River into the mountains in the face of the Afrikaner "freebooters" who pushed their way into what is now the Orange Free State, they have lived on the sidelines of development. Only one-eighth of the country is arable, and most of that land lies along the western border.

The situation has hardly improved in recent years. The Basotho men alleviated their poverty by going to the diamond and gold mines of South Africa as migrant laborers, and even to work on the farmlands which their ancestors had once possessed. Now, black South Africans want those jobs, and instead of 60 percent of the labor force going as migrant workers to the republic and providing a large share of Lesotho's national income in remittances, these men will remain at home on a land of dwindling resources.

The resources are dwindling because population growth is already high at 2.3 percent (and will presumably rise with more men at home), and because the farmland has become badly eroded over the last fifty years. In the 1930s a prolonged drought destroyed much of the vegetation, and violent rains later washed away topsoil. Thousands of gullies, which were then created, have expanded over the years, and overgrazing by cattle and goats has speeded the process. Deforestation and the fact that few farmers terrace their land are further causes of erosion. The punishing drought of the last four years has added further to the basic problem, and since 1974 the country's need for food aid has tripled, to forty-four thousand metric tons in 1984.

There are many ways to respond to this deteriorating situation, and the USC has tried to help in several. One is the most direct course of controlling the gullies (or *dongas*) and reclaiming the land, work that the Ministry of Rural Development is now organizing through its Soil Conservation section. The USC has been funding a large manual effort at Masite, in a medium-size valley. Some five hundred workers were brought in on a Food for Work program to build thick stone walls across the *dongas* with the help of village volunteers. USC funds of twenty-one thousand dollars went to pay for wheelbarrows, pickaxes, and other tools. Silt will pile up behind the walls, and then quick-growing *kikuyu* grass can be seeded. Another technique, used where enough soil remains, is to collapse the sides of the *dongas* into gentle slopes, and plant trees. The USC is also funding courses on soil conservation for school teachers at the Lesotho Agricultural College, leading to widespread community efforts at land reclamation.

Another direct course is through planting forests and fruit trees in the thin topsoil of mountain areas. The forests of cypress, cedar and pine are needed for hut construction and also fuelwood, as villagers are now reduced to burning cow-dung instead of using it to fertilize their farmland. One such forestry project has started at Semongkong under a Canadian priest, Father Latremouille, and all the primary schools in these isolated areas are receiving seedlings with which to start their own woodlots.

What the military might call a flanking attack on the land problem has been the growth of "egg circles" in many communities around Lesotho. The USC has supported these producer cooperatives from their earliest days, and it has probably been the agency's most effective contribution to the country so far. Poultry farming was popularized by the government in the mid-1960s, to improve levels of nutrition among villagers and to provide income for women. By 1976, according to Dr. Gordon Merrill, there were 1,450 chicken farmers in Lesotho, and many of the women had five hundred or more. He quotes the typical case of a Mrs. Maitia of the Teyateyaneng egg circle, who was making a profit of forty rand (then fifty dollars) a week as a chicken farmer.[5]

[5]*Report to the USC board*, March 1976, p. 5.

USC's contribution so far has been to pay for construction of stores and equipment – refrigeration, grading instruments, and storage facilities – in more than a dozen places where the producers' association has built a depot from which to sell eggs on a year-round basis. The Lesotho government has supported these efforts strongly, and the country has become almost self-sufficient in eggs through a network of these depots. It has meant a considerable investment by USC, but the large donors were not interested in supporting what to them (in Gilles Latour's words) are "piddling little efforts." So the agency's help has been essential.

Two brief accounts of the opening of new egg circles will illustrate the enthusiasm they fire. Charles Gray wrote of being the guest of honor when the Butha Buthe egg circle was officially opened in February 1978: "There were delegations from every egg circle in Lesotho, and the prime minister's wife turned up unexpectedly. She put on the traditional poultry producer's white coat and blended in with the crowd. There was a great deal of enthusiasm shown for the USC."[6]

Gilles Latour writes more dramatically about a 1984 opening at Qacha's Nek:

It is difficult to describe the excitement and pride that these events created throughout the country. Small egg producers from as far away as the northern districts of Leribe and Butha Buthe...spent as much as two full days in crammed buses, travelling over hazardous roads to meet in Qacha's Nek for a truly rousing celebration...It had the makings of a revival meeting with singing, hollering, tooting and dancing and of a political meeting with an endless roster of speakers drawing cheers and jeers from the festive crowd. The celebration went long and hard into the night....[7]

The broadest approach to the development crisis – for it is nothing less – facing Lesotho lies in education, and it is "education" used in the widest sense. That includes awareness of problems, identification of some solutions, and a willingness to take part in trying to solve them. This type of education starts in secondary school, and in December 1983 there were only ninety-six secondary schools in the whole country. Most of these are boarding schools run by missions, and the fees are

[6]*Report to the USC board,* April 1978, p. 1.
[7]*Report on USC Program in Lesotho,* February 1984, p. 58.

beyond the reach of poor families. From the outset, USC has been sponsoring such students through its Foster Parent scheme, and today, scholarships of $375 a year are helping 120 students in Lesotho, 100 in Botswana, and 60 in Swaziland.

There remains the question whether many of these projects can be drawn together into a form of integrated community development similar to the RDP in Bangladesh.

After looking closely at the program in Bangladesh and the situation in Lesotho and Swaziland, Gilles Latour concluded that "while [the RDP] can be an inspiration,...little more than the general approach can be transferred and translated into African terms."[8] For example, in contrast to Bangladesh, most people in Lesotho have their own land and are literate. As well, there is more of a network of government and NGO extension work at village level, so there is not the same need to train development workers as prompted the establishment of the center at Thakurgaon in Bangladesh. Finally, rural development has to be based on communities, rather than on small groups of ten or twelve families.

The hope, however, is to move towards integrated community development (ICD) in Lesotho and Swaziland, while respecting these differences, and make them the mainstay of the whole country program of the USC. A first step was taken in Lesotho in 1982, when the villagers of Ha Sets'abi wanted to improve their creaky system of water supply (basically, a pump that frequently broke down). With USC funds, they built a large water tank for the community and dug a borehole. The entry-point to development, it may be noted, is exactly the same as Dian Desa has found in Indonesia: water supplies. From there, thirty-four families in the small village moved to form an agricultural cooperative, farming 49 hectares with successive crops of maize, beans, and peas. They are proud of the way they covered the costs of tractor-ploughing, fertilizer and the rest, in contrast to nearby farmers who were enrolled in the government's Food for Self-Sufficiency Program and who pay nothing.

They also plan to cooperate in raising pigs and chickens, making cement blocks and running a store, and in 1984 they planted five hundred eucalyptus trees on a slope above the

---

[8]*Report on USC Program in Lesotho*, February 1978, p. 13.

village to control erosion. They suffered badly from crop failure in the drought, and the USC paid off some current debts and provided eleven thousand dollars for a revolving fund that can be used for future drought relief.

This example of taking broad initiatives at Ha Sets'abi has led to a more ambitious experiment being launched in 1984 with the 240 families of Majaheng village, in Berea district. Again, water and agriculture are the first priorities the people mention in a needs assessment survey. The university's Institute of Extra-Mural Studies has been active in training and supervision, as it had been at Sets'abi, but the villagers have taken the lead in organizing themselves into various committees – school, agricultural, water – to tackle problems communally. Building a one-room schoolhouse, planting a woodlot of sixteen thousand trees, were two early results. USC funds will take the ICD project further, with boreholes and a tractor.[9] If the project is successful at Majaheng, its expansion can follow in parts of the district where the same chief has responsibility.

Swaziland: change and the cyclone

A similar movement has begun in Swaziland. The Swazi tradition has been for families to maintain isolated homesteads surrounded by their own fields. But this tradition is being reversed as families group together to organize basic services: water, health, schools. Sometimes the focal point for the regrouping is a school, where people begin meeting and forming functional committees. Sometimes it is a clinic at a mission station, like St. Philip's Mission in the low-veld area, where cholera and malaria add to the hardships of a subsistence life.

One strand of this movement is the development of farmers' associations to cooperate in irrigating their lands for a second, or even a third, crop. The Ministry of Agriculture and Cooperatives has recently helped set up several farmers' cooperatives, with which it shares the cost of irrigation. Two of the most

---

[9]The issue of tractors versus oxen comes up frequently in these countries. Two reasons are advanced for the replacement of oxen: many have died for lack of grazing, especially during the drought, and they do not plough deeply enough or fast enough to catch the spring rainfall and to retain the most moisture.

successful – both in terms of crops and farmers' contributions – have been at Phophonyane and Ntamakuphila, and they are now moving to the stage of wanting their own tractor in order to complete their ploughing and ridging in time for this intensive farming. USC's part has been to underwrite the bank loans for the farmers (who are not "established" customers in the eyes of bank managers). This will form a revolving fund, so that when the two cooperatives have repaid their loans to the bank, there will be enough money to underwrite a third tractor loan.

In two other villages – Bulunga and Asiphilisane – the USC has been helping community projects since 1980. But, as Latour quickly concedes, "they have mostly developed haphazardly, from year to year, without following a plan clearly endorsed by a majority of the local population."[10] Actually, the successful efforts at Bulunga have added up to a well-rounded contribution and can retrospectively be called "integrated community development." But it was not planned that way in this remote village of grass huts. The string of projects involved all ages – children keeping a bean patch, women planting a communal vegetable garden, men using high quality seeds and building a storage shed. A tractor was bought, and the government joined in by sending teachers to the new primary school and an agricultural officer, and by providing a road instead of a track to this hilltop community. The road was wiped out by the cyclone in January 1984, but the spirit of cooperation survived, to judge from the pantomime performance put on by farmers for Gilles Latour in their shed soon afterwards.

> The women had prepared a few sketches to dramatize the development of their organization and the help received from USC. The pantomime, accompanied by song and dance, celebrated cooperation and collective work. It dramatized the situation of one person in difficulty who discovers the advantages of joining the group... Another sketch illustrated the hard work involved in fetching water in past days and the new reality, all done very humorously. A third sketch showed the problems of farmers when they had to plough with oxen (the oxen teams were played by women moving about on all-fours on the floor of the shed) and the process by which the farmers discussed their needs, got together and asked for help.

---

[10]*1984 Report on USC Program in Swaziland*, p. 10.

[They indicated] the advantages which came with the tractor and the gratitude they feel.

This form of popular theatre, all done with few accessories, much good humor and deep conviction, was more eloquent than any report or documentary which could have been assembled on this project.... No project imposed from the outside could have generated so spontaneously this type of popular expression."[11]

In the same way as at Bulunga and Asiphilisane, a number of projects within a 30 kilometer radius of St. Philip's Mission in Lubombo district have touched nearly every aspect of community life: sanitation, gardening, sewing activities, carpentry work, schooling, training, and larger-scale farming through irrigation. The women in that area show a pride in the solid advances made in their tough struggle against disease and poverty. One slide shown by Gilles on his fund-raising tour that usually raises a sympathetic laugh from Canadians is of some of these Swazi ladies standing in a field around a toilet, complete with wooden seat, that is mounted on a concrete slab. Well may they be proud! They had by then installed more than one thousand such latrines over pits lined with stones. In an area where cholera is a threat, this was an important step towards better health.

As well, the mission clinic, under the energetic Sister Raphael Sharkey, is the center of much activity. A government doctor visits twice a month, malaria and TB control officers call, and the clinic itself operates four outreach clinics in a seventy-kilometer radius, with a team of three nurses or midwives touring the countryside. Some three thousand patients are seen every month at the mission or at these clinics. Until 1984 the mission had only a pickup van to do this work and take the sick to hospital. But now, with USC funds, the nursing sisters have a mobile clinic ambulance.

The isolation of such places was highlighted after Cyclone Damoina had blown the countryside into near chaos in January 1984, destroying (among other things) many bridges. St. Philip's Mission was cut off for weeks. When Gilles and the lively USC representative, Thabisile Mngadi, eventually reached it by roundabout routes and sought the way to some outlying projects, they found themselves fording a river on foot "only

---

[11]*1984 Report on USC Program in Swaziland*, p. 23.

half reassured by Sister Sharkey's promise that there were no crocodiles in the immediate area."

Coordinating these diverse efforts of community development began about 1982, when Sister Sharkey made Gilles' visit the occasion to gather all the groups together for a general consultation and the presentation of a list of requests for assistance that had been coordinated. But this still falls short of a real community plan to deal with their problems.

The prospect for truly integrated community development has been advanced, however, by a proposal from four hundred farming families in the Guquka area, not far from St. Philip's Mission. They began planning communally only in 1983, after many of them regrouped their houses around a primary school. They now have plans to build an eight-kilometer pipeline to supply fresh water to the school and families. Until now, they drew water from a stagnant dam – and suffered for it, with gastroenteritis and other diseases. They also plan to build a storage dam for irrigation, clear the bush, and prepare the land for regular crops, instead of hoping for a year of good rainfall. And they want to expand the small school into a community center, because two hundred women have organized themselves into a production group. By generating some jobs and income locally, they hope to stem the exodus of young people to the towns. The USC has committed the relatively large sum of $72,775 to this experiment in its first year, and Gilles Latour writes: "Motivation and enthusiasm are high in this community...I hope it may also develop into a model that will inspire others throughout the country."[12]

Making a life in towns

But what of those young people who have left their villages for the uncertain life in towns? Despite the strictures of conservative leaders in Swaziland, there is a transition taking place to a western, urbanized life style. This transition is bound to have its gawky stages, with a breakdown in family relationships and the flailing around of youthful energies, out of school and out of jobs. Many people, including those running the Family Life Association, have tried to find alternatives, for the

[12]*1984 Report on USC Program in Swaziland*, pp. 15-16.

young people, to petty crime, alcoholism, drug abuse, prostitution – and, finally, imprisonment – all of which are on the rise in the main towns, Mbabane and Manzini.

The Manzini Youth Centre was one alternative. It took over an abandoned building in 1979, repaired it, and set about providing facilities for sports, skills training, and family life education. It also made links with the Swazi Works Camp Association, to encourage its own members to take part in small-scale development in rural communities.

It is an ambitious program, which the USC has backed, and there are mixed views about its performance. Trevor Hall, the youth leader at the heart of it, was a surprising figure from the International Voluntary Service in Britain. He is of Jamaican origin and Rastafarian faith, a good musician as well as a carpenter and a zealous exponent of brotherly love. While no one disputed that his exotic personality had attracted many young people to the center, there were murmurings that vocational training was being neglected in favor of sessions at the coffee bar, which was somehow failing to be the money-spinner envisaged. While USC management has considered it a good program and has thought that support should be continued, Trevor Hall was urged to produce some worthwhile results from the training courses.

A more established alternative to child vagrancy and delinquency is the Zakhele Home and Reception Centre set up by Father Larry McDonnell, who is also headmaster of the Salesian High School in Manzini. The first shelter he could find for the street children referred to him by local police was in the abandoned Manzini morgue, and their dining-room was the gutted frame of an old bus in a nearby vacant lot. Since then, Zakhele has moved into decent quarters in a residential area, and the older boys helped build a house for themselves. There are always setbacks, with some boys doing what Father McDonnell calls "the annual disappearing act." But more than 150 children have passed through Zakhele and have also attended the high school. Some move on to two-year courses to learn carpentry and building skills at another institution started by the Salesian community, the Manzini Industrial Training Centre.

The USC has supported Zakhele and the MITC, and has also used its Foster Parent scheme to help some of the brightest children from villages and towns who need scholarships to go all the way through high school. I have a shining memory of the final image in the slide presentation that Gilles Latour has used for fund raising across Canada. It is of a girl in a tunic, sitting at her desk in St. Theresa's High School, Manzini. Three years before, Ntombgiesa Ngozo had been a nine-year-old kid in Bulunga who had never had a chance to go to school. Then the primary school was built, and Ntombgiesa, among the first fifteen children to enter it, sailed through 7 years of primary schooling in 2½ years. The next year she was top of her class at St. Theresa's and, through Gilles's camera, giving a galvanizing stare (together with a warm smile) to Canadians who doubtless take for granted the provision of high school education. The point of the slide was not just to show the benefit to her but to indicate the tremendous waste of potential there is in countries with inadequate facilities, like Swaziland, Lesotho, and Botswana.

The cost of providing training has been tiny, compared with expenditures in Canada. For example, in 1983 the USC helped to train three hundred health workers in Lesotho at a cost of less than a hundred dollars per village (there were several trainees from the same villages). And the annual cash support which the USC gave during the first four years of community projects in Bulunga, which helped bring Ntombgiesa's village up from a lethargic bunch of neglected people to a proud and active community, amounted to no more than twelve thousand dollars.

Canadians have responded to such stories of success and cost-effectiveness. Gilles wrote a lively account of Bulunga's progress and told the tale of Ntombgiesa in a *Letter from Swaziland*, which was mailed out to USC friends. He wrote: "I am still astonished by what I saw. Their new sense of purpose, unity and commitment...is paying off." It garnered a second harvest, too. For the *Letter* drew gifts of $130,000, more than ten times the annual contribution USC had been providing to Bulunga. The response helps pave the way to greater efforts to help break the chain of poverty in southern Africa.

CHAPTER 12

The Fifth Decade

The long journey

IT HAS BEEN A LONG and extraordinary journey, these forty years. In 1945 Dr. Lotta could never have supposed that it would last so long or take her so far. It began as a modest program to help European refugees while they found their way back to their homes and to a livelihood, and she believed at the outset that it might be finished in three or four years. But it has lasted ten times that period, and the need for such an agency is as great now — in other parts of the world — as it was in Europe in those first years.

Although she herself appeared unchanging, in her olive-green uniform and the questions she put to everyone in her clear Czech accent, the programs she launched and monitored, inspected annually and came home to tell donors about with drama and compassion, did change in nature and scope. Throughout her years as executive director, she remained deeply concerned with the welfare and training of young people. The medallion figure of her bending over some scrap of a child with a bowl held out has become almost her stamp, but feeding and affection was always only a first step in helping them to a school, to a skill, to some level of self-reliance. It is wrong to think of her at any time as simply giving relief aid. The motherliness in her made her enjoy enormously the welcomes she received from the youngsters at children's homes, but she expressed a more profound joy when the children left these homes with assured jobs. And when some of them asked her to bless them before marriage, she was moved with pleasure beyond words. These young people in France and Korea, India and Bangladesh, were indeed the family of her own she never had. And she succeeded magnificently in helping bring them up and in leading them to self-development.

Before many other agencies, she was particularly concerned with the improvement of the position of women. In Greece she supported special courses for village girls in Thessaloniki, and she set the widows of Mesovouno moving to better times with the famous Cockshutt tractor; in India she launched the women leaders' meetings in the villages around the Karnatak Health Institute. But it was only halfway through this period — in 1965 — that she recommended the first USC support for a program of family planning, in Hong Kong. To say that is not to suggest she was behind public opinion; she rarely, if ever, was. Rather, it is a reflection of general attitudes of that time. She moved as soon as she calculated that she had the bulk of her constituency behind her. Although she claimed that she and the USC kept clear of politics (which, in a strict sense, is true), she showed all the attributes of a sharp-sensed politician.

The USC program in Greece was a first step into community development and broad-based support for farmers, especially in Evritanias prefecture. The response to the famine in Bihar — relief supplies first, followed by the farsighted establishment of the Ranchi agricultural training center and the follow-up work of extension with the tribal farmers — was the agency's next major effort in what is now acknowledged as the first priority in rural development: self-sufficiency in food production. That may seem belated recognition of a prime need, and slow action upon it. But one should remember, that several years after Ranchi was set up, the Canadian International Development Agency was giving such a low priority to stimulating food production in developing countries that only 3 percent of its government-to-government budget in 1973 was being allocated to this sector. Again, the first large project USC funded in Botswana was the afforestation work of the Kweneng brigade. And growing eucalyptus trees on the edge of the Kalahari Desert was not only a pioneering venture but also surely the kind of battling against odds that Dr. Lotta understood and, most of the time, enjoyed.

While she extended the scope of USC programs into more developmental work in the thirty years when she was vigorously in charge – for her bout of amoebic dysentery in 1975 was the start of her deteriorating health – she never altered her stance on some basic principles. First among these (to stress this point once again) was her determination to work through nationals of the country, or at least the region, where the project was located. The search for efficient partner agencies, for trustworthy contacts and soon for local USC representatives, was a crucial part of her early investigations in a new country.

Sometimes she made a misjudgement and a poor selection, but in nearly every important case the USC was splendidly rewarded by the sensitive and skillful management of projects by local directors. Her perseverance with partner agencies and local direction – something no other foreign agency had then done – for example, in Korea – was amply justified by results.

I doubt that Dr. Lotta would ever have described herself as a feminist at any stage of her life. The interesting figures in her university years had been men of literature older than herself. The USC board and Projects Advisory Committee have been headed by men all these years. But it is intriguing that the staff she worked with in Ottawa for twenty-five years were all female, that most of the USC representatives she chose in Asia were women – Mrs. Aiyar in India, Mrs. Jahanara in Bangladesh, and Miss Nirmala Bhattarai (Mrs. Pokharel on marriage) in Nepal, and that a surprisingly high number of project leaders were also women. As well, the USC branches and working groups across Canada were mostly headed by women, while men cheerfully headed for the background and basement where the packing cases were. It is not that men found it difficult to work with such a strong-willed ascetic woman; some indeed enlisted her as an ally in the problems they were having with a woman above them (as Mr. Nambudiri did in Madras). Rather, it seems to have been an instinctive desire on her part to bring out the leadership qualities she knew were in so many talented women she met, and an intuition that their ideas on human development would match her own. The recent recruitment of three women to be USC representatives in the countries of southern Africa shows she has not been alone in holding these views.

Since her retirement from the role of executive director, significant changes have been made in the shape of projects. They are still directed to some of the poorest countries, like Bangladesh, Nepal, or Lesotho, or to the more neglected parts of slightly richer countries like Indonesia, Botswana, and Swaziland. But whereas she saw merit in keeping the size of projects small, the present USC team has worked to make them many-sided, and therefore considerably larger. Her instinct was to keep a project "at a manageable level," which meant that a brief annual inspection would reveal any shortcomings, and that the human element (which was the sustaining part for her own spirit and the core of her eloquent reports back to

Canadian donors) would not be swamped by the sheer size of the program under way. On the other hand, the new team grasp, more than she ever seemed to do, the interlocking parts of underdevelopment which go to make up "the chain of poverty." As Gilles Latour often said, "this has to be attacked at every link." Hence the move towards projects of integrated community development of a size which would have worried Dr. Lotta in years past.

Another significant change has been in the relationship of USC Canada with other Canadian voluntary agencies. The agency did become, during the 1970s, a member of the Canadian Council for International Cooperation (CCIC), the umbrella organization serving the more than one hundred Canadian voluntary agencies working overseas. Charles Gray was a member of the CCIC executive. But Dr. Lotta herself had literally no time for a body whose job was to coordinate some agencies' efforts and represent their common interests in talks with CIDA officials, and which also busied itself with forms of development education with the Canadian public that went beyond her pattern and were not directly linked to fund raising. To spend precious time talking to other Canadian voluntary agencies, when she and the USC had their own plans and programs worked out, was almost as wicked a waste as to take hours away from an inspection tour of Indian projects to visit a waterfall.

Her successor, Raymond ven der Buhs, is a more gregarious person, and takes a quite different attitude. His views about cooperative efforts were probably formed during his boyhood in a farming community around Englefeld, Saskatchewan. For he was the eldest son in a family of five girls and four boys, and his father farmed wheat and kept a thousand pigs during the difficult years by dint of organizing the daily work of his sons to the last detail. Indeed, he had decided ideas about how each of the sons would continue to work for the family's farm holdings, and Raymond's part was to train as an accountant. Today, three brothers are farming three sections (of 259 hectares) cooperatively and combining on winter work in farm machinery plants, but Raymond, in his own words, "threw a wrench in the works by going to the ministry." Yet he never left a collegial setting. As a Catholic priest, he taught philosophy at Ottawa University and agriculture back home at St. Peter's Abbey, the boarding school he had earlier attended, and he worked in parishes in

Saskatchewan. When he came to USC in 1969 as Dr. Lotta's personal assistant, he had no experience of overseas development, but he brought this collegial spirit which is now the style of USC administration.

Raymond has projected this collaborative approach to work in South Asia and has been a leading figure in the South Asia Partnership (SAP), an experiment in helping smaller NGOs in that region find partners among Canadian agencies. The South Asia Partnership owes its creation to Romeo Maione, then the director-general of CIDA's NGO division, and the equally ebullient Aloysius Fernandez, the NGO liaison officer in the Canadian High Commission in New Delhi. When Romeo visited India in 1980, he was struck by the large number of indigenous NGOs engaged in training and development work. They could do a good deal more, and do it more effectively, he argued, if they made links with a Canadian agency that could provide funding and other support. He knew of the Australia-based Asian Partnership for Human Development (APHD), a Catholic consortium that linked church groups in Australia, Belgium, Britain, and Canada with similar groups like Caritas operating in Asian countries, and pooled project funds. Romeo, who is always asking original questions, asked why Canadian nonchurch NGOs couldn't do something similar to draw the smaller indigenous NGOs into a network. A somewhat rambling meeting followed in 1981 in Bangalore (known to SAP veterans as Bang-1), which, however, produced the idea of a partnership that included shared decision-making throughout the process.

SAP was slow to take off. In its first two years, only fourteen and then twelve projects were funded by Canadian agencies. A Canadian committee was set up to coordinate which Canadian agency would take on any particular project request, and the committee's administration was handled as an additional task by the agency to which the chairman belonged: first, Tim Brodhead of Inter Pares, and then John Laidlaw of Canadian Hunger Foundation. A structure was evolving in the three countries participating in SAP – Bangladesh, India, and Sri Lanka – with one established organization in each country acting as a "service committee" to check on and refine requests before sending them on to an international executive committee of the four countries that met twice a year to compile a single "international list" of projects which the Canadian committee would later share among themselves. There were excellent organizations involved in this work, like the Marga Institute in Sri Lanka and the Asian Institute for Rural Development in India. But the procedure was becoming too elaborate, with as many as fourteen steps to take from start to finish, and a number of projects did not begin until two years after first identification.

Early in 1983, Raymond became chairman of the Canadian committee and was joined on the executive by Nazeer Ladhani, administrator of the Aga Khan Foundation Canada, and Maria Hulme, program director of the Vancouver-based Food for the Hungry – Canada. They concluded that SAP would not advance, and would probably wither away, unless it recruited an "anchor" person in Canada, and the process of refining and funding projects was greatly speeded up. So Richard Harmston, CCIC's executive director for the past seven years, took on the new job of executive director, SAP-Canada. An effort was put behind enlarging the flow of projects, and in 1983-84 Canadian donors were found for seventy-six projects (of which USC took on twenty-six), while in 1984-85 a total of ninety projects was in the pipeline. CIDA's role in multiplying the funds raised for these projects by individual NGOs was critically important. In 1984-85, for example, CIDA was advancing $1.6 million to SAP, against the $325,000 which the Canadian agencies would themselves raise. Of this figure, only about 10 percent had to be used for administration at either end, and for the meetings at which the agencies and representatives of the four countries gathered. The rest went directly to the projects.

It is instructive, and cheering, to sit in on one of the international SAP meetings, as I did in January 1984. Early on in the meeting, two proposed projects in Sri Lanka were on the table for examination. A village on its dry eastern coast had formed the Natpiddimunai Welfare Society and wanted to sink two eighteen-meter deep tube wells to tap the underground water. They needed fifty-five hundred dollars to engage expert assistance from outside the village. Another village wanted funding for outside help to repair the road that led to a main highway. Both these project proposals were subjected to a barrage of questions, from other Asian participants as strongly as from Canadians. Would the tube wells be dug in the compound of the welfare society's chairman, a retired district judge, and thus benefit the well-to-do most? Would there be any other spinoffs for the village: any plans for literacy classes, or any way to coalesce a society of part-Tamil and part-Portuguese background? Mr. Mohideen, from the Marga Institute, assured everyone the judge wasn't rich, and the wells wouldn't be near his house.

As for the road project, participants asked whether the poor of the village had other priorities. Only the upper class usually ask for roads; the poor don't have shoes and a paved road hurts the feet. Mr. Mohideen told the meeting that the request had been signed by all sorts of villagers, that the sick had at present to be carried in chairs to the highway and to hospital, that minor efforts at repair had failed, and that a proper road could galvanize a lethargic community. Raymond, for one, was not satisfied. He said a road might be thought a "safe project," but in many countries it was considered the responsibility of someone else, some level of government. The villagers might not repair it next year. Wouldn't an income-generating project be a better start in stimulating a lethargic community? He produced the example of Bulunga in Swaziland[1], which had also been lethargic and had begun with literacy classes and better crop production. The people of Bulunga themselves went on to build a nineteen-kilometer road, he said.

The discussions went on for two days. They asked questions about helping a potters' cooperative in Bangladesh to set up their own factory (Was a group of a hundred potters unmanageably large? Who is going to look after marketing? What arrangements were there for a bank loan?), and about resettling thirty-eight families of bonded laborers on land in Tamil Nadu. The government was giving them land, digging an elephant trench, building them houses and a community center. Donors were being asked for funds for land reclamation and water supplies, and also for the planting of fruit trees and trees for fuelwood, banks were being asked for loans to provide the families with bullocks. Mr. Alwa, of Myrada in Bangalore, who presented the request, soon found it was being criticized as much by Bangladeshi participants as by Canadians. Raymond liked the integrated nature of the project, although he felt too much was being done for the settlers; and Ruth Vikse, of the Camrose One World Institute in Alberta, thought the animal husbandry component could interest her people. But it was

---

[1]See Chapter 11, pp. 236-237.

Ataur Rahman of Bangladesh who firmly said they must "avoid spoonfeeding."

These meetings may be unique. They bring together agencies in South Asia that have had no other previous connection. In a round-table style, the requests are screened by Asian representatives, who have experience of similar efforts in their own countries, and by Canadians, who bring examples from elsewhere. An unusual amount of cross-fertilization of ideas takes place.

The advantages to the smaller NGOs in Asia go beyond the immediate funding of their first project request. For example, Mozammel Haque, who is field director of SAP-Bangladesh, heads a team of seven people who ease these requests past government officials and also advise the NGOs on future directions. SAP is beginning to get a second or third round of requests from such NGOs, but, in the meantime, some of the first hundred or more NGOs who have benefitted from the system have made a continuing link with a particular Canadian NGO (and more than a dozen Canadian agencies are now enrolled in SAP) and do not need to go through this multi-lateral channel.

The cross-fertilization process within SAP is being taken a further stage in 1985 with a month-long tour of projects in the three countries of fifteen representatives of Asian agencies, together with some Canadians. With the memory of a program from his CCIC days, Harmston named this traveling seminar LEAP, standing for Linkage Exchange Animation Partnership; no doubt this tour will serve to advance all four objectives. Another imminent step is to extend SAP to two other countries in the region, Pakistan and Nepal.

The bottom line: fund raising

The strong CIDA support of this SAP experiment, as well as its more direct support of projects funded solely by USC, brings up the issue of whether a Canadian agency should set a limit on the amount of "matching" funds it accepts from the government. Ten years ago the USC board faced this issue squarely for the first time. Until about 1969, when the NGO division of CIDA got into stride under Lewis Perinbam, the matter had not arisen. USC had certainly been the recipient of

Canadian government funds or supplies (milk powder, dried fish, etc.), but it was usually an in-and-out matter of being the channel for distribution. In the early 1970s, more and more CIDA NGO funds became available for development, as opposed to relief projects, and at the same time, councils for international cooperation in Alberta, Saskatchewan, and Ontario were starting to match funds raised in their provinces, while the British Columbia government had its own fund for agricultural development.

Were there dangers in this weight of government support? The USC board considered the question carefully in 1975 and eventually issued a statement in September announcing that it would limit its acceptance of governmental funds in any fiscal year to 25 percent of its total cash budget. It welcomed the willingness of all these governments to "share Canadian wealth" with poorer nations but thought there were potentially adverse effects of governmental funding on voluntary agencies. It explained its view in the following terms.

The USC drew its financial support from several hundred thousand Canadians, and in turn, supported "a wide variety of self-help projects in the Third World in the name of these donors, with an absence of red tape and at low administrative cost." Independence and the ability to remain flexible were essential to success in "assisting many small but excellent projects that often yield amazingly important returns." Procedures required by CIDA and other governmental agencies on the use of public funds were appropriate for large and costly projects, but not for the many small ones USC then supported. Also, USC did not have the administrative staff to prepare detailed reports for CIDA – and resisted the idea of adding such staff for this work, because it would "jeopardize the USC's most significant attribute – the ability to act swiftly and without red tape."

• Ten years later there is a very different situation. In 1983-84, the USC cash budget (that is, excluding contributions in kind of food and clothing) amounted to $5,022,346, and of that total, government grants came to $2,781,817 – or 55 percent. In 1984-85, the figures were an estimated total budget of $6 million, of which governments would contribute $3.5 million or 58 percent.

What has happened during those ten years is that the USC has moved into supporting much larger projects of rural development, on which detailed reports have, in any case, to be compiled. As well, there are three CIDA projects for the reconstruction of water systems in Swaziland following the devastating cyclone, for which USC has been asked to act as agent because of its effective local organization. The funds behind these projects amount to $440,000. So the issue is more complex than it seems at first sight. But attitudes have altered. Raymond ven der Buhs expresses the view that, as long as the development effort is effectively carried out, no particular ratio should be set between governmental funds and those directly raised by a voluntary agency.

This does not, of course, relieve USC of the responsibility to raise as much money as before, and indeed to increase the amount. This has become an important way to maintain a broad base of Canadian support, now that the collection and packing of clothing has been phased out. Conversely, the agency needs support across Canada, not simply for fund-raising purposes but also to be able to call on a core of committed people who will help spread word of the needs in developing countries and keep USC in the public eye. It is literally a circle of support, each part maintaining the next.

The success that branches and groups have had in turning from the work of collecting and packing clothing to that of fund raising[2] suggests that the USC structure is surviving what has been the biggest change to its organization in Canada. Reorganization of the board, following Dr. Lotta's decision to step down, has been a vital part of that change. The bringing of new people onto the board — some, like Robert McKinnell, having wide overseas experience — and the formalizing of regional representation, with three board representatives from Western, Central, and Eastern Canada locally chosen, were important steps. So were the revival of its executive committee, which now holds monthly meetings with staff members present, and the strengthening of the Projects Advisory Committee. These changes have allowed a thorough examination, over the last three years, of every aspect of USC operations, to help the staff look ahead.

Overseas, changes are becoming equally visible. There is now a local USC representative in each of the six countries. The next step must be more effective communication among these

---

[2]See Chapter 9, p. 200.

representatives within a region. Already, the three representatives in Lesotho, Swaziland, and Botswana have begun to meet, to share experiences, and work on joint solutions. Both they and their counterparts in Asia are forming advisory committees of prominent local people to help their own work. More direct global communication with the board has also been shown to be worthwhile, starting with a visit to Ottawa in 1984 of the Swaziland representative, Thabisile Mngadi, and of the three representatives from Asia in 1985.

Everything is not changing, of course. The agency is trying to maintain the guiding principles by which Dr. Lotta worked for so long: keeping a personal touch, continuing to be economy-conscious (the office is still a crowded and industrious place), and remaining independent of political influence. And it is still at 56 Sparks Street.

Forty years is a landmark in a person's life, when by popular notion, one is either reaching the "sunlit uplands" of maturity or else sloping down into the shadows. There is uncertainty in the tone of people who repeat the phrase, "Life begins at 40." The USC did not wait forty years for life to begin, and I do not suppose anyone connected with the agency feels that it is lacking in vigor today. The years with Dr. Lotta may be past; but, as she herself said in 1983, a new generation has taken over, and "we have passed a turning-point." Much excitement and many challenges lie ahead.

Appendix I

Chairmen of the USC Board

June 1945	Dr. Lotta Hitschmanova
May 1949	Mrs. Rita McConkey
January 1954	Mr. Bower Carty
January 1956	Dr. David B. Smith
June 1963	Mr. Bower Carty
June 1965	Dr. David B. Smith
June 1966	Mr. Harry Bolster
June 1969	Mr. W.A. McKay
June 1971	Mr. F.J. Holmes
June 1973	Dr. Gordon Merrill*
January 1974	Mr. Harry Bolster
June 1974	Mr. Harry Wood
June 1977	Mr. Bower Carty
June 1981	Mr. Jack Todd
June 1983	Dr. Gordon Merrill

* Dr. Merrill resigned after six months as chairman, on being appointed to a staff position for two years. Mr. Bolster filled out his year's term.

Chairmen of the Projects Advisory Committee

from 1959	Dr. James Gibson
1964	Mr. Jack Todd
1979	Dr. W.B.C. Robertson**
1980	Mr. Harry Bolster
1983	Mr. Pierre Barbeau

** Dr. Robertson resigned as PAC Chairman on moving to Halifax.

Appendix II

Funds raised and gifts-in-kind received

			(Current $s)	(1984 $s)
Year	Cash	Value of gifts-in-kind	Total	Total
1945	$ 64,000	$ —	$ 64,000	$ 429,000
1946	46,000	133,708	179,708	1,165,000
1947	50,000	64,660	114,660	680,000
1948	57,000	65,340	122,340	634,000
1949	46,500	144,000	190,500	958,000
1950	48,000	124,273	172,273	841,000
1951	100,000	143,650	243,650	1,076,000
1952	132,000	128,322	260,322	1,123,000

| | | Value of | (Current $s) | (1984 $s) |
Year	Cash	gifts-in-kind	Total	Total
1953	$ 150,000	$ 257,152	$ 407,152	$1,772,000
1954	165,000	240,152	405,152	1,753,000
1955	158,500	248,414	406,914	1,758,000
1956	163,500	185,600	349,100	1,486,000
1957	177,393	160,178	337,571	1,392,000
1958	207,000	466,575	673,575	2,705,000
1959	242,325	476,000	718,325	2,854,000
1960*	286,289	246,560	532,849	2,091,000
1960-61	309,974	374,590	684,564	2,662,000
1961-62	321,525	408,700	730,225	2,805,000
1962-63	363,108	500,000	863,108	3,260,000
1963-64	471,072	407,030	878,102	3,258,000
1964-65	467,909	513,838	981,747	3,556,000
1965-66	559,230	481,091	1,040,321	3,633,000
1966-67	567,448	503,433	1,070,881	3,610,000
1967-68	655,469	636,860	1,292,329	4,187,000
1968-69	731,323	703,859	1,435,182	4,447,000
1969-70	890,763	548,462	1,439,225	4,318,000
1970-71	645,577	592,682	1,238,259	3,611,000
1971-72	952,488	708,273	1,660,761	4,621,000
1972-73	901,737	630,401	1,532,138	3,964,000
1973-74	1,470,253	625,579	2,095,832	4,889,000
1974-75	1,626,410	1,003,265	2,629,675	5,537,000
1975-76	1,412,162	1,104,813	2,516,975	4,929,000
1976-77	1,650,252	1,114,926	2,765,178	5,014,000
1977-78	1,606,363	1,224,088	2,830,451	4,711,000
1978-79	2,085,565	1,721,292	3,806,857	5,806,000
1979-80	2,187,149	1,668,607	3,855,756	5,339,000
1980-81	2,581,955	2,100,849	4,682,804	5,764,000
1981-82	2,821,753	2,308,048	5,129,801	5,698,000
1982-83	2,484,561	2,290,431	4,774,992	5,016,000
1983-84	4,976,368	526,469	5,502,837	5,503,000
Grand total	34,833,921	25,782,170	60,616,091	128,855,000

* There was a change in fiscal year accounting in 1960. The figure for "1960" covers only four months; and that for "1960-61" the next 12 months.

Note: The totals in constant 1984 dollars have been calculated on the basis of the average consumer price index for that year. The CPI, of course, rose much more steeply during the 1970s than in earlier, less inflationary, years.

253

Appendix III

Honors and Awards conferred on
Dr. Lotta Hitschmanova, C.C.

1983 Rotary International Award for World Understanding (only two previous recipients).
      Officer of the Most Meritorious Order of Mohlomi, Lesotho.
1980 Companion of the Order of Canada (C.C.).
1979 Royal Bank of Canada Award (Outstanding contribution to Human Welfare and the Common Good – medal and $50,000).
1978 Order of Civil Merit, Camellia Medal, Government of South Korea.
1976 Special Honor by Prime Minister Indira Gandhi of India ("in appreciation of her outstanding service to India").
1972 Officer of the Order of Canada.
1967 Athena Messalora Gold Medal, Government of Greece.
1964 Gold Cross, Hellenic Red Cross.
1962 Public Welfare Medal.
      Public Service Medal (Government of South Korea).
1958 Gold Medal, Hellenic Red Cross.
1952 Medal of St. Paul, Government of Greece.
1951 Medal of Gratitude, Government of France.
1950 Chevalier of Public Health, Government of France.
      Gold Medal, Red Cross of France.
      Silver Medal, Hellenic Red Cross.

Dr. Hitschmanova has also received numerous other national and civic citations.

Appendix IV

Countries in which USC has supported projects

Czechoslovakia	1945 to 1949
France	1946 to 1980
Austria	1948 to 1958
Greece	1950 to 1979
Italy	1950 to 1964
South Korea	1952 to 1978
Hong Kong	1952 to 1980
India	1953 to 1975
Gaza Strip	1956 to 1975
South Vietnam	1969 to 1975
West Bank of Jordan	1970 to 1975
Bangladesh	1971 until...
Botswana	1971 until...
Lesotho	1971 until...
Swaziland	1971 until...
Indonesia	1975 until...
Vietnam (Hanoi)	1976 to 1979
Nepal	1976 until...
Cyprus	1977 to 1980

Index

Aga Khan Foundation Canada, 246

Agriculture: in aid programs, 9; in Greece, 67-69; Vietnam, 108; India, 119-122, 242; Indonesia, 179-182; Bangladesh, 213-219; Lesotho, 234; Swaziland, 235-236

Aiyar, Mrs. Sarojini, USC representative in India, 116, 117, 243; in Nepal, 207, 208, 224

Alamgir, Dr. Muhiudin Khan (Bangladesh), 212

American Friends Service Committee, 25, 27, 77; British Quakers, 29, 71, 99; Swedish/Danish Quakers, 58

An, Mr. Tran Dinh, 103, 104

Appleton, Christine, 146, 147

Arnould, Irene, 33

Australia: aid in Vietnam, 108; in Asia, 245

Austria: historical, 1, 12, 13; Nazi occupation of, 19; USC program in, 54, 57-59

Balderson, Ted (hotel manager), 148

Bangladesh: general, 1, 6, 114, 224; conditions after 1971 war, 204, 209; landlessness, 211; rural development, 8, 196, 202, 213-219, 224, 234; USC training centre, 218; Proshika movement, 210, 213, 214; other NGO programs, 213, 248; USC "Stitch a Shirt" campaign, 204; milk program, 203, 204

Barbeau, Marius (folklorist), 32, 35, 36, 44, 158

Barbeau, Pierre (PAC Chairman), 252

Barber, Mrs. H.G., 42

Barber, Richard (USC solicitor), 141

Barr, Dr. Margaret (medical missionary), 122, 153, 195

Barzin, Betty (journalist), 20

Belgium: Lotta, refugee in, 20; Nazi attack on, 20-21; church groups' aid to, 245; Belgian Congo, 33

Bell, Max (newspaper proprietor), 155

Bellido, Dolores, 49

Beneš, President Edvard (Czechoslovakia), 18, 19, 55

Bhatia, Dr. (Mrs.) S. (India), 126, 188

Boggs, Mamey Maloney (columnist), x, 136

Bolster, Harry (USC chairman and board member), ix, x 145, 146, 198, 252

Borgford, Mrs. Elsie (USC vice-chairman), 40

Borgford, Dr. Ingi (Unitarian minister), 42

Botswana: general, 2, 6; characteristics, 226-227; brigade system, 227, 228, 229, 230, 242; schools, 228; afforestation, 229-230; problems of cooperatives, 230

Bragg, Raymond (USC Boston), 61

Bremner, Eric (cameraman), 136

Britain: attitudes to Hitler, 19, 20; freezes Vietnam aid, 108; church groups' aid, 245

Brock University: Chancellor's Lecture, 187, 188, 194, 196, 199

Brodhead, Tim, 245

Brooks, Rev. Howard (USC Boston), x, 56, 140, 142, 195

Bulgaria, 62

Buss, John (cameraman), 121, 136, 168, 192, 197, 204

Cahill, Rev. Edward (USC Boston), 44

Calgary Albertan, 155

Cameron, Lorraine (USC projects

officer), x, 148, 154, 155

Camrose One World Institute, 247

Canada: aid from provinces: Alberta, 106, 113, 249; B.C., 60, 88, 98, 107, 108, 120, 203, 249; Nova Scotia, 60; Ontario, 113, 249; P.E.I., 205; Saskatchewan, 79, 249

— Action and aid from cities/towns: Brandon, 142; Brockville, 200; Calgary, 99, 124; Campbell River, B.C., 64; Camrose, 247; Charlottetown, 64; Clinton, Ont., 135; Deep River, Ont., 59; Duncan, 8, 149; Edmonton, 167; Exshaw, Alta., 59; Eyebrow, Sask., 137; Flin Flon, 53; Halifax, 84; Hamilton, 53; Ile d'Orleans, 38, 158; Kingston, 83; Lethbridge, 97; London, Ont., 200; Moncton, 62; Montreal, 5, 31-32, 44, 47, 156, 158, 200, 220; Moose Jaw 137, 142, 148; Nanaimo, 4, 5, 6, 10, 135, 146 Nelson, B.C., 134; North Bay, 3, 55; Oshawa, 200; Ottawa, 32, 36, 46, 97, 99, 102, 103, 147, 200; Pincher Creek, 200; Regina, 137; St. Catharines, 136; St. John's, 135; Saskatoon, 53, 55; Toronto, 2, 44, 46, 53, 157, 220; Truro, 147, 148; Vancouver, 41, 44, 45, 55, 57, 137, 148, 156, 200, 205, 246; Vancouver Island, 4, 8; Victoria, 8, 91, 136, 148, 200; Winnipeg, 41, 44, 45, 57, 146, 200

Canada World Youth, 5

Canadian Broadcasting Corporation, 45, 168

Canadian Council for International Cooperation, 160, 244, 246

Canadian Government: help to USC, 198; action on Vietnam, 189

Canadian Hunger Foundation, 197, 245

Canadian International Development Agency (CIDA): matching funds for NGOs, 5, 119, 134, 135, 152, 173, 203, 249; relations with NGOs, 250; aid freeze in Vietnam, 108; CIDA in Bangladesh, 210, 211, 216; low priority given to agriculture, 242; supports South Asia Partnership, 246

Canadian Pacific Railways, 44, 84

Canadian Teachers' Federation, 5

Canadian Women's Club, 44, 45

Caritas (aid agency), 245

Carroll, Madeleine (film star), 51

Carty, Bower (USC chairman and treasurer), ix, 135, 144, 145, 149, 252

Casanueva, Manuel (Spanish Loyalist), 30

Catley-Carlson, Margaret (CIDA President), 134

Chafid, Dr. Achmad (Indonesia), 184

Chalufour, Aline, 33

Champsaur, Gwenydd, 47, 48

Children: care of, 10; in Czechoslovakia, 55; Austria, 58; France, 48, 49; Italy, 59; Korea, 86; Lotta's plan for European children, 34, 38, 40, 45; malnutrition and hunger, 2, 6, 7, 8, 47, 52; diarrhoea, killer of, 99, 173; Canadian Appeal for Children (1949), 142, 160

China: and Vietnam, 108; and Hong Kong, 162, 163, 164

Cho Ki Dong (USC Korean director), 85, 94, 195

Chowdhury, Dr. Zafrullah (Bangladesh), 171

Clark, Andy (cameraman), 136

Clarkson, Ida (television host), 136-137

Clothing: appeals for, 5, 10, 41, 42, 44, 46, 137; aid to France, 48, 51, 53; Spanish refugees, 49;

Czechoslovakia, 55, 56, 57; Italy, 60; Greece, 62, 63, 64; Korea, 92, 147; Middle East, 96-98, 99; India, 119; Bangladesh, 206; Cyprus, 220; packing, 46, 141, 146, 147, 243, 250
Cloutier, Edmond (King's Printer), 34, 83
Cockburn, Bruce (folk singer), 156
Cogan, Martha (USC Boston): work in Czechoslovakia, 25, 43; work in Vichy France, 26; smeared in U.S. Congress, 61; (see Waitstill Sharp)
Coleman, Jennifer, 113
Community development: in Greece, 73-76, 77-79, 79-80, 129, 193, 242; Korea, 93; India, 129-130, 131-132 193; Indonesia, 183-184; Nepal, 223-224; Lesotho, 234-235; Swaziland, 236, 238
CUSO (Canadian University Service Overseas), 134, 135; in Bangladesh, 210; Botswana, 230
Czechoslovakia: general, 1, 12; Nazi moves against, 19, 20, 26; refugees from, 27, 31, 32; Lotta's memories of Prague, 3, 11, 12-15, 17-19; her books on, 34; studies in, 186; relief proposals for, 35, 40; children's homes in, 42, 55; Lotta's visits to (1946), 46, 55, (1947), 56; USC Boston medical mission to (1948), 140
Cyprus: elderly refugees in, 219; USC clothing and hospital aid to, 220

Denmark: and Vietnam, 108
Deshamukh, Mrs. Durgabai (India), 129
Dewar, Anne (USC Ottawa), 147
Dexter, Dr. Robert (USC Boston), 25, 31
Dewey, Milton (constitutional reviewer), 143, 144
Dobson, Wendy (USC staff), 155
Doherty, Mrs. D.K., 115

Donald, Margaret (artist), x, 146
Dong, Dr. Nguyen Van (Hanoi official), 105, 106, 107

Earthquakes: in Greece, 63, 66, 77, 79
Evans, Dr. John, 3

Family planning: debate on USC support of, 157-158; programs in Korea, 92; Gaza Strip, 98; India 110, 122-124, 128, 157; Hong Kong, 158, 165-168; Indonesia, 171, 177; Bangladesh, 212; Family Planning Association of India, 123, 158; FPA of Hong Kong, 158, 165-168; FPA Bangladesh, 205
Feuchtwanger, Lion (novelist and refugee), 26
Field, Noel (USC Boston), 26, 48, 51, 61
Fisheries: Pacific, 5; Indonesia, 182; Nepal, 222
Flower, Theresa (USC publicity officer), 153, 154, 155
Food for the Hungry — Canada, 246
Forestry: in India, 130, 247; Indonesia, 179-181; Botswana, 229-230; Lesotho, 232, 234; Greece, 62, 70, 80
Foster Parents schemes: general, 40, 42, 153, 155; in France, 50, 51, 52; Czechoslovakia, 55, 57; Austria, 58; Italy, 60; Korea, 87, 95; South Vietnam, 102; India, 117; Indonesia, 170; Cyprus, 220; Botswana, Lesotho, Swaziland, 234, 240
France: general, 33, Lotta as a student in, 16, 17; as refugee in, 19, 21-24; attitudes to Hitler, 19, 20, 22; postwar conditions in, 47, 48; concentration camps in, 26-27, 30; relief plans for, 40, 46; Limoges, 21;

258

Les Andelys, 47; Sèvres, 51;
Marseilles, 1, 23-25, 28, 47;
children's homes in, 43, 49, 51, 52,
100; Lotta's visit to (1946), 46,
(1947), 51; USC program overlong
in, 189
Fried, Antony (UNRRA official), 35
Fullerton, Douglas (USC volunteer),
147

Gandhi, Indira, 116, 121, 190, 208
Georgacopoulos, Constantinos
(Hellenic Red Cross), 72
Germany: pre-war, 17; refugees from,
27; prisoners-of-war, 32; war events
in, 45, 52, 54, 66
Ghana, 9
Gibson, Dr. James (PAC chairman),
197
Gingras, André (CIDA officer), 152
Globe and Mail, 155
Gokarn, Mrs. Nirmala (India), 115
Golstein, René, 20, 21, 23, 37
Goussi, Mrs. Effie (Hellenic Red
Cross), 70
Grace, John (newspaper publisher),
155
Gray, Charles (USC projects officer),
152, 233, 244
Gray, Douglas (Vietnam), 102
Greece: general, 1, 82, 143, 160;
effects of civil war on, 62, 63, 156;
"Bread for Greece" campaign, 10,
65, 66, 67; projects in Mesovouno,
62, 66-69, 242; Marathon, 62, 71,
72-73; Karpenissi, 65, 77-79;
Karpero and Doxera, 70; American
Farm School, 71-72, 74, 76;
Thesprosia, 79-80; Gold Medal
award, 186; program thought
overlong in, 189
Guerrera, Professor Maria (Italy),
60
Guild of Service (India, also *Seva
Samajam*), 110, 111, 114, 115, 152

Hagnauer, Mme Yvonne (France), 51,
52
Hall, Dr. Marian (medical
missionary), 157
Hamilton Spectator, 156
Hanidis, Julie (Greece), 67
Hardiker, Dr. Narayan (India), 124,
125, 126, 132
Harmston, Richard, 246, 248
Haspl, Dr. Karel (Unitarian minister
in Czechoslovakia), 56, 57
Health care: Marathon well-baby
clinic, 72; health centres in Middle
East, 98, 99; Vietnam post-polio
clinic, 101; in Assam, 122; Karnatak
Health Institute, 124-125; in
Central Java, 171; Swaziland, 237
Hébert, Jacques, 5
Heim, Lotte, x, 41
Helliwell, John (Vietnam), 102
Henderson, Lorna, 135
Hendrata, Dr. Lukas (Indonesia), 170,
171, 172
Hewett, Rev. Philip, x
Hicks, Henry, 84
Hinds, Mrs. A.C., 97
Hitschmann, Else (mother of Lotta):
background of, 12; on holidays, 15;
death of, 38
Hitschmann, Lilly: *see* Steen
Hitschmann, Maximilian (father of
Lotta): career of, 13, 18; views on
children's upbringing, 15; death
of, 38
Hitschmanova, Dr. Lotta: childhood
in Prague, 13-15; parents, 13, 18,
38; student in Paris, 16-17;
journalist in Prague, 17-19; in
Belgium, 20; refugee in Belgium,
20-21, and in France, 21-23;
wartime work in France, 23-25; in
Portugal, 28; voyage on SS *Guiné*,
29-31; censor in Ottawa, 32; work
in Washington, 35; planning USC,
38, 41-43; immigration of, 37;

declining health of, 143, 199, 242
— Vistis to: France, 46, 51;
    Czechoslovakia, 46, 55, 56;
    Austria, 58; Italy, 60; Greece,
    63, 64, 65, 67, 69, 72, 73, 75, 77;
    Korea, 82, 83, 87, 88, 89, 90, 92,
    193; Norway, 90; Middle East,
    97, 99; India, 109, 111, 116, 118,
    122, 126, 129, 131, 190, 192, 194;
    Vietnam (Saigon), 100, 103;
    (Hanoi), 105, 106, 107; Cyprus,
    219; Hong Kong, 163, 168;
    Indonesia, 169, 170, 177;
    Bangladesh, 203, 204, 205, 206,
    207, 208; Nepal, 224; Botswana,
    229
— Speech at Brock University, 186,
    192, 196; Lotta as broadcaster,
    33, 45, 136; skill with words, 135,
    150-153; as fund raiser, 4-5, 45,
    65, 148, 159-160
— Her relations with USC Boston,
    35, 41, 42-43, 61, 140; with USC
    branches, 138-139, 151; with the
    media, 136, 155, 156, 168;
— her attitudes to staff, 137, 153-155;
    to uniform, 150; to family
    planning, 98, 122, 157-158, 168;
    to local leadership, 10, 54, 164,
    195, 243; transplanting ideas,
    129, 193; to training of women,
    241, 243, and of young, 71, 87,
    196, 241; to community
    development, 79, 129; to
    economising, 149-150, 153, 154,
    199; to work in Quebec, 159
— Her personal approach, 134, 191,
    201; assessment of character, 11,
    14, 199, 241, and of her work,
    241-243
Holdrinet, Gérard (USC projects
    officer): x; reports on Bangladesh,
    217, 218, 219; on Botswana, 227,
    228, 230
Holland, Carroll (writer), 159

Holmes, F.J. (USC Chairman), 252
Hong Kong: 108; population
    pressures in, 162-164; USC
    program in (1960-80), 164-168
Hopkins, Mrs. Louise (quiltmaker),
    200
Huddlestone, Mrs. Rita, 135
Hulme, Maria, 246
Hutchison, Bruce (editor and
    columnist), 83

India: general, 2, 9; USC projects in
    children's homes, 110, 192; in
    Madras training centres, 112-115;
    in Bangalore, 115-118; in Ranchi
    118-121; in Kodai, 2, 123; Karnatak
    Health Institute, 124-133, 152, 188,
    222, 242; Indian complaint at USC
    film, 190; phase-cut decision, 189;
    endowments for four programs,
    191; aid to Bangladesh, 203; as
    participant in South Asia
    Partnership, 245, 247
Indonesia: general, 6; network of
    women leaders, 168; USC projects
    at Ciputat training centre, 170;
    Central Java nutrition scheme, 171;
    Dian Desa water projects, 174, 222,
    234; outer islands development,
    176-184; group fishing scheme,
    182; community development in
    Nagapanda, 183
Inger, David (Botswana), 229
International Development Research
    Centre, 134, 180, 193
International Labour Organization,
    34
International Planned Parenthood
    Federation, 124
International Red Cross: 26, 34;
    British Red Cross, 82; Cyprus Red
    Cross, 220; Hellenic Red Cross,
    72, 73; Swedish Red Cross, 38;
    Swiss Red Cross, 27; Canadian Red
    Cross Society, 34

260

International Voluntary Service: in Swaziland, 239
Inter Pares, 245
Irving, Judy and Janice, 200
Italy: USC program in, 59-60
Iwamura, Dr. Noburu, 2

Jadhav, Mrs. Mary Clubwala (India), 110, 111, 115, 190, 220
Jahanara, Mrs. Syeda (USC representative in Bangladesh), xi, 208, 210, 213, 243
Japan: general, 2, 106, 150, 217; invasion of China, 163; occupation of Hong Kong, 163
Jefferson, Jack (USC Vancouver chairman), x, 148
Jewish Children's Aid Society: work in France, 27
Johnson, Vera (singer), 156
Jolliffe, A.L. (immigration official), 37
Joy, Rev. Charles (USC Boston): work in Europe, 28, 29, 30, 35, 36; plans for Canadian branch, 41, 42, 43; in Czechoslovakia, 54, 55
Jugoslavia, see Yugoslavia

Keate, Stuart (newspaper publisher), x, 136, 137, 155, 156
Kehayias, Chrys (Greece), 78
Kenya, 8
Kershaw, Howard (Quaker worker), 29
Khalikane, Mrs. Maletele (USC Lesotho representative), 227, 251
Kinsmen Clubs, 160
Kiribati, 8
Kirloskar, M.S. (India), 126, 130
Korea, Republic of: general, 1, 150; Canadians defend, 81; USC's largest program, 81; feeding programs, 82, 84, 92, 193, 196; Seoul rehabilitation centre, 87, 100; Mokpo TB children's hospital,

89-92, 100, 193; problems of islanders, 93; four social service centres in, 92, 193; phasing out of, 189
Koskinides, A. (Greece), 63, 64
Kusnadi, Dr. Hadji (Indonesia), 170-171

Ladhani, Nazeer Aziz, 246
Laidlaw, John, 245
Lam, Mrs. Peggy (Hong Kong), 165, 168
Lang, Robert (film-maker), 214n
Lansdale, Bruce (American Farm School, Greece), xi, 74, 75, 76, 152, 195
Latour, Gilles (USC projects officer): general, x, 5, 244; fund raising on Vancouver Island, 4-8, 10; extends Quebec support, 159; reports on Indonesia, 171; on Lesotho, 226, 233, 234; on Swaziland, 236, 237, 238, 240
Latremouille, Father (Lesotho), 232
Latrines: in Swaziland, 7, 237; Greece, 75, 78; Indonesia, 173, 184; Bangladesh, 218, 219
Legge, Dorothy (USC Truro chairman), x, 147, 148
Lesotho: general, 2, 6, 7; characteristics, 226, 231; land problem, 231; schools, 231; food production, 7; award to Lotta, 186; egg circles, 194, 226, 233; community development, 234
Lethbridge Herald, 155
Literacy, 6, 123, 183, 216, 221, 224, 234, 247
Litsas, Theodore (Greece), 74, 75
Long-Landry, Dr. Marie (France), 24, 28, 37
Lown, Dr. Bernard, 2
Lutheran World Service: in Bangladesh, 208, 209

MacCallum, Elizabeth, 198
Macdonald, Mrs. (USC Montreal chairman), 143
MacRae, Pamela Lee (USC information director), x, 136, 155
Mader, Marjorie (teacher), x, 36
Magann, Mrs. George: in Greece, 139
Maione, Romeo (CIDA officer), 245
Malawi, 227n
Malone, Brigadier Richard (newspaper chairman), 155
Maltby, David (film-maker), 136
Mann, Arthur (USC Duncan chairman), x, 8, 149
Mannan, M.A. (Bangladesh architect), 218
Martin, John (CIDA officer), 216
Mary, André (writer), 17, 23, 37
Masitara, Thantshi (USC Botswana representative), 227, 251
Mason, Deborah (now Cowley, former USC staff), xi, 154, 155
Mavrina, Mrs. Sophia (Greece), 68
Mboi, Mrs. Nafsiah (Indonesia), 169, 184
McBroom, Robert (teacher), 36
McConkey, Mrs. Rita (USC founder member), 46, 147, 252
McConkey, T.A., 46
McDonnell, Father Larry (Swaziland), 239
McEwen, Charlotte (activist), 97
McKay, W.A. (USC Chairman), 252
McKee, Neill (film-maker), 134
McKinnell, Robert (USC board member), 250
McKinnon, Ruth (physiotherapist), 53, 100
Mennonite Central Committee: in Bangladesh, 213
Merrill, Dr. Gordon (USC chairman and special adviser), ix, 95, 104, 146, 147, 166, 170, 252
Middle East (Palestine): Lilly Steen in, 12, 35; USC projects in Gaza Strip, 95-99
Miles for Millions walks, 98, 124
Milk, Mrs. Ethel (Lotta's landlady), 34
Miller, Persis (USC Boston), 48, 49, 50
Mngadi, Thabisile (USC Swaziland representative), 227, 237, 251
Molina, Dr. Olimpia (Italy), 60
Mondal, Dr. Amitava (Bangladesh) 206, 207
Morgan, Mrs. J.R., 57
Mowers, Cleo (newspaper publisher), 155
Muenter, Claus (journalist), 10
Mukasa, Dr. Hirojo (Rotarian), 2
Mulla, Awamma (India), 131, 132
Muller, Henry (USC Boston), 41
Musiol, Mme Marie-Jeanne (translator), 159

Nambudiri, M.S.S. (India), xi, 112, 113, 114, 243
Narayan, Jaypradesh, 119
National Film Board of Canada, 38
Nepal: general, 2, 6, 7; terrain of, 221; USC projects in terracing, 7; safe water in, 221, 223; snack foods in, 224
Netherlands, 123
Ngozo Ntombgiesa (Swazi student), 240
Nicholson, Mrs. Frances (USC Nanaimo chairman), x, 146
Norway: cooperation in Korea, 89; in Bangladesh, 208, 209
Nuclear war, 2, 3

O'Connor, Mary Jo, 101
Oldham, W.F. (USC Winnipeg chairman), 141, 142
O'Leary, Senator Grattan, 44, 45
Ottawa Journal, 155, 189
Oxfam, 133, 182

Pakistan, 198, 202, 203
Pavlasek, Dr. Frantisek
  (Czechoslovakia), 32
Pearson College of the Pacific, 8
Pearson Commission on International
  Development, 161-162, 166
Pearson, Lester B., 35, 161
Perinbam, Lewis (CIDA vice-
  president), 248
Petursson, Rev. Philip (Unitarian
  minister), 141, 142
Phuong, Mme Nguyen Khanh (Hanoi
  official), 105
Picasso, Pablo: as refugees' champion,
  48
Pilowski, Iona (USC Winnipeg
  chairman), x, 149
Pilowski, Alex, 149
Plowman, Shirley (USC publicity
  officer), x, 154, 155
Pokharel, Mrs. Nirmala (USC Nepal
  representative), 224, 225, 243
Poland: Nazis invade, 20, 26; wartime
  conditions in, 33; refugees from,
  27, 32, 36
Pollution, 6, 221, 223
Polychronidou, Maria (Greece), 68
Pono, Dr. Radja (Indonesia), 182,
  184
Poole, Christopher (journalist), 10
Pope John Paul II, 2
Portugal, 22, 28-29
Potter, Theresa (former USC staff),
  82-83, 150
Potulika, Countess Marie, 33
Prager, Eva (artist), 156
Presbyterian Church (in Korea), 93
Princess Alice, 33
Purcell, Mrs. R.G. (Ontario Women's
  Institute), 67

Queen Victoria: statue in Madras,
  112; appeal from Lesotho, 186

Radja Haba, Dr. Frans (Indonesia),
  178, 179, 180, 181, 182, 184
Rama Krishna Mission: in India, 119,
  121, 122, 152; in Bangladesh, 202,
  203, 205; difficulties with, 205, 206,
  207
Ramin, Jeff (USC projects officer):
  sacred dance participant, 192;
  reports on Indonesia, 179, 181,
  183, 184; on Bangladesh, 207; on
  Nepal, 223
Ramstad, Dr. Herman (Norway), 90
Ranger, Richard (translator), 159
Ransom, Mrs. E.J. (USC Winnipeg
  chairman), 57, 138
Rashid, Syed Mohammed (USC
  Bangladesh staff), 218
Reader's Digest, 155, 159
Reale, Mrs. Guiseppina (Italy), 59
Reid, Mrs. Escott: in India, 139
Rekkebo, Gotfred (Norway), 85, 89,
  90
Reza, Humayun (USC Bangladesh
  staff): xi, 8, 213; adventurous life
  of, 209-210; and Jagarani Club,
  210; rural development program,
  213-219; leadership, 218
Rockingham, Brigadier J.M., 82
Rotary International: Toronto
  meeting, 2, 3; Cyprus, 220
Royal Canadian Legion, 59
Rumania, 18
Rusk, Dr. Howard, 88

Sadanand, S. (India), 116
St. Laurent, Louis, 141
Samuel, Edgar (conductor), 8
Sarjono, Mrs. Roesiah (Indonesia),
  169, 177
Sarton, Edgar (as censor), x, 32
Schinz, Marie-Thérèse (wartime
  friend of Lotta), 24, 28, 37, 38
Scott, Fred (USC treasurer), 141, 149
Sharkey, Sister Raphael (Swaziland),
  237, 238

Sharp, Rev. Waitstill (USC Boston): work in Czechoslovakia, 25, 26, 43; in Vichy France, 26, (see Martha Cogan)

Skaller, Hans (George) and Ruth (friends of Lotta from student days), x, 16, 18, 23

Small, Mrs. John (in Hong Kong), 139

Smith, David B. (USC chairman), 144, 147, 157, 252

Smith, Norman (editor), 155

Soedjarwo, Anton (Indonesia), 174, 175, 176

Soepardjo, Mrs. (Indonesia), 169, 173

Soulioti, Mrs. Stella (Cyprus), 220

South Africa: and Lesotho, 227, 231; customs union, 226

South Asia Partnership, 160, 245-248

Soviet Union: hunger in, 10-11; wartime contribution, 33; pledge to Czechoslovakia, 19; and Vietnam, 108

Spain: Loyalist refugees, 26, 30, 48-50, 61

Speaking tours: by Lotta, 4, 45, 83, 148, 203; by Gilles Latour, 4-8, 237, 240

Sprague, Helen (USC treasurer), 40

Sri Lanka, 245, 246, 247

Steen, Lilly (Lotta's younger sister): x; childhood, 12-15; marriage to Charles Steen, 12; life in Prague, 18, 20, 56; sketches for Lotta, 35; life in Palestine, 37; emigrates to Canada, 56

Steward, Newell (Quaker worker in Greece), 77, 78, 79

Swaziland: general, 2, 6, 197; characteristics, 226; schools, 7, 196; Lotta's frustrations with, 227; clinics, 237; urbanisation, 238; USC revolving fund for farmers, 236; scholarships, 239; rehabilitation of water systems, 250

Switzerland: 12, 38; Swiss Red Cross, 27; refuge for French children, 34

Tainsh, Euphemia (USC Winnipeg supporter), x, 146, 151

Tanzania, United Republic of, 229

Tempi, Mme Jo (USC Boston), 51, 61

Thapa, SS (Nepal), 223

Thérive, André (critic), 17

Thibert, Dr. Marguerite, 34, 35

Todd, Jack (USC chairman), ix, 146, 252

Tracy, Jack M. (USC Toronto chairman), 157

Trebert, Leon, 43

Trimis, Antonio (Tony): xi; in Greece, 74, 75, 76, 77, 129, 193, 198

Trudeau, Pierre, 4, 156

Tuberculosis, 89, 90, 91, 95, 124, 125, 237

Unitarian Church: and American Unitarian Association, 25, 42, 140; and Unitarian Universalist Alliance, 145; and Canadian Unitarian Council, 140, 145; British Unitarians, 122; support for USC, 40, 42, 44, 141, 145; relationship issue debated, 139-145; family planning issue, 158; Lotta's lecture to First Unitarian Congregation, 187, 191n

Unitarian Service Committee — Boston: clinic in Marseilles, 25, 26, 36, 48; other wartime work in Europe, 25-27, 28, 31; work with Spanish refugees, 48; with Czech orphans, 56; clothing drive, 41; help to USC Canada, 40, 41-44, 46, 140, 142; attacked in U.S. Congress, 61; "affiliation" with USC Canada, 141; Lotta's criticism of, 195

Unitarian Service Committee — Canada: registration, 44; principles,

3, 7, 10, 187-191, 192; constitutional review, 143-145; significance of "Unitarian", 145; relations with Unitarian Church, 139-145; with USC branches, 138-139, 143, 157; with other NGOs, 159, 244; programs (see under various countries); Board's hesitation about programs or projects in Greece, 189; in Cyprus, 220; in Bangladesh, 203; and in Vietnam, 108. Role of Projects Advisory Committee, 197-199, 250; of Board and executive committee, 46, 198-199, 250; attitude to CIDA "matching funds", 249-250

United Church of Canada (in Korea), 81

United Nations: 6, 33, 161, 196; UN Security Council, 108; UN forces in Korea, 81; peacekeeping in Cyprus, 219

United Nations Korea Reconstruction Agency, 82, 84, 85

United Nations Relief and Rehabilitation Administration, (UNRRA), 35-36, 195; clothing drive, 41

United Nations Relief and Works Agency (UNRWA), 95, 96, 97, 98, 99, 199

United Nations Children's Fund (UNICEF), 35n, 58, 85, 99, 160, 177n, 196

Vaidya, Dr. M.K. (India), xi, 124-128, 133

Vaidya, Dr. Kiran, 125, 132

Vaidya, Mrs. Vatsalabai, 129, 131, 132

Vancouver Sun, 124n, 137

van Rensburg, Patrick (Botswana), 228

Vegetable gardens, 7, 121, 163, 223, 230, 236

ven der Buhs, Raymond (USC managing director): 3, 138, 160, 184, 188, 196: Saskatchewan background of, 244; views on concentrating program, 197; on funding, 250; work with South Asia Partnership, 245, 246, 247

Victoria Daily Times, 83, 137, 155, 156n

Vietnam: general, 1; USC program in South, 100-104; in North 104-8; abrupt end to program, 108, 189

Vijayarghavan, Lt. Col. A. (India), 114

Vikse, Ruth, 247

Walmsley Dr. Norma (as PAC member), 198

Water: clean supplies of in Nepal, 7, 221, 223; India, 131, 132, 133, 247; Greece, 76, 78; Indonesia, 174-176, 182; Bangladesh, 212, 219; Lesotho and Swaziland, 234, 235, 238

— Irrigation projects in Greece, 75; India, 120, 121; Indonesia, 181; Bangladesh, 211, 212, 213, 215, 217; Botswana, Lesotho and Swaziland, 230, 235, 238

Watson, David (television host), 10

Webster, Howard (as newspaper proprietor), x, 156

Whyte, Ronnie (USC founder member), 40

Wickenden, Dr. Robert (USC Calgary chairman), 46, 138

Willard, Mrs. N. (champion knitter), 137

Wilson, Senator Cairine (honorary chairman of USC), 40, 43, 44, 67; work with refugees, 33

Winnipeg Free Press, 155

Women: role in development, 162, 169, 227; training of, in Greece, 71-73, 241; Palestine, 95; South Vietnam, 103; India, 110, 114-115, 125, 126, 129-131; Bangladesh, 207, 213, 217; Nepal, 222, 223;

Swaziland, 240; Lesotho, 233
Women's Alliance (General Alliance
    of Unitarian Women), 41, 42
Women's Institutes: 160; in Ontario,
    67; in Alberta, 64
Wood, Charles (Quaker worker in
    Portugal), 29
Wood, Harry, 252
Woods, Marjorie (champion knitter),
    137
Woodward, Hazel (USC Victoria
    chairman), x, 146, 148, 152
World Bank, 3, 6, 9, 161, 211
World Food Program, 196

Yugoslavia: 66, 204; in Petite Entente,
    18; Lotta's UNRRA posting in, 35
Yuktananda, Swami: x; in India, 119,
    121; in Bangladesh, 203, 204, 206,
    208
YWCA: in Korea, 82

Zimmer, Dr. René, 26-27, 30, 31
Zissis, Michael (Greece), 79-80